Guidance
in the
CURRICULUM

Guidance

in the

CURRICULUM

1955 Yearbook

ASSOCIATION FOR SUPERVISION
AND CURRICULUM DEVELOPMENT

A department of the
National Education Association
1201 16th Street, N.W., Washington 6, D. C.

From the Association

YEARBOOKS of the Association for Supervision and Curriculum Development deal with issues of special concern to educators. They are timely, vital and frequently controversial. Their topics are chosen because they are important to the profession and because thinking about them and doing something about them constitute primary responsibilities of education in this country. ASCD yearbooks deal with issues of mental health, conservation, social class, economic education, classroom practices, democratic administration, public relations, the role of supervision in the teaching process, group planning in education, creating a good environment for learning, and the changing nature of the curriculum. Sometimes the issues are pressing and dramatic growing out of the fears and struggles of the immediate present; sometimes they emerge from long years of careful study and experimentation and years of careful testing in terms of human growth and human values. Though the philosophy and practices set forth may seem revolutionary, these volumes have come from insights and understandings gained by psychologists, psychiatrists, sociologists and educators working over the years. In this latter category falls the 1955 Yearbook GUIDANCE IN THE CURRICULUM.

In this yearbook the integral relationship between guidance and teaching is clearly set forth, both as philosophy and as method. The guidance-centered philosophy on which the book is based is not new; it has been growing in this country for over thirty years. But its expression in the life of American schools is seriously retarded. Its growth can be accelerated, however, by putting into practice ways already well developed for studying individual children, for recording findings on useful, cumulative records, and for using knowledge of behavior and its motivations to increase the quality of human relationships in all aspects of school life, especially in the relationships between pupils and teachers, which determine very largely the direction and degree of learning.

"With individual differences as our starting point," write the authors, "we view guidance as relating to all those things which adults do *consciously* to assist an individual child to live as fully and effectively as he is able." This concept of guidance as inseparable from curriculum is illustrated here again and again with specific, day by day activities planned and carried out by classroom teachers, supervisors and administrators who believe that "wholesome guidance and effective learning go hand in hand." In this yearbook we see teachers using the three basic resources of curriculum building: studies of contemporary society, studies of learners, and studies of the contribution of subject fields to the special and general education of children and youth. We see teachers using these resources to build programs which fit with increasing adequacy the unique needs and interest of every child and which, at the same time, help every child to adjust with maximum benefit to the demands that are made upon him by the society in which he lives.

Balance is the keynote of the yearbook: balance between competition and cooperation in motivation and learning, balance between the needs of individuals and the needs of society, and balance between firsthand experiences and vicarious experiences provided through abstractions and symbols. Teachers are urged to help children find balance between their liabilities and their assets and to see their academic achievement in relation to their total growth.

The authors have made helpful distinctions between the general guidance responsibilities of the classroom teacher and those of specialists in guidance who provide expert assistance beyond the skill of the classroom teacher to perform. The services of school psychologist, evaluator, counselor, school physician, dentist, nurse and social worker are defined and illustrated. The part of administrators and supervisors is developed extensively, as well as the responsibility of parents and community. In this volume each reader may find himself and discover his own part in helping to build a functional and flexible curriculum through which guidance of children may be fulfilled.

This yearbook is a result of the cooperative effort and thinking of leading educators in several sections of the United States. The Executive Committee of the Association for Supervision and Curriculum Development, NEA, expresses sincere appreciation to each of the members of the 1955 Yearbook Committee and to the members of the Writing Committee who prepared the final manuscript.

Especial recognition is due Camilla M. Low, of the University of Wisconsin, who served as the able and devoted chairman of the Yearbook Committee and editor of the manuscript.

The ASCD Executive Committee also makes the following acknowledgments: George W. Denemark, executive secretary, ASCD, read the manuscript in its several stages and made many constructive suggestions regarding its development. Robert R. Leeper, associate secretary, ASCD, worked with the original manuscript, did final editing on the volume and was in charge of its production. Cover and title page are the work of de Graffenried W. List, NEA Publications Division. Florence O. Skuce, of the Editorial Unit of the NEA Publications Division, assumed major responsibility for proofreading, paging and other technical aspects of production. Stella S. Clark and Glenda L. Jones, ASCD staff assistants, helped at various stages in preparing copy and in proofreading. Henry Rule, copy editor with the National Publishing Company, Washington, D. C., gave critical assistance in the several stages of production of this volume.

The ASCD Executive Committee proudly accepts this 1955 Yearbook and commends it to all persons who are concerned with the integral relationship between guidance and teaching.

PRUDENCE BOSTWICK, *President*

For the Executive Committee

The 1955 Yearbook Committee

CAMILLA M. LOW, *professor of education,* University of Wisconsin, Madison, Wisconsin, *Chairman.*

MILDRED L. FISHER, *principal,* Maplewood Junior High School, and *director of the Child Study Department,* the South Orange-Maplewood Schools, Maplewood, New Jersey.

HAROLD C. HAND, *professor of education,* University of Illinois, Urbana, Illinois.

ETHEL KAWIN, *director, Parent Education Project,* University of Chicago, Chicago, Illinois.

KENNETH J. REHAGE, *associate professor of education,* University of Chicago, Chicago, Illinois.

AMELIA TRAENKENSCHUH, *assistant superintendent in charge of curriculum and instruction,* Rock Island Public Schools, Rock Island, Illinois.

The Writing Committee

MILDRED L. FISHER, *principal,* Maplewood Junior High School, and *director of the Child Study Department,* the South Orange-Maplewood Schools, Maplewood, New Jersey.

MARGARET GRIFFITHS, *dean of girls,* Neenah High School, Neenah, Wisconsin.

HAROLD C. HAND, *professor of education,* University of Illinois, Urbana, Illinois.

EARL H. HANSON, *superintendent of schools,* Rock Island Public Schools, Rock Island, Illinois.

DOROTHY HAYES, *director of elementary education,* State Teachers College, New Paltz, New York.

ETHEL KAWIN, *director, Parent Education Project,* University of Chicago, Chicago, Illinois.

CAMILLA M. LOW, *professor of education,* University of Wisconsin, Madison, Wisconsin.

KENNETH J. REHAGE, *associate professor of education,* University of Chicago, Chicago, Illinois.

BERNICE SCOTT, *guidance counselor,* North High School, Sheboygan, Wisconsin.

AMELIA TRAENKENSCHUH, *assistant superintendent in charge of curriculum and instruction,* Rock Island Public Schools, Rock Island, Illinois.

Foreword

THIS book is primarily about one aspect of guidance—that part which can and should be done by teachers on all school levels and in all of the many classroom and out-of-class contacts they have with children. Thus it is addressed to teachers and to those within and outside the school who are in a position to help teachers best accomplish their guidance aims. It does not underestimate the services of counselors, psychologists and various other guidance specialists in the clinical and social case work fields but limits discussion to the ways in which these members of the guidance staff can assist teachers.

The terminology used in the volume needs some explanation since it may differ slightly from that currently used in books on guidance and counseling. In an effort to stress and to dignify the important role of the classroom teacher in guidance, the term "guidance workers" is used to include teachers as well as all other guidance personnel. The term "specialist" is used to apply to all staff members who have guidance functions calling for personnel training or psychological background over and above that typically required for classroom teaching. The authors recognize that there are different levels and kinds of specialization. The general school counselor may be a specialist in administering and interpreting certain types of standardized tests, in providing certain kinds of information regarding posthigh school educational and occupational opportunities, and in counseling with respect to certain kinds of social and academic problems. The psychologist may be more highly trained than the counselor in the use of certain diagnostic and therapeutic techniques, yet less specialized in the areas of college and occupational counseling. Similar differences in amount and kind of specialization would be represented by the nurse, the reading specialist, the speech correctionist, the social caseworker and others. The assumption made by the authors is that each member of the school staff will give to boys and girls the kind of guidance service for which he is qualified and will have a lively sense of the dangers involved in attempting to help children with problems which call for a different kind or a higher level of counseling skill than he possesses.

"Group guidance" has not been discussed under this appellation since the general philosophy of the authors is that all classroom and other group learning situations afford opportunities for guidance. It is felt that designating certain areas of subject content such as "orientation to the new school" or "choosing a vocation" as appropriate for group guidance, while other areas such as "science in everyday living" or "effective communication" are not so designated, sets up a false dichotomy. The authors take the position that no subject matter which is not related to the needs of boys and girls should remain part of the school curriculum and, conversely, that all content which does serve to meet individual needs is appropriately included in what we call group guidance.[1] The major part of the guidance role of every teacher, therefore, is in the area of group guidance.

In Part Three of the yearbook the authors faced a choice of addressing the teacher and indicating where he might go for assistance with the various types of guidance problems he meets, or of analyzing separately the role of several kinds of guidance workers as helpers of teachers. The latter method of organization was selected to make it easy for each of these specialists to find himself and to review the whole range of services which he might be in a position to give to teachers. This emphasis was considered important even though overlapping services resulted in some repetition in chapter content.

While a brief discussion of the organization of guidance services and the newer patterns of curriculum organization is included, these matters are not dealt with in detail. This is not to underrate the importance of a well-coordinated program of guidance and of a curriculum setup which provides maximum opportunity for discovering and meeting individual needs. The authors, however, believe that there is no magic in any administrative arrangement. Good guidance goes on in classrooms in which there are good teachers—teachers with insight and human understanding

[1] The term "needs" is broadly defined to include not only the developmental and psychological needs of boys and girls but the needs which arise from the demands which the society makes upon them.

as well as teaching skill. Opportunity for good guidance far beyond that which now obtains is possible in the highly departmentalized pattern of organization as well as in the "core," and in the school which has no "organized" guidance program as well as in the one which boasts a full complement of special services.

In general this volume attempts to give the rationale for conceiving the whole teaching-learning process as inextricably related to guidance, and the teacher as the central figure in developmental guidance. While many brief illustrations have been given to clarify this position, it has not been possible to include the longer diary-type accounts of teachers on various grade levels and in various subject areas who are implementing this point of view in their day-by-day teaching. This might well be the content of a subsequent yearbook.

The authors hope that GUIDANCE IN THE CURRICULUM will prove useful to teachers, counselors and supervisors who are on the "firing line" as well as to students in college courses in guidance, curriculum and general teaching method.

CAMILLA M. LOW, *Chairman*
Committee for the 1955 Yearbook

Contents

Part One
A Point of View

Part Two
Implications of This Viewpoint
for Teachers

Part Three
Resources Available to Teachers
in Guiding Children

Part Four
Integrating Guidance with Instruction

Part One

A Point of View

CHAPTER I

Relationship of Guidance to Instruction

THE common responsibility of all school personnel, under whatever title they operate, is to see to it that the school program in its entirety is of maximal benefit to the pupils and to the supporting society. How classroom teachers may cooperate with other school personnel and with parents to discharge this common responsibility in respect to that aspect of the school program which we call guidance is the problem of this yearbook.

In many schools this problem has not been resolved very satisfactorily, with the consequence that the pupils are not as well served as either their needs or those of the supporting society require. The character of the instructional program in these schools makes guidance a *separate* service *supplementary* to the instructional program. In these schools classroom teaching and guidance are regarded as separate functions, to be carried on by separate groups of staff people—teachers and guidance workers.

Guidance as a Supplementary Service

In schools in which guidance is viewed as a supplementary service the content of the subjects taught is largely set in advance and permits of but little flexibility. On the elementary school level this means, for example, that children promoted to the fourth grade are tacitly assumed to be ready for fourth grade work. If the work in reading, arithmetic or other subject content proves too difficult for a given child, or if for any other reason he fails to make a satisfactory adjustment to the prescribed fourth grade pattern, he is generally referred by the teacher to someone who is supposed to be responsible for the guidance of pupils. In many schools, this person is the principal. In some he may be the school psychologist, a remedial reading specialist, or a speech correctionist. The usual expectation is that after referral the child will be able better to measure up to fourth grade standards. If, as too frequently happens, this does not work out as it is supposed to, the teacher may resolve the problem by simply allowing the child to sit and fail, then send him on to the next grade where he may again sit and fail. This unhappy experience often encourages the youngster to leave school too early. All too frequently this is what happens in elementary schools in which classroom teaching and guidance are separated, and in which the pupil is expected to do most if not all of the adjusting while the subject content remains relatively inflexible.

Similar unhappy consequences result when the separatist philosophy operates at the secondary school level. Here it is the task of the classroom teacher to see that the predetermined content of his subject is learned by the pupils who come to him. The task of the guidance counselor in such situations is to help the pupil select and enroll in the subjects, or the particular sections of given subjects, which are suited to his purposes, interests, needs and capacities—to see to it that the pupil and the subject "fit."

The casualties which result when this "fit" is bad are principally the responsibility of the counselor. It is his job either to help the pupil adjust himself to the situation in which he had his difficulties or, failing in this, to steer the pupil (if he can) to some other subject, or some other section of the subject, in which it is hoped that his adjustment will be more satisfactory. Too often there is no such possibility. The only alternative then seems to be the addition of new courses in the hope that they will be better adapted to the interests and capabilities of the youth in question. But as long as classroom teaching and guidance are regarded as separate functions the new subject content is likely to be just as inflexible as the old. There is then a precedent as well as pressure for providing still other courses for the pupils for whom this new content is later found to be ill-suited. The present hodge-podge proliferation of high school courses is in no small measure the result of this well-intentioned effort to resolve the problem of "fit." Although the addition of new high school courses is at times desirable, the needs of youth cannot satisfactorily be met in this manner alone.

Even if a course such as English is obviously important for a given pupil to take, and even if he is placed in the section of English with others of similar academic achievement, inflexible subject matter content cannot serve him and all the other pupils in his section equally well. Even if metal shop, a new course in the curriculum, seems to relate to the particular interests of a given boy, there is little chance that his insights and skills, as well as those of all the other boys, will be developed if the course content prescribes virtually the same number and kind of projects for all, and assumes that the same method of learning will work for all.

When adjusting to individual differences is solely the responsibility of counselors and other guidance specialists and the problem of "fit" is removed from the teacher's hands, the educational experiences offered to boys and girls cannot be well suited to the pattern of purposes, interests, needs and capacities uniquely characteristic of each pupil. It is for this reason that the authors of this yearbook subscribe to the point of view that teachers and guidance specialists must share the functions of guidance.

Making Instruction Inseparable from Guidance

In schools which operate in harmony with this point of view the instructional program is sufficiently flexible to enable the teachers to make substantial adjustments in it the better to meet the needs of each of their pupils. The teacher has the dual role of making these necessary adjustments in the instructional program and of helping pupils adjust themselves to those of its aspects which societal need renders less flexible. Classroom teaching is regarded as inseparable from guidance; the teacher guides as well as teaches.

There is a reciprocal relationship between guidance and instruction in the hands of such teachers. One has the effect of modifying the other in a way which both enriches learning and assures better help to each pupil as he faces and tries to solve his problems. The inclusion of an illustration may be helpful at this point. Miss Best has been observing and talking informally with each of her fifth graders during the first few days of school. Already she knows that Kathy's handwork is meticulously done but that she is quite limited in the academic aspects of her work. Doris attaches herself to the teacher but is ignored by the other children. Beth is bright but overweight and self-conscious about accepting prominent leadership roles. Peter's father is disappointed in his son's mediocre school record and tends to blame the school. Max is especially good at building things with tools. Ted seems long on ideas but short on "carry-through." Fred devours *Popular Science*

Magazine and is interested in experimentation. Esther has just entered this northern community from the south and seems quite fearful and withdrawn. Richard is noisy and simply cannot sit still for long in a schoolroom seat.

There is much more that Miss Best needs to learn about these and the other children, but as she does her initial planning for the science study on "weather" she keeps in mind what she does know. She figures out how she can create an environment for these children so that each child can find activities to suit his interests and to challenge his efforts. She thinks about the possible committee groups which might be set up to extend the friendships of those who need friends and to utilize leadership in constructive ways.

The first learning activity for which Miss Best plans is the planning period itself. As children and teacher pool ideas and consider the books the children might read, the people they might talk to and the places they might visit, the teacher learns many other things about the children which modify her initial plans. These facts not only will enrich the unit but will assist her pupils as individuals in their social and emotional adjustment and hence in the learning of the subject content of the unit.

Miss Best learns, for example, that Peter's father is a weatherman at the local airport. Peter is pleased when Miss Best approves his idea that he talk to his father about arranging a class trip to the weather bureau. Doris thinks her dad, who is a building contractor, might get some scrap materials for Max and Fred to use in building a weather tower. Miss Best had not realized before how nervously active and yet how thin and pallid Ted appears. She must refer him for a thorough physical examination. Richard has more background knowledge in science than Miss Best realized. She must be sure to help him build on this background by suggesting reference materials and investigations on a level mature enough for him. She notices now that Esther's fingernails are bitten to the quick. She must get more background information about Esther.

Each day, as the children proceed with the study, the teacher becomes better acquainted with them and is able more intelligently to provide the kinds of learning experiences which are most suitable for them as individuals.

It is clear that no outside person—principal, school psychologist or counselor—could accomplish what is taking place in Miss Best's classroom and in every classroom on all school levels in which the teacher effectively assumes his role as a guide to individual boys and girls. All that such a teacher, through his activities as a guide to children or youth, discovers about them, he utilizes to modify his teaching to insure a better "fit." This results in instruction which is more effective and satisfying to the teacher and the pupils alike—and to their parents no less. And what he learns about his pupils through teaching them makes the teacher more competent to guide the children or youth in his charge. Thus do the benefits to pupils spiral when instruction is made inseparable from guidance.

Role of Specialized Guidance Personnel

Not all of the guidance services needed by children and youth can be supplied by classroom teachers. There is definitely a place for specialized guidance counselors and for a planned guidance program. Both are needed and should be provided. An important aspect of this planned guidance program should be its direct services to classroom teachers. The specialized guidance personnel should supply specialized resources and services to teachers, work with them and deal directly with such deviate pupils as the teachers, unaided, are not competent to help.

To make certain that we will not be misunderstood, let us put this in different words. To say that all classroom teaching should be inseparable from guidance, which is the position taken by the yearbook committee, is not to say that all guidance should be inseparable from classroom teaching. Some aspects of guidance must be separated from instruction for the reason that teachers are not especially trained or do not have the time to deal with them. The committee recognizes that there will probably always be some deviate pupils whose problems require the direct services of specialists of various sorts—problems with which teachers can deal unaided only at the certain risk of being accused of operating as "quacks." It also recognizes that a considerable number of pupils have certain problems such as serious speech and reading disabilities with which only specialized personnel are competent to deal. When it comes to the application of technical therapeutic techniques, the yearbook committee is confident that the undertaking should be in the hands of a person trained especially in psychology, guidance and therapeutic work. Rarely if ever is a classroom teacher so equipped by his training.

The yearbook committee recognizes the need for specialized guidance personnel. It believes that all children and youth can be served adequately by the school only if such personnel is provided. The committee emphasizes, however, that the providing of guidance specialists may work to the disadvantage of the pupils if what we have called the separatist philosophy of guidance is permitted to prevail in the school. If, prior to the employment of such personnel, the teachers were sufficiently disturbed about the lack of adaptation to individual differences in their classes to do something about it, but now feel free of any such responsibility because there are specialized staff members to whom the "problem pupils" are to be referred for guidance, it is obvious that desirable adaptations are now less likely to be made in their classroom practices than was formerly the case. Especially is this likely to be true if the teachers are led to believe that adequate guidance is being provided outside their classrooms. Because of the possible hazard to pupils when specialized guidance personnel are provided, it is especially important to make clear the central role of the teacher both in sensitizing himself to individual pupil needs and in meeting these needs.

Conversely, it is equally important that the roles of specialized guidance personnel be made clear to all staff members. In later chapters we shall take note of the important services which these specialists can render the pupils through aids provided for classroom teachers. We shall not, however, attempt to treat those aspects of guidance which only specialized guidance personnel are competent to handle. Instead, this yearbook is concerned with making clear what is involved when classroom teaching is made inseparable from guidance, and with giving what assistance it can to teachers who would thus better serve their pupils.

Why Separation of Instruction from Guidance Continues To Exist

In urging that classroom teaching be made inseparable from guidance the yearbook committee recognizes that it is recommending against what appears to be at the present time a rather common practice. Unsatisfactory though it is, the practice of separating classroom teaching from guidance—in fact, if not in theory—prevails in many elementary and in a clear majority of secondary schools. The factors which operate to make this the prevailing practice are not difficult to detect. Probably the most pervasive and compelling is the feeling on the part of many teachers that they are at fault if they do not strive to bring all pupils in a given grade group or in a given high school course "up to standard"—that, regardless of what the range of individual differences may be, they are somehow guilty if they do not attempt this impossible task and that they have failed if all or nearly all their youngsters are not "up to the norm" in respect to subject matter achievement. These feelings are appreciably heightened if the teacher has reason to believe that the principal and the people of the community are judging him chiefly in terms of his pupils' success in achieving the prescribed subject matter content.

These pressures from the community usually increase as children progress through the grades. In the early elementary school years the teachers usually feel that they have considerable leeway in varying the classroom activities to take account of individual differences in maturity, capacity, background, interests, needs and consequent readiness to learn. The result is that instruction and guidance are both quite capably carried on in the lower elementary grades. Later the pressures mount, partly because of a misunderstanding and consequent misuse of standardized achievement tests. Too frequently, adminstrators, teachers and patrons alike overlook the fact that a norm is simply an average, that only about one-half of the youngsters on whom the test was standardized came up to or exceeded this average, and that any teacher who succeeds in getting half of a cross-section group of pupils up to or above this average or norm is teaching subject matter as capably as the teachers in whose classes the test in question was standardized. But whether it stems from this misunderstanding or from other sources, the false idea that all youngsters can and should "measure up to standard" gains ground as one progresses up the elementary school ladder —with the result that the teachers increasingly feel restricted to a fairly narrow range within which to make adjustments in their classroom work to fit the individual capacities and needs of their pupils. This feeling on the part of the upper elementary school teachers is, of course, heightened when high school teachers tend to place blame upon the elementary school for pupils who are poor readers, who are deficient in arithmetic fundamentals or who fail in other respects to measure "up to standard" when they enter the secondary school.

There are going to be as many who achieve above the standard as there are who fall below it. Preoccupation with the standard leads teachers to strive for the impossible with the less academically capable, on the one hand, and, on the other, to fail to give sufficient attention to those who should be encouraged to achieve at levels often vastly higher than the average.

The forces which make for relative inflexibility in classroom work are appreciably greater in the secondary than in the lower school. The high school teacher's training as a subject specialist makes it especially difficult for him to feel comfortable about varying his expectations to insure a better "fit" with the capacities, interests and needs of individual students. Despite the fact that the providing of this "fit" is a requisite for effective subject matter achievement (see Chapter II), the making of such accommodations is often perceived as the "lowering of standards" and hence is rejected.

The outside as well as the intramural pressures which make for the separation of classroom teaching from guidance also become greater at the secondary school level. Among the pressures exerted by the local community are those which emanate from businessmen for employees of excellence and from the community for finished performances in vocal and instrumental music and in athletics. The strongest of these outside pressures on the secondary schools, however, comes from professors in the colleges and universities. With the accusing cries of anguished college professors recurrently in their ears, it is not strange that high school teachers feel impelled to give attention to the frustrating task of bringing their pupils "up to standard."

Given the pressures to which we have alluded, there is little wonder that the state of mind induced in the teachers leads many to become preoccupied with prescribed subject matter and tends to blind them to the personal factors in the lives of their pupils—factors that, as will be shown in Chapter II, prevent the very achievement which so many well-intentioned teachers are single-mindedly attempting to encourage.

As we have just implied, some teachers make the necessary adaptations in their classrooms, but many do not. All undoubtedly do some adjusting to individual differences, but most introduce only a small fraction of the flexibility which the individual capacities, interests and needs of their pupils require. The truth of the matter is that typically at all school levels it is only the unusually courageous and ingenious teachers who modify the prescribed subject matter content sufficiently to insure an adequate "fit" for all their pupils.

It is not realistic to expect a majority of the elementary or secondary school teachers so to modify their classroom work until they come to see clearly that the making of these adaptations is a necessary precondition for maximum subject matter achievement by the pupils in their charge. In Chapter II we will demonstrate that achievement in mastery of subject matter which represents each child's maximum can be had only if boys and girls are considered as individuals; only if what they are asked by their teachers to do *now* provides them with the basic feelings of success and recognition which encourage their active effort to tackle the problems which keep them from doing their best to meet whatever the outside standards may be. If and when this is done, classroom instruction will be indeed inseparable from guidance.

We turn now to Chapter II in which the point of view of the yearbook committee is elaborated by an operational description of the teacher who makes his classroom teaching inseparable from guidance. As implied, this description is in terms of what such a teacher values, believes, knows and has made himself competent to do.

Setting Our Sights

OPERATIONALLY, the task of guidance differs from school to school. In one, the relative inflexibility of the instructional program makes guidance a service supplementary to classroom teaching. In schools of this kind it is the responsibility of one group (the teachers) to give the instruction; that of another (the guidance counselors) to provide the guidance. As was noted in the first chapter, the needs of children and youth cannot be well served in schools in which this separatist philosophy and practice prevail.

In the other type of school, there is no thought that teaching can possibly be adequate if it is separated from guidance. In these schools teachers guide as well as teach. There are specialized guidance workers in such schools, but they see their role as that of (a) helping teachers become ever more competent in the guidance of children and youth and (b) dealing directly and individually only with those pupils whose problems the teachers cannot resolve without the help of those with special training. As Chapter I indicated, the needs of pupils and of the supporting society can most adequately be met only if this concept of guidance is practiced in the school.

In the remainder of this yearbook the authors take the position that classroom teaching should not be separated from guidance; that, instead, guidance should be regarded as an essential aspect of the work of every classroom teacher. Further analysis of the implications of this position will now be made.

A Concept of Guidance

In the first place, the need for guidance derives from the existence of individual differences. If all boys and girls were equally alert and vigorous, equally intelligent, adjustable and interested in school learning, there would be no case for curriculum flexibility and far less need for guidance. The knowledge that each child presents a unique pattern of characteristics and requires unique treatment lies at the heart of our guidance philosophy. With individual differences as our starting point, we view guidance as relating to all those things which adults do *consciously* to assist an individual child to live as fully and effectively as he is able.

Such assistance on the part of school personnel may take an almost endless variety of forms—from studying some aspect of a child's life to understand him better, to devising learning situations from which he can gain a needed experience, to conferring with his parents to understand their expectations for the child, to being a sympathetic listener when he wants to talk, to giving him the consistent psychological support which encourages wiser self-direction. Guidance involves both helping the child adjust to a required pattern and adjusting the pattern better to fit the child. Since both of these adjustive aspects have the single objective of developing a human being who is capable of self-direction in a democratic society, the child's freedom of choice, commensurate with his maturity, must be protected. Helping each child to help himself and make his own decisions is inherent in such a concept of guidance.

Parents, teachers, supervisors, counselors and many other people both inside and outside the school share in the child's guidance. The teacher, however, stands second only to the parents in the weight of his responsibility for guiding the development of the pupil. It is with the teacher and his activities and resources in guiding boys and girls, as he helps them with their learning, that this volume is chiefly concerned.

A Concept of the Curriculum

The authors of this yearbook conceive of the school curriculum as comprising all of the opportunities for learning which the school provides for children and young people to meet their varying needs. These opportunities relate to much more than the course of study. Just as the selection of text and reference material is part of curriculum planning, so are arrangements for a properly run program of extraclass activities, plans for the choice and display of foods to be served in the cafeteria, and decisions about such things as grading systems, promotion policies, the height of the bubblers and the intramural sports activities. This planning results in a certain range of opportunities available to boys and girls if and when these become appropriate for the children or young people.[1] These opportunities from which learning experiences accrue constitute the school curriculum.

In a well-planned curriculum for a whole school, or a single class group, there are many times more learning opportunities than a given child can or should take advantage of. A large element of choice enters in as far as *the child's own curriculum* is concerned. It is in all these matters of choice that guidance is important. What the teacher does to help the child in scores of choice-making situations determines the teacher's role as a guidance person. The teacher's adequacy in carrying out his guidance function relates, in turn, to what he knows about children and the social demands required of them.

The Orientation of the Teacher Who Guides as He Teaches

A teacher who effectively integrates guidance with his classroom teaching knows that all children face a variety of adjustment problems in the normal course of growing up and that it is in the resolution of these problems that all children need guidance. When guidance and instruction are largely separate, there is a tacit assumption that many children need little or no guidance. Except on the high school level for such matters as the selection of courses and extra-class activities, decisions relating to the continuation of formal education, the choice of an occupation and the finding of suitable employment, a pupil who does reasonably well in the prescribed curriculum of such a school is usually not considered a subject for guidance. The guidance services are reserved largely for those who are misfits, and guidance is primarily remedial and corrective in nature.

The process of human development is, of course, characterized by the meeting and resolving of a continuous series of adjustment problems. The life of no child is free of these problems. Many are concomitant with growth; many more arise as the individual attempts to cope with the prescriptions and the restrictions of his environment and to take advantage of its opportunities.

---

[1] Curriculum planning takes place at various times and involves various people. Considerable planning must, of course, be done before the arrival of the learners in anticipation of their needs. The crucial planning, however, stems from personal knowledge of the children, and must indeed involve them. A discussion of the important ways in which the pupils share in curriculum planning is included in Chapter IV.

For example, six year old children typically face the problem of conforming to first grade school routines. This may involve varying degrees of adjustment from the security and informality of home or kindergarten life. Other problems for six year olds relate to learning to read, to count, to respect the property rights of others, to control outbursts of emotional response, to expend energy in better organized play and to use their bodies in such coordinated skills as manuscript writing and jumping rope. Some of these problems they have already been working on during younger years but have still not attained the degree of mastery appropriate for this age level. At each successive level of growth the problems become somewhat more complex, commensurate with the heightened level of expectation set for the child by society.

Much further up the developmental ladder, in the junior high school years for example, some of the adjustment problems have to do with the acceptance of rather dramatic changes in physical growth, with social adjustments to members of the opposite sex, and with the often painful efforts to break away from family supervision. Still further along, in the senior high school, there come such problems as choosing an occupation, learning how to earn, budget and spend money for good family living, and preparing for active citizenship as an adult.

The satisfactory resolution of these and all other developmental problems depends to a marked degree upon the wise guidance of adults. Within the school, providing guidance of this kind should be primarily the function of the teacher whose continuing contact with a given youngster makes it possible to know him well.

The adjustment problems of some children will, of course, be more severe than those of others. If there has been lack of wise guidance over the years, or if there are special conditions in the life of the pupil which have hampered him from the satisfactory handling of developmental tasks at younger levels, then guidance to correct and remedy unwholesome behavior patterns and to compensate for inadequate background may be in order. The services of guidance specialists are often needed for such problems for they frequently require special competence which teachers do not possess. Preventive guidance, however, is largely the province of the teacher, as is what we might term *developmental guidance* wherein the teacher's role is to guide the child, as he grows, to make full and effective use of his talents and capabilities.

The authors of this yearbook maintain, therefore, that *all* children need guidance and that, of all school personnel, the classroom teacher is best situated to help them with their developmental tasks.

A teacher who effectively integrates guidance with his classroom teaching knows that children of the same chronological age are at different levels of readiness for a given learning experience. Much of the academic and social content of the school curriculum is planned to meet outside criteria. As already suggested, the nature of our social institutions and our methods of communication make it vital for boys and girls to acquire certain kinds of information and to become skilful in the use of certain tools. These constitute the basic reason why we teach such subjects as reading, spelling, the social studies, science, arithmetic and physical education. Society also decrees that its members live up to prescribed social standards in their relationships with others. Certain basic freedoms must be protected. These are the reasons why the school provides a variety of social situations both in the classroom and in extraclass activities to help children learn to protect the rights and property of others, to work cooperatively with others and to give respect to differing ideas. All good teachers conscientiously strive to help each child meet these criteria.

Children at any grade level, however, represent a range of individual differences in their readiness to accept the learning tasks which society may demand of them and which are typical for that chronological age group. It is not uncommon, for example, for a given classroom of boys and girls to represent a span of seven years in reading level. Certainly all of them are not ready to comprehend a science textbook appropriate for the average reader in the group. Nor are all of them stimulated by reading material geared to the typical child. In respect to social, intellectual and physical factors, the typical class group will probably present an equally diverse picture.

Moreover, each individual represents different maturity levels within himself. Because of his background and his level of intelligence, a given pupil may be ready for mathematical experiences much more complex than those typical for his age group. At the same time, in motor coordination and physical strength this youngster may lag behind many of his classmates. In sociability and leadership he may be at still different levels of maturity. And to add another complicating factor for the teacher who guides learning, every youngster has his ups and downs in feelings and moods; he has problems on certain days which demand so much of his attention that he is not ready on those days for the experiences planned by the teacher.

Actually, no teacher who reads these lines ever doubts the fact of individual differences. Every teacher knows of the existence of a wide range of maturity and readiness levels both among individuals and within each individual. The question is whether such knowledge makes a difference in what the teacher *does* in the classroom. If, operationally, the teacher appears to assume that all first grade children are ready to read by December, or all seventh graders are ready to learn to dance, or all tenth graders are ready to make an occupational choice, or all twelfth graders are ready to appreciate Macbeth, then in spite of intellectual acceptance of individual differences, guidance does not enter into classroom teaching to any appreciable degree. Conformity to a single standard, with some adjustments in methods of approach, is the operating formula of such a teacher. The individual child cannot be well served under this formula.

A teacher who effectively integrates guidance with his classroom teaching is skilful in gathering and using the data needed to determine readiness. The teacher who consistently tries to apply his knowledge about individual differences appreciates, first of all, the need to know each child as fully and intimately as his own skill and time and as the resources of the school and community will allow. As will be noted in a later chapter, the special services of the guidance and supervisory personnel can do much to assist the teacher in assembling and interpreting information about the child. A good cumulative record based upon the pooling of information about a given youngster over a period of years can likewise be an invaluable help and time-saver for the teacher in acquainting himself with the developmental history of each child.

Even in a departmental high school situation, the teacher has more continuous personal contact with a given group of boys and girls than does the principal or counselor or any other member of the school staff. This means that he is in the key position to discover many important things about the way a given child is developing and about the special problems he may be facing.

As indicated, if guidance is to enter into classroom teaching, the teacher must engage in careful observation of pupil behavior. This is a skill which calls for considerable self-discipline on the part of the teacher. A person who is preoccupied with himself and his own difficulties is likely to be quite blind to the subtleties of behavior and the feelings of others. The things which such a teacher does notice about a given child are likely to be the aggressive acts which threaten the teacher's security. He may overlook recessive behavior far more indicative of need for guidance. Similarly, a teacher who places subject matter mastery above all else is likely to be insensitive to differences in individual capabilities and interests in his single-minded approach to the academic job to be done. His perception of his pupils is likely to be restricted to how much or little they know about the subject he teaches, and how well or poorly they prepare the academic work he expects or requires of them.

The teacher's major preoccupation should, of course, be with the children themselves in an effort to sense their feelings and discover the motives for their reactions to situations and people. If he has the interests of children at heart, his vision will include a wide range of personality factors. Furthermore, his purpose in observing his pupils will not be to label and to pigeonhole them, but to see what constructive adjustment he might make to encourage more wholesome development on their part.

The art of listening is another quality which effective guidance-minded teachers possess. We would probably agree that "talking too much" is one of the occupational diseases of teachers. Unless we can "cure" ourselves of this malady, we not only deny the youngsters many fine learning opportunities but cut ourselves off from their thoughts and feelings. Actually, listening involves much more than merely "stopping talking." A listening attitude is evidence of *outward* orientation to the boy or girl, and of a willingness to accept and respect him as one whose ideas count for something. Forgetful of self, this kind of teacher can develop a relationship of trust and confidence with boys and girls which will encourage them to talk freely and frankly about themselves and their problems. Through this active kind of listening in which the teacher tries to discover how the world looks through the child's eyes, many important factors relating to readiness will be revealed.

A teacher who effectively integrates guidance with his classroom teaching is also fully aware that what happens to a child during his out of school hours is reflected in the goals which he sets for himself at school and in the efficiency with which he works to achieve them. Either personally or through cooperation with the special school and community guidance services the teacher needs to "get around" for purposes of discovering the degree of opportunity afforded each youngster in his home, the nature of his relations with members of his family, the satisfactions he receives from his gang or his playfellows, the interests he exhibits during his leisure hours, and scores of other items of personal information which provide added insight into his character and personality make-up.

Only if he understands the child in his school, in his home and in the wider neighborhood and community, can the teacher estimate how far the pupil has progressed in each aspect of his growth and what next steps are appropriate for him.

A teacher who effectively integrates guidance with his classroom teaching knows that success in school work is intimately related to the way a child conceives of himself as a human being, and to the emotional satisfactions he is achieving in his relationships with others. Children carry around pictures in their heads. Each child has his own picture of what a teacher is like, what a police officer is like, what a father is like, or what a youngster who goes to the church across the street is like. He also has "pictures in the head" of himself as a pupil, a son or daughter, or a pal. Each picture is a generalization compounded of many past experiences. These pictures may be based on faulty perceptions and be distorted by emotion, but all are powerful guides to the child's conduct.

The picture which influences a child's way of life most profoundly is the one he carries around of himself. A teacher who assumes his guidance responsibilities must somehow discover what this picture is, and the experiences in the life of the child which have contributed to its detail and clarity.

If a youngster conceives of himself as a person who is reasonably successful in the things he undertakes, he will approach new situations—new developmental tasks— with confidence. If he thinks of himself as a failure, he will be fearful of new situations. If he accepts himself as a reasonably likeable and friendly person, he will approach each new social situation in ways which encourage a friendly, warm response from others. If he thinks of himself as "not much good" or as a person who is disliked or merely tolerated by others, then he will behave in harmony with this self-concept and tend to perpetuate and reinforce his record of failure and of social rebuff.

There are certain general conditions which must be met to assure the development of a wholesome self-concept. A youngster must feel, first of all, that he is very *important* to somebody else—so important that nothing he could do would be so wrong as to take away the support and faith of this person. That "you're-with-me-all-the-way" feeling which a child has about his parents who love him, or his teacher who accepts and respects him, does much to guarantee that the major elements of his self-portrait will be wholesome and acceptable to the youngster. The components of a wholesome picture-of-self are the resultants of the tasks which the child has been able to perform with reasonable success, of the recognition he has been able to gain for worth-while contributions to his group, of the friendly acceptance he feels from his own classmates and his neighborhood gang, and of his developing sense of competence that he can make choices more intelligently and face failure more constructively.

These, then, are the kinds of experiences which the teacher must provide if he is to guide the child wisely. If the teacher is able warmly to accept each child regardless of his I.Q. score, or his ill-advised behavior, or his race, or his unkempt appearance, he offers the youngster the very best insurance that school life under his guidance will be a happy and profitable experience. If, in addition, the teacher can set his level of expectation for each child at a point where successful achievement is possible, yet must be striven for, the child will develop the underlying confidence needed for future success at more difficult tasks. If, finally, the teacher can devise classroom activities to encourage friendships and to give each child a chance to "shine" and receive the commendation of his classmates for doing well something that needed to be done, then the frame of mind with which each child attacks the job at hand will be that which is most conducive to effective learning.

The yearbook authors believe that the maximum wholesome development of children is impossible unless guidance and classroom teaching proceed hand in hand. To bring this about, teachers must understand the springs of human conduct and their implications for school learning, and must be versatile in adjusting subject matter content and teaching methods to help meet the fundamental personality needs of each boy and girl.

A teacher who effectively integrates guidance with his classroom teaching knows that children learn many things within a given context, and plans with reference to the whole constellation of possible wholesome learnings. The effective guidance-minded teacher is oriented with reference to the total best adjustment of each boy and girl. He knows that youngsters learn their attitudes, their appreciations and their behavior *while* they learn academic knowledge and skills. In each case one learning task is in the center of focus, and the others are on the fringe.

The teacher has two jobs: to allow a shift of focus for a given child when it appears appropriate, even though other children in the group have a different focus; and to make the fringe learnings in every instance as wholesome as possible. The teacher is, therefore, always faced with such alternatives as deciding whether at this time for this boy resting his head on the desk is more important than doing the arithmetic problems, or whether for this girl attending the rehearsal of the school play is more important than staying after school to make up history deficiencies. The question is, what is going to mean the most to a given youngster in the long run? The answer, of course, is in the nature of a best guess in the light of all the teacher knows about the particular individual's needs and desires. Inevitably, however, whatever the teacher tries to encourage the child to make his focus brings in its train other learnings which may or may not be equally constructive and wholesome.

The good teacher also realizes that personally satisfying and socially desirable experiences on the fringe tend to reinforce the central learning. Failure to plan for wholesome fringe experiences may detract from or completely negate accomplishment of the central learning. For example, while seven year old Sally is learning to subtract she is also learning to like or dislike her teacher, to gain a sense of achievement or failure, to feel comfortable or uncomfortable in her associations with the other children, and to learn a number of good or poor ways to gain acceptance. The attitudes, feelings and behavior patterns learned *along with* subtraction are, if positive and pleasantly toned, the supportive structure which helps make possible the learning of arithmetic.

Similar examples might be cited at any other level of maturity. Ralph, a senior in high school, was failing in chemistry. Eventually it was discovered that a major factor in the failure was lack of stimulation commensurate with the critical and inventive capacities of this bright boy. While the teacher, with conscientious but narrow single-mindedness, was laboring to get Ralph to read the chemistry textbook and do the prescribed experiments, all the fringe learnings were operating against the accomplishment of the so-called central goal. He was *learning* to escape a boring situation through daydreaming. He was *learning* to withdraw socially from his classmates and to feel that he had no responsibility for contributing anything for the good of the group. The disciplinary measures of the teacher, which actually amounted to no more than an occasional exasperated remark about his laziness, made this sensitive, unhappy and bright boy lose face with his peers and *learn* that he was pretty much "no good" and a failure. He *learned* poor posture reflecting the hangdog picture he had of himself. And finally he *learned* to escape the whole unhappy classroom situation through truancy.

A teacher with more sensitivity and perception and one capable of exercising greater flexibility in adjusting learning experiences to individual needs could have capitalized on Ralph's potential leadership in chemistry to reverse this snowballing of negative learnings. He could have created a situation for Ralph in which many excellent social, physical and intellectual habits and attitudes would have accompanied and reinforced the learning of chemistry.

Sensitive awareness of the fact that learning takes place in an integrated and patterned manner, and care in planning learning experiences for a given child with reference to what should be his focus of attention and what fringe benefits should accrue, are characteristic of a teacher who guides as he teaches.

A teacher who effectively integrates guidance with his classroom teaching appreciates that the true measure of his success is the degree to which children come to understand themselves more fully and to direct themselves more wisely. The philosophy of guidance accepted in this yearbook is in harmony with the democratic way of life. Respect for people, even though they be little children or confused adolescents; faith in their growing capacities to make intelligent choices, even though in the process they make mistakes and show poor judgment—these are central in any constructive guidance relationship.

If the curriculum is relatively inflexible and the teacher's job is somehow to get the child up to standard, there must of necessity be considerable prescription and many devices used to encourage and goad him toward achieving academic respectability. Disciplinary measures are apt to be employed more frequently in this situation; so also are the incentive of high grades and the threat of low ones. In a prescriptive, authoritarian atmosphere, children become pawns and are not accorded the respect which encourages self-respect and do not develop the initiative which leads to self-direction. Even if general school policy is liberal and opportunities exist for adjusting learning experiences to individual needs, some teachers still feel that they should make most of the decisions for the pupils. Such a teacher hampers a child's growth in self-direction and thereby handicaps him in facing the many unpredictable problems of tomorrow.

So, while guidance implies adult influence on children and young people, it also must insure that each child, on his own level of development, is given rewarding opportunities to set his own goals, make his own decisions, measure his own progress and, in the process, understand himself better. The teacher helps the youngster gather information for making a choice, he helps to clarify the possible consequences of alternative choices, he gives the child psychological support when failure results from an unwise choice, and he helps him analyze the situation so that next time he will make a better choice. But the child, to the degree that his maturity will permit, is encouraged to operate as a free, thinking agent. Guidance includes helping the child learn what is involved in facing and solving a problem, sensitizing him to the resources available for its solution, and stimulating him to utilize these resources wisely. Yet the child, and not the teacher, does the resolving of whatever the problem situation may be. The active involvement of the child in every aspect of the learning situation, with increasing responsibility for the consequences of his choices, helps him to grow in self-assurance and to face with greater confidence the complex problems of adult life.

The effectiveness of the teacher in guiding the pupil is measured by the degree to which he is able progressively to make himself *less* necessary to the youngster.

A teacher who effectively integrates guidance with his classroom teaching is able to accept diversity "in stride" and to retain perspective in spite of confusing variations in pupil behavior. Teaching in which guidance and instruction are inseparable is a complex operation. There seem to be but few routine factors in the classroom situation that can be dealt with by the teacher in a uniform manner. When teachers permit themselves to employ such methods as confining reading to a single textbook, making a single assignment to be measured on a single standard, setting rigid deadlines for work due, or establishing rules for behavior applicable without exception, there is probably corresponding lack of adjustment to the needs of some boys and girls, and therefore an absence of adequate teacher guidance.

Sometimes the difficulties faced by the teacher in attempting

to teach children as a group, and at the same time vary the content
and the approach to individuals, relate primarily to lack of acquaintance with teaching materials and project ideas. When this
is the case teaching experiences may contribute to competence.

In the course of their experience many teachers develop a store
of challenging alternative learning activities. Projects and assignments which have worked out well for gifted children, or for those
who are mentally retarded, are noted for use at some future time.
Pamphlet and other reference material well suited to the poor
reader, or for youngsters with special interests and hobbies, are
collected. Methods of organization found satisfactory by the
teacher for providing flexibility and some diversity in classroom
activity are other items which the teacher remembers for future
use. Ways of utilizing community resources and for extending
learning beyond the limits of the classroom are likewise remembered if experimentation with them has encouraged wholesome
growth on the part of some youngsters. With experience, the
teacher also becomes more appreciative of the many interesting
and workable ideas which boys and girls themselves have to offer
for achieving their goals. If they are given the opportunity to participate in planning, these children will contribute helpfully to solving
the problem of providing for individual differences.

The ability to accept diversity in stride, especially as it concerns
social behavior, also relates to the teacher's own feelings of personal security. The teacher is better able to make the adjustments
required to meet individual needs if his own pattern of living and
his own system of values offer him the basic satisfactions he desires.
If he is in good physical health and is not too preoccupied with
personal worries and concerns, he will be able to accept the im-
maturities of boys and girls without regarding these as a personal
threat. If he can strike a happy balance between emotional involvement and detachment, he will be able to give each youngster the
psychological support he needs and, at the same time, the perspective he needs to go about solving his problems.

Even the best of teachers will sometimes "fumble the ball" in
his relationships with his pupils. His humanness, with all that it
implies of both weakness and strength, may actually be an important element in the warm, friendly response which he receives from
children. They can accept his occasional shift of mood and his
occasional impatience or authoritative action if he is basically consistent in his treatment of them, and if they are certain that he

likes them and would "go to bat" for them when they are in trouble. What is requisite is that the teacher have sufficient emotional integrity to create a classroom environment which furnishes security for children and, at the same time, provides the degree of flexibility and freedom which encourages wholesome growth.

This chapter has dealt briefly with some of the understandings and characteristics which teachers should possess in order that consideration be given to the needs of individual children. It is the belief of the authors of this yearbook that these needs can adequately be met only if guidance and classroom teaching are regarded as interrelated. They believe that teachers who are equipped to accept their responsibility for guidance must understand how children grow and develop and how they differ one from the other in the process. They also believe that such teachers must be skilful in studying children to discover their needs and in guiding their growth with reference to all the personal and cultural factors which relate to wholesome adjustment. Finally, they are persuaded that the teacher who guides wisely must himself be mature in outlook; that he must be able to accept each child, no matter what his behavior, as worthy of his faith and respect.

Part Two

Implications of This Point of View for Teachers

CHAPTER III

Deciding Upon Objectives

THE two preceding chapters have sketched the broad outlines of the general point of view held by the yearbook committee. In the balance of the yearbook the committee has sought to be as explicit as possible as to the implications of this point of view. The next three chapters direct the attention of the reader specifically to the kinds of questions that concern each classroom teacher as he plans the instructional program for and with his pupils.

How would the point of view taken by the committee affect a teacher's decisions about the objectives of instruction? How would it influence his decisions in selecting and evaluating learning experiences? How would it be reflected in the ways in which a school might be organized and a total faculty might work together? Chapters III, IV and V seek to explore these questions in some detail. The first question under consideration deals with the objectives of instruction.

Objectives of Instruction

In any effort to improve an instructional program there comes a time when some attention must be given to the problem of objectives. Curriculum development projects often begin at this point, for it is a logical starting place. But even when a faculty group elects to begin its work by making an appraisal of the present program, or perhaps by exploring ways in which learning can be made more effective, it will not get far without some recognition of the need for an adequate statement of objectives. Someone is almost certainly going to ask in what terms the appraisal is to be made, or what particular learnings are desirable. At this point the problem of objectives has to be faced directly.

The question to be considered in this chapter relates to the ways in which the general viewpoint of the yearbook committee would influence the approach to the problem of determining objectives. If a staff rejects the "separatist" view described in Chapter I, and subscribes instead to the notion that teaching should be made inseparable from guidance, would the staff members then approach the problem of objectives in any particular way? Perhaps the best way of looking at this question would be to analyze what is involved in the making of decisions about objectives. If we can see clearly what the essential elements of this problem are, we may be able to see more easily how the viewpoint of the yearbook committee is related to that task.

Determination of objectives is not a simple problem, especially for those who are inclined to view the curriculum in the broad sense described in Chapter II. Indeed, this procedure is exceedingly complex. One must take into account in some way the varied nature of the school population, the presence or absence of opportunities for learning outside the school, the many and varied pressures currently operating to affect the school program, the wide social and economic differences within and among communities, the limited amount of time available for elementary and secondary education, the different conceptions of the ultimate purpose of education, and the like. While the task is a complex one, no serious-minded teacher, administrator, curriculum worker or guidance worker can turn from it.

Schools cannot expect, nor should they be expected, to provide all the needed opportunities for learning. To a greater or lesser degree learning goes on also outside of school, and it goes on continuously throughout life. Nevertheless schools by their very nature are in a unique position to provide a highly favorable setting for learning. Certain kinds of skills, understandings, attitudes and generalized patterns of behavior can be learned far more effectively and economically through well-planned school experience than through the informal and unorganized experience provided by life itself. By giving systematic attention to the identification of the particular learnings which can and should occur primarily as a result of school experience, the school is in a much better position to organize its instructional program so that the opportunities for such learnings are maximized. Without giving careful attention to the identification of these learnings the school can easily slip into the serious error of allowing its instructional program to be guided solely by tradition and of remaining relatively insensitive to the potent and dynamic forces that affect the lives of boys and girls it is trying to educate.

When one considers the range of possible objectives it is perfectly clear that a major problem facing teachers is that of making wise and appropriate choices. This problem of making choices is enormously complicated by the often conflicting points of view within the profession as well as outside of it. The matter is further complicated by the fact that choices appropriate for one school community are not equally suitable in another. The rapidity of both technological and social change serves to bring new additions to the list of possible objectives. Therefore, schools that would be sensitive to the social realities of our time must examine these newer objectives, and, if these are deemed important, should find a place for them. In order to find such a place it is often necessary for the school staff to decide whether or not less emphasis should be given to objectives formerly thought to be essential. Perhaps some objectives should no longer be sought at all. It is never easy to make such decisions.

The problem of determining objectives, then, involves answers to questions like these: What particular learnings are desirable? For which of these learnings is it appropriate to have the school assume a major responsibility? For which of these learnings should the school be expected to provide experiences that tend to reinforce learnings primarily acquired elsewhere? For which of these learnings is it inappropriate for the school to assume any responsibility? These are fundamental questions. The answers to them are never completely final. The answers may not be the same in one decade as they were in a preceding decade. Because of such considerations curriculum study becomes a continuous process, and a school faculty can hardly escape the responsibility for frequent re-examination of the objectives toward which its instructional program is directed.

It is possible to approach the problem of determining objectives in terms of three separate but related questions:[1] (a) How may likely objectives for an educational program be identified? (b) How may appropriate selections be made from among the possible

---

[1] For a fuller treatment of these questions, particularly the first two, see R. W. Tyler. *Basic Principles of Curriculum and Instruction*, syllabus for Education 360, Chicago: University of Chicago Press, 1950. The writer acknowledges his indebtedness to Professor Tyler for the concepts which form the core of the presentation of this chapter.

objectives? and (c) With whom does the responsibility rest for the identification, selection and formulation of objectives?

What Are Possible Sources of Objectives?

Studies of Contemporary Society. With respect to the first of these questions it is necessary to identify possible sources of objectives and to determine how these sources may be effectively used. One such source is the vast array of information which can be found in studies of contemporary society. The justification for turning to such studies is primarily found in the fact that our educational enterprise is firmly rooted in the society of which it is a part. It is inconceivable that sound educational programs could be developed without giving considerable attention to the essential characteristics of the society in which the school is so deeply imbedded, and which indeed is the source of support for the school. Furthermore, society now makes, and will continue to make, certain demands upon young people. It expects them to be able to meet these demands effectively, for upon their ability to do so the future health and vigor of the society will largely rest. Analyses of contemporary society underscore some of those demands.

Some of these analyses focus primary attention upon the international and national scene. We may use the latter to illustrate here how wide a variety of generalizations and insights with important implications for the school program may be obtained from such sources. Studies of population movements, for example, call attention to the nature and extent of internal migration from rural and urban areas, and from central cities outward to the periphery of large metropolitan areas. Many consequences flow from these developments, and some of them suggest matters that may be of considerable import to the school. Studies of the changing characteristics of family life serve to identify trends toward which the school cannot easily remain indifferent. Similarly, studies of political behavior, of economic aspects of contemporary life, of leisure time pursuits, of the effects of mass media of communication, to mention only a few further examples, permit characterizations of our society in terms of its various aspects. Each of these analyses can suggest possible objectives for an educational program.

Other studies of contemporary society deal more explicitly with local communities. Some of these point out generalizations found to apply with little variation in most communities. Problems relating to health, government, community planning, recreation, welfare, and the like are sufficiently common so that insights obtained from studies in certain selected communities are generally applicable. These insights often suggest important objectives for education. At the same time, the particular conditions found to exist in any single community may differ significantly from those found elsewhere. For example, in some localities the problem of maintaining even a minimum standard of living, as far as food, clothing and shelter are concerned, may be the most crucial matter facing the people of the community. In others this particular area may be of relatively little consequence. Instead, the large majority of the people, and particularly the youth, may face problems of making wise choices as consumers. In some communities antagonisms between various ethnic and social groups may be practically nonexistent, while in others this problem may be so acute that its consequences may be felt in almost every classroom. Studies of these and other aspects of life in local communities, analyses of the kinds of activities carried on in the community, community surveys, and the like provide a wide variety of information which may be examined to see what implications there are for educational objectives.

It is important to note at this point that studies of contemporary society, either at the national or international level or at the level of the immediate local community, do not directly yield objectives for the educational program in a given school. They merely indicate possible directions and emphases in that program and need to be considered with suggestions obtained elsewhere.

Studies of Learners. We may turn, then, to a second source of possible objectives, namely, the studies of learners themselves. Justification for using this source for identifying possible objectives is found primarily in the fact that these studies focus our attention upon the child in terms of the factors which may either positively or negatively influence his learning. Such studies can tell us what children are like—their interests, their potentialities, their needs, their concerns. If a teacher knows his students well enough to be able to determine what learnings have already been attained, he can take steps to avoid wasteful duplication of learning effort. Similarly, if the teacher is able to identify significant gaps in the students' previous learning he can make provisions for closing such gaps.

Unless these and other characteristics of students are taken into account, the school can easily fall into the error of determining objectives and planning educational experiences which are not meaningful to those for whom they are intended. If the school's educational program holds little or no meaning for the pupils, the chances are very great that the learning which occurs will be negligible and that it will not be long retained. This may be the result even when a teacher has worked hard with every resource available to him to "put it across" to the students. As a matter of fact, teachers probably complain more about this unhappy state of affairs than any other one thing. While it is by no means easy to solve such a problem, it usually helps to understand the matter more fully if a teacher can ask, "In what ways is this particular lesson, or this particular course, relevant to the things that really matter to these particular pupils?"

Quite obviously, such a question can be answered only if the teacher knows a great deal about these pupils. What the teacher knows, or is able to find out through continuous evaluation of the instructional program, may help him to re-examine the objectives he believes to be important, to clarify them, to reformulate them in more realistic terms, or perhaps even to substitute other goals for them. It should, of course, be clear that studies of learners can also furnish important clues as to what means are appropriate to help pupils attain these objectives, as well as to indicate what the objectives should be.

There has been, in recent years, a tremendous increase in the number and kinds of studies of children and youth. Some of these studies are concerned primarily with general characteristics of children at various age levels—early childhood, middle childhood, adolescence or even with finer breakdowns within each of these broad age categories. Other studies focus primary attention upon selected characteristics, as in the case of the work of Jersild and Tasch on children's interests.[2] Many such studies are undertaken and, to the extent that one is inclined to believe that the characteristics in question apply quite generally to American children, the findings are indeed useful for suggesting objectives. Increasingly, however, teachers are recognizing that such findings need to be supplemented by information that can be obtained about the particular children in a given school or class.

[2]Arthur T. Jersild and Ruth J. Tasch. *Children's Interests and What They Suggest for Education.* New York: Bureau of Publications, Teachers College, Columbia University, 1949. 173 p.

It is therefore desirable for teachers, curriculum workers and guidance specialists to strive to collect systematically the kinds of information about the children in their schools which can be useful in suggesting objectives. This can be done through observation, interview, questionnaire, various kinds of tests, to mention but a few of the more commonly used techniques.

A great deal of work done in this area to date has been primarily concerned with the characteristics of individual learners and the extent to which these characteristics are found to exist among large numbers of young people. In recent years much more attention has been paid than formerly to the fact that groups of learners may exhibit characteristics that develop, in part at least, because of their association as a group. Thelen and Tyler, for example, have outlined important group factors to be taken into account.[3] Further studies by Thelen and his associates, and by others working in the general field of group dynamics, illustrate the fact that group characteristics, as well as individual characteristics, have implications for what is to be learned and how effective the learning will be.[4] Since practically all instruction in American schools occurs in a group situation and since group factors are known to have a powerful influence on learning, it appears that teachers would do well to study carefully characteristics of their classroom groups in order to get further suggestions for objectives.[5]

It may be well to point out here that it is often difficult, and perhaps not necessary, to draw a sharp distinction between the two sources for objectives mentioned thus far. Obviously the studies of individual learners need to be interpreted in terms of some social context in order to have maximum meaning. Correspondingly, the studies of society need to be interpreted in the light of their significance for particular groups of individuals. The work of Havighurst and others in analyses of the "developmental task" concept serves to illustrate how the individual's motivations, the demands of society, and the maturing of the physical organism combine to set tasks which, in Havighurst's view, may properly be

[3] Herbert A. Thelen and Ralph W. Tyler. "Implications for Improving Instruction in the High School." Learning and Instruction. Forty-ninth Yearbook. Chicago: National Society for the Study of Education, University of Chicago Press, 1950. Chapter 12, p. 304-35.
[4] See especially the collection of papers by Professor Thelen and others in the October 1951 issue of The Journal of Educational Research, Volume XLV.
[5] See, also, Ruth Cunningham and others. Understanding Group Behavior of Boys and Girls. New York: Bureau of Publications, Teachers College, Columbia University, 1951.

considered as objectives of education.[6] Studies of developmental tasks, therefore, become a particularly useful source for identifying possible objectives, because they explicitly take both the learner and society into account.

The Subject Specialist. A third source of possible objectives to be considered here is the subject specialist. It has long been the practice to organize knowledge in terms of "subjects," and to many people education consists of learning the contents of these various subject fields. This is particularly true of those who have spent a great deal of time in becoming specialists in one or another of the subjects.

Subject specialists are often inclined to suggest objectives that are appropriate chiefly for those who are also to become specialists in a given field. To the extent that this is true the specialist is helpful primarily in identifying objectives appropriate for a limited group, but not for all students. Each of the specialists tends to think that schools should give more attention than they now do to matters he believes to be of crucial importance. What this usually means is that if he is an historian the specialist will be prone to suggest objectives that could only be attained by adding more history to the school curriculum. The same would hold for the specialists in mathematics, science, language and other well-known subjects. Such a situation can lead only to confusion and, as almost any secondary school teacher knows only too well, to open rivalry and competition among the adherents of the various subjects for the students' time.

If, however, the subject matter specialist is asked to suggest the ways in which his speciality can make a distinctive contribution to the general education of a wide variety of young people, his answers can indeed be helpful and can yield suggestions which are more realistic in terms of the total educational task confronting our schools. Fortunately, there are increasing numbers of subject matter specialists who are giving attention to this problem. We therefore have access to a number of statements that are extremely useful to teachers. It is now nearly fifteen years since the Commission on Secondary School Curriculum of the Progressive Education Association published a series of reports on the place of science, social studies, mathematics, language and other subject fields in general education. These reports have been widely used and have

[6] Robert J. Havighurst. *Human Development and Education*. New York: Longmans, Green and Company, 1953.

been found generally very useful to teachers. The recent curriculum bulletins of the National Council for the Social Studies are further illustrations of helpful statements from those with competence in a particular subject field.[7] Perhaps the most comprehensive effort in recent years to get suggestions for objectives from subject matter specialists, as well as from other sources, is that of the Mid-Century Committee on Outcomes in Elementary Education.[8] Recognized authorities submitted to the committee their statements of desirable outcomes in subject matter learning and intellectual competence. These were taken into account, along with other authoritative statements on personal development and social maturation, by the committee in preparing its final recommendations.

It is possible for specialists in the various subject fields to indicate not only the particular contributions that are unique to their own field, but also to suggest how their own field, along with other subject matter areas, may make a substantial contribution to the total educational program for youth. In either case, the subject matter specialist is seen as a valuable source to whom educators may turn in their quest for possible objectives.

In the degree that a school looks solely, or even primarily, to one or another of the above mentioned sources in its efforts to identify objectives, it opens itself to criticism. If suggestions are taken primarily from the analyses of contemporary society, or from studies of the learner, or from reports of subject matter specialists, the resulting statement of objectives will lack both the comprehensiveness and balance that are needed to develop a well-conceived instructional program and to meet the needs of individual boys and girls.

[7] Mary Wilcockson and Ernest Horn, editors. *Social Education for Young Children*. Curriculum Series Number Four. Washington, D. C.: National Council for the Social Studies, a department of the National Education Association, 1946. p. 119.

Loretta E. Klee, editor. *Social Studies for Older Children*. Curriculum Series Number Five. Washington, D. C.: National Council for the Social Studies, a department of the National Education Association, 1953. p. 139.

Julian C. Aldrich, editor. *Social Studies for Young Adolescents*. Curriculum Series Number Six. Washington, D. C.: National Council for the Social Studies, a department of the National Education Association, 1951. p. 87.

Eunice John, editor. *Social Studies in the Senior High School*. Curriculum Series Number Seven. Washington, D. C.: National Council for the Social Studies, a department of the National Education Association, 1954.

[8] Nolan C. Kearney. *Elementary School Objectives*. Report of the Mid-Century Committee on Outcomes in Elementary Education. New York: Russell Sage Foundation, 1953.

The process of identifying possible objectives from such sources as those mentioned involves a good bit of analysis and interpretation. As has been pointed out earlier, objectives are rarely directly identifiable from the sources themselves. The analyses of contemporary society and studies of the learners, for example, can give us a great deal of information about things as they now are. Such information can suggest objectives only when we have some notions about how things *ought* to be, and can then compare and contrast the conditions found with what we believe ought to obtain. If there is a gap between these two, and if we believe it is the function of the school to help close such a gap, we have a clear indication of a possible objective.[9]

How To Approach the Determining of Objectives

Let us now return to the question raised initially in this chapter. Does the point of view that instruction is inseparable from guidance influence the way in which teachers and other guidance workers approach the task of determining objectives?

First of all, curriculum workers who appreciate the central role which the classroom teacher plays in guiding individual boys and girls are not likely to restrict their investigation to less than the full range of the sources of learning objectives. The teacher or supervisor who never loses sight of the functioning human being as he approaches the professional problem of determining objectives cannot limit himself to a single school of thought. He understands that if objectives are derived largely from studies of the contemporary society with insufficient reference to the capacities, interests and motivations of the learners, the resulting instructional program is not likely to include classroom experiences which will help boys and girls resolve problems of social adjustment important to them. Similarly, he recognizes that to conceive of objectives as stemming largely from the inner psychological and growth needs of human beings is to forget that wholesome personal growth can be achieved only within a social context and only through behavior which meets in all essential respects the requirements of contemporary society. He further appreciates that when objectives are

[9] Ralph W. Tyler. "Translating Youth Needs into Teaching Goals." *Adapting the Secondary School Program to the Needs of Youth.* Fifty-second Yearbook, National Society for the Study of Education, Part I. Chicago: University of Chicago Press, 1953. p. 215-29.

limited to the mastery of academic content a fairly high level of interest and intellectual capacity is required to attain them. All growing boys and girls do not readily share the specialist's enthusiasm for his subject. Such objectives will fail to encompass for many boys and girls both their personal needs and the societal demands made upon them.

The importance of a broad attack upon the problem of investigating sources of objectives—complex though the problem may be —can be readily accepted by those who are convinced that the ultimate goal of all classroom experiences is to help each pupil learn what he needs in order to function with social effectiveness and personal happiness.

In the second place, does the position of this yearbook with reference to the integral relationship between guidance and instruction have implications for the ways in which the above mentioned sources for objectives might be utilized? Learning is commonly viewed as the acquiring of desired patterns of behavior. Presumably among the kinds of behavior desired by both the learner and the school are those which facilitate a socially acceptable adaptation to a continuing succession of problem situations. It is the student, however, who must *learn* to make this adaptation, this adjustment. The effective guidance worker, correspondingly, would view his contacts with students as opportunities for this kind of learning to occur. An important implication would therefore seem to be that both the teacher in performing his "guidance" function and the specialized guidance worker in performing his "teaching" function need to develop a knowledge and understanding of the kinds of situations to which society requires young people to make satisfactory adaptations.

A third and related implication grows out of the fact that such situations are by no means unchanging. For this reason both teachers and guidance specialists must periodically examine the demands society makes in order to enlarge their understanding of the adjustive behavior required.

Fourth, the necessity for studying learners individually and collectively in order to identify possible objectives places a considerable obligation upon the classroom teacher. It is not likely that this work will be accomplished in anything more than a superficial way if a teacher regularly must see a hundred or more different pupils each day. But, even where the number of individual pupils with whom a teacher has daily contact is such as to make these studies feasible, the teacher may wonder whether efforts to study his pupils somewhat systematically are really worth while. It might be interesting for such a teacher to experiment a bit. He might try for a month or so to accumulate as much information as possible about individual pupils in one of his classes, and about the structure of the group. Meanwhile, in another class, he would follow his usual procedures. He might ask the help of counselors and other specialized guidance personnel both in the accumulation and interpretation of data collected. He might communicate his own information to others, particularly to guidance specialists, so that their work with these pupils might also be more meaningful. At the end of the month he might ask himself whether or not the experience of collecting and studying a wide variety of these data had influenced his teaching practices appreciably, or whether it was easier for him to help pupils attain certain objectives in one case than in the other, or whether he tended to view the problems of learning encountered by one group any differently than those encountered by the other. He might ask whether greater knowledge of his pupils did in fact make it possible for him to do a more creative, more satisfying job of teaching. The yearbook committee believes that the findings would be affirmative, but the argument would be much more persuasive if a teacher's own experience led him to a similar conclusion.

Finally, it can be pointed out that involving the learners themselves in the process of determining possible objectives is a useful means of providing teachers with valuable insights as to matters that are important to children. Many teachers, in trying out this aspect of pupil-teacher planning, have found that the joint efforts of teachers and pupils can provide both with a clearer understanding of what the objectives mean and why they are worth pursuing. Not only is the teacher here helping to guide pupils toward desirable goals, but the pupils' observations and judgments are helpful in guiding the teacher's actions. At this point it is indeed difficult to distinguish between "guiding" and "teaching."

Selecting and Stating Educational Objectives

In general, two kinds of considerations become relevant as the problem of selecting objectives from among those identified is approached. The first has to do with what *ought* to be learned, and the second with what *can* be learned.

What Ought Young People To Learn?

Let us assume that a junior high school language arts teacher identifies the following as being among the potential objectives for his class: learning to appreciate and enjoy poetry, developing skill in creative writing, understanding certain aspects of formal grammar, learning how to locate information, learning how to read a newspaper, broadening reading interests. Let us say that the existing program in this school provides for some instruction focused upon these, as well as other language arts objectives. Taking a realistic view of what is possible in the time available, the teacher chooses to give major emphasis to the first three of the objectives mentioned even though he thinks that to do so will preclude much, if not all, attention to the last three. In some way he has convinced himself that the former are more important than the latter. He has made a decision on the basis of what he thinks *ought* to be learned.

When the teacher asks the question, "What ought young people to learn in school?" he can answer it only in terms of some concepts about the worth of the individual, about the nature of the good life, about the place of education in helping young people to find that good life, about the role of formal schooling in this regard, and about the role of the school in society. Many teachers may say that they do not have time to give much attention to matters of this kind, and indeed this may be true. Nevertheless, in every decision a teacher makes about educational objectives (and in most schools the classroom teacher's decisions on this point are the ones that really determine the nature of the educational program) he is acting as though he entertained real convictions on these broad questions of educational philosophy. Whether or not he is aware of the strength of these convictions, his decisions about educational objectives are, nevertheless, based upon them. He selects from among potential objectives those that are consistent with his own views in these matters. If these views are not themselves internally consistent, it is highly probable that the objectives selected will reflect this inconsistency.

If everybody's views were the same, or if the range of possible objectives were so small that all could be accepted, there would be no very serious problem. But neither of these conditions obtains. Not infrequently one sees in the same school instruction that reflects sharply contrasting views of the purposes of education. Differences in viewpoint are to be expected, and even encouraged, provided that the total effect of such differences is not to diminish the effectiveness of instruction as far as the children are concerned. Nevertheless, a staff ought constantly to work toward the point where there is sufficient agreement so that the instructional program is not guided wholly, or even partially, by an educational philosophy that is inconsistent.

Viewed in this light, the effort of a staff to build a sound educational philosophy is not seen as an academic exercise merely to satisfy the requirements for a mimeographed page to hand out to visitors or for a high-sounding preface to a curriculum report. The educational philosophy of a school becomes a useful tool to guide the deliberations of the staff as it considers a variety of important educational questions. One of its most valued uses is to serve as a means of selecting objectives. It can call attention to objectives that ought to permeate the whole school program so that important learnings are reinforced at many points. Even more importantly, it can help to prevent situations in which various members of the school staff actually work at cross purposes. In order that it may be continually useful in this way, the statement of educational philosophy itself needs to be scrutinized from time to time to see whether the beliefs upon which it is based are still tenable. It ought not to be a rigid, inflexible statement, but rather one which can be modified or extended when it becomes apparent that the existing formulation is no longer completely adequate to serve its purposes.

What Can Young People Learn?

By considering also the question, "What *can* be learned?," the teacher is helped materially in the selection of objectives. This question can be answered in terms of our knowledge of how learning takes place, the factors which tend to motivate and encourage learning, those which inhibit learning, how much learning may reasonably be expected and the extent to which transfer of learning can occur. In short, it is at this point that the teacher can make effective use of his general knowledge of educational psychology and learning theory. Here again the teacher may say that he has little or no time in a busy day to give thought to such matters as these. But once more we may note that every day he makes decisions that are based in part on his conception of how learning takes place and what learning is appropriate for the children with whom he works. If these concepts are inadequate, if they are based upon faulty notions of the learning process, it is quite likely that he will make some decisions about objectives that are unrealistic.

On the other hand, if the teacher were to make explicit his ideas on the nature of the learning process, or if a school staff were to develop a statement of learning theory that squares with what is now generally well known, there would then be available a second very helpful tool for the selection of objectives. For example, such a statement would be helpful in distinguishing between those learnings which are generally known to be attainable at given age levels and those which are not. Experimental evidence thus far available suggests that intensive efforts at the middle grade levels to have children master certain time and place concepts are not justifiable.[10] Such learning appears to be more likely to occur, and with considerably less effort, in the junior high school grades. Similarly, such a statement would help teachers to distinguish between learnings which are acquired slowly, over a long period of time, and those which may occur much more quickly. Thus, the understanding of basic concepts, such as "interdependence" and "justice," appears to grow very slowly and only after repeated exposures to appropriate learning experiences over a long period of time. The same is true for attitudes and for many of the skills associated with critical thinking.

When potential objectives have been identified in some such fashion as that described, and when selections from among them have been carefully made, there remains the problem of stating them in a form which will be most useful in developing the instructional program. This is an important problem, for unless the objectives are genuinely useful they will readily be filed away unused and the instructional program is quite apt not to reflect in any visible way the effort that has gone into the formulation of appropriate objectives. The two ways in which objectives are most commonly used will be considered here. The first is to facilitate the selection and organization of learning experiences, and the second is to give explicit direction to a program of evaluation designed to appraise the effectiveness of instruction. There are obviously other uses for well-formulated statements of objectives, but these two are of paramount importance. If the objectives are not func-

---

[10]Alice Flickinger and Kenneth J. Rehage. "Building Time and Place Concepts." *Improving the Teaching of World History.* Twentieth Yearbook. Washington, D. C.: National Council for the Social Studies, a department of the National Education Association, 1950. p. 107-16.

tional in that they serve at least these two purposes, it is not likely that they will be used at all in any significant way.

When learning is viewed as a process of changing behavior, objectives may be taken as descriptions of the kind of changes desired. When one learns, he has really acquired new ways of responding to particular situations—new ways of thinking, feeling and acting. Learning is an active process, involving action on the part of the learner. An important kind of learner action is practice, for learnings are most likely to be acquired if there are frequent opportunities to practice the behaviors sought. It is important, therefore, for statements of objectives to include a clear indication of the behavior desired. But these behaviors occur in some particular context. They are carried on with reference to some particular content. The clearest direction to the teacher, then, comes from a statement of objectives which describes both the behavior desired and the content in which such behavior is believed to be appropriate.

When objectives are stated so that both these elements are present it is generally quite easy to see what kind of learning experiences must be planned, and the kind of content with which these experiences should deal. For example, the objective, "to develop skill in critical thinking," is hardly explicit enough to give direction to the planning of an instructional program. The behaviors associated with critical thinking need to be specified more clearly, and the kinds of problems with which this critical thinking is to deal need to be delineated in general terms. Thus, the objective, "to be able to determine the basic assumptions in opposing points of view on social issues," gives immediate and clear direction to the teacher in planning learning experiences. Students would obviously need to have practice in the determination of assumptions in situations involving controversial points of view with respect to social problems.

In the same way this degree of explicitness in the statement of objectives can be suggestive with respect to the development of various means of appraising the instructional program. Generally speaking, teachers are of the opinion that evaluation of pupil progress in terms of objectives other than knowledge and understanding of subject matter is extraordinarily difficult, if not impossible. As long as this belief is widely held there is little reason to expect that much effort will be made to appraise growth in the direction of other kinds of objectives. If this were the case, we might never have more than the most subjective judgments as to the effectiveness of instruction with reference to attitudes, interests and the like. To be sure, it is not a simple matter to develop means of appraising these kinds of behavioral changes. But an effort to be clear and precise as to the nature of the behavior desired and the situations where such behavior is likely to be manifested—in other words, a clearly formulated statement of objectives—is a necessary first step in approaching the problem of evaluation of instruction.

Setting Realistic Objectives

In this section we have seen that the job of selecting objectives involves at least two critical questions: what *ought* to be taught, and what *can* be taught? We have seen also that answers to these questions are more readily obtained if a staff has given thought to the educational philosophy upon which it wants to build an instructional program and to the ways in which effective learning takes place. How would the point of view expressed in this yearbook affect a teacher's decisions which relate to selecting and stating educational objectives?

When teachers accept the interrelationship of guidance and instruction they deal with the question of what *ought* to be learned from the viewpoint of the effect of their answer upon the lives of the boys and girls they are teaching. The question can never become purely academic or impersonal. This is not to say that the problem of "ought" can be approached uncritically. It is rather merely to stress that there is bound to be a predisposition on the part of a teacher who conceives of himself as both instructor and guide of children to be sensitive to pupil needs and to the whole problem of individual differences. As he and his colleagues who hold a similar view attempt to think through a satisfactory educational philosophy to guide their choice among alternative objectives, it must of necessity be centered in the conviction that human beings of whatever age or condition are eminently important in our society and that, as pupils, each deserves the respect and trust and help of his teachers. Such conviction would fundamentally influence their choices.

In decisions relating to what *can* be learned, the teacher who supports the point of view presented in this yearbook would find it congenial to accept and use the major findings of psychology relative to growth sequences and their meaning for readiness, and those relating to the principles of learning. Both make possible a selection of learning objectives more wisely related to the needs of each student than would be true if these findings had been disregarded. Such individualization is of the essence of guidance.

A further implication for those who agree that guidance and instruction are inseparable is that the task of selecting objectives is one which requires a good measure of cooperative effort among teachers in a given school, and that guidance specialists must also be involved. This cooperative effort might well be directed toward the formulation of basic beliefs about what ought to be learned and toward the development of genuine insight into the conditions under which various kinds of learning are most likely to occur. The context provided by such beliefs and insights should be materially helpful to individual teachers in selecting the kinds of objectives that are most appropriate for the boys and girls in their classes.

The task of stating objectives in terms of behavior and content likewise calls for cooperative effort among teachers. Only when he knows in what areas of content a particular type of behavior has already been applied can the teacher guide and extend the subsequent experience of his pupils in most meaningful ways. Thus, the more one tends to view guidance and instruction as inseparable the more one is required not only to accumulate a considerable fund of knowledge about the total instructional program but also to participate with others in the development of that program.

Who Determines Educational Objectives?

We may now turn briefly to the third major problem to be faced in connection with the determination of objectives, namely, the question of who is to assume responsibility for the tasks that have been thus far described. Implicit throughout the discussion thus far is the notion that society in general, parents, pupils, as well as professional educators, all have a considerable stake in the answers to the questions that have been raised.

The representatives of society, the state and the local school boards, are the legally constituted authorities charged with the responsibility of providing an adequate education for youth. Generally this responsibility is discharged through setting down quite broad limits within which the schools are to operate, although state legislation sometimes makes very specific requirements. Recent years have seen an intensification of interest in the objectives of the school on the part of extralegal but, nonetheless, influential organizations. Such organizations may function at the national, state and local levels. Parent groups and citizens groups are examples of organizations at the local level that are quite properly concerned with the objectives of education in their respective communities.

The legally constituted agencies can and must give careful consideration to the *general* character of the education to be provided for youth. The extralegal agencies can and should do likewise. It is becoming increasingly apparent that both kinds of groups are speaking to this point, often with many voices. Whether they do so in a way that is calculated to make the schools a servant of special interest groups, or in a way that takes the broader view of the interests of the whole of society, should depend upon the nature and extent of the information used as a basis for decision. One of the very real services of the professional educator—administrator, teacher, curriculum worker, guidance counselor—to society is that of providing accurate data and informed judgments upon which to rely when broad questions of educational policy are being considered.

Within the broad limits thus established, however, there can be little doubt but that the responsibility for deriving and formulating objectives and for building an instructional program consistent with those objectives rests with the professional educator. This is not to say that the professional staff will not need to counsel frequently with nonprofessional groups in order to make a continuous check upon the validity of its basic decisions. The point at which these decisions are directly implemented, however, is the classroom. In a very real sense, therefore, the classroom teacher is the key person in this whole process. He, more than any other one person, is in a crucial position to translate the school's educational objectives into appropriate instructional goals in his own classroom. As was pointed out in Chapter I, it is he who will have to work out the details of the solution to the problem of developing an instructional program sufficiently flexible to insure "a good fit" with the purposes, interests, needs and capacities of each of his pupils.

While recognizing that the teacher is central in the dynamic process of developing a sound program of classroom instruction and guidance, it is necessary to realize also that he is by no means expected to undertake this responsibility alone. The very nature of the tasks outlined in the preceding pages indicates clearly that the demands are such that no individual could hope to meet them without extensive aid from others. Moreover, it is very likely that the most important objectives identified through the processes described will be ones which can be achieved in appreciable amounts only over a period of years. The learning that goes on in any particular classroom will be profoundly affected by what has gone on previously and ought to take into account learning opportunities likely to be available in subsequent years. It is perfectly clear, therefore, that the task of determining objectives is one that *requires* cooperation and shared responsibility. Cooperative activity is not merely desirable in this case. It is essential.

Few people would admit that the development of an instructional program should be regarded as an end in itself. Yet our practices often make it appear that such is the case. We often engage in child study without ever asking explicitly what implications such study holds for matters pertaining to instruction. We set up elaborate organizational arrangements for something called "guidance" without ever asking how the activities carried on there could or should be related to the on-going program of instruction. We sometimes are able to identify problems with obvious implications for the classroom (such as those relating to drop-outs or irregular attendance) and then say, "That is a problem for the counselor or the Child Study Department to consider." Staff members thus often expect that the specialized guidance personnel will not only consider the problem but that they will also deal with it in such a way as to lessen its importance and thus remove one more source of frustration for the classroom teacher. These and other practices seem well calculated to maintain a separation between guidance and instruction. They tend to confirm the suspicion that guidance and instructional activities are often very close to being regarded as ends in themselves.

One way of giving emphasis to the integral relationship between guidance and instruction, and to the fact that neither can be properly viewed as an end in itself, is to analyze in some detail the major instructional tasks. In this chapter we have tried to do just this with reference to the instructional task of determining objectives.

We have seen that the determination of objectives is no simple task. We have seen that it involves broad questions of social and educational policy. We have seen that the staff of a school must develop a sensitivity both to the demands of society and to the needs of individual pupils. We have seen that the determination of objectives requires cooperative effort. This cooperation will, at different points and for different purposes, involve the professional staff of the school and various interested nonprofessional groups, teachers of different subjects and grade levels, teachers and guidance specialists, teachers and parents, teachers and pupils.

The classroom teacher is central in all this activity, for it is in the classroom that the instructional program designed to achieve these objectives takes its ultimate form. It is there that we see the extent to which the objectives are in fact selected so that individual boys and girls may meet both their personal needs and the expectations of society. When this happens we can be relatively certain that guidance and instruction are viewed as inseparable.

To test further the validity of this conception of the relationship between guidance and instruction we turn in the next chapter to an analysis of another important instructional task—the selection and evaluation of learning experiences.

CHAPTER IV

Selecting and Evaluating
Learning Experiences

T HE preceding chapter has stressed the fact that, for instruction to be inseparable from guidance, learning objectives must stem from needs of children—needs which relate to the social demands made upon them as well as to the interests, desires and capabilities of the boys and girls themselves. Certain purposes and goals are important for *all* children, others are common to those of a given developmental level, and still others relate to the special needs 'of each youngster. For effective learning to take place, all of these goals and purposes must be accepted by the learner as objectives which are important in his own life.

Defining Learning Experiences

We usually think of learning experiences as the means by which an educational objective is gained. There is, of course, no clear-cut separation of means from ends or of learning experiences from goals. If a sixth grade girl says, "I want to make a cake," and thereupon sets about the activity of making a cake, it is hard to separate goal from learning experience. If, however, she says, "I want to learn how to cook" and bakes a cake in the process, this learning experience is one of many which advance her toward her goal. For purposes of this chapter we will think of a goal or objective as sufficiently generalized and long-range to demand a variety of learning experiences for its achievement.

To define "learning experience" further, we can say that it is the reaction or the response which an individual makes to an environmental situation of which he is a part. What appears to be the same classroom situation or learning activity is "internalized" in a somewhat different way by each individual who is exposed to it.

What each actually *experiences* depends upon the lifetime of previous experiences he brings to it, as well as his particular pattern of physiological and mental characteristics. A learning experience, therefore, is in actuality a highly individualized thing. While in common educational parlance we speak of a "learning experience" as building the grocery store or participating in the panel discussion or doing the arithmetic problems, these are, actually, the activities from which accrue as many different learning experiences as there are pupils in the classroom. The *reactions* of the pupil to such things as the books he reads, the music he hears, the places he visits, the children with whom he associates, the ideas he thinks about, the objects he creates with his hands, the disciplinary methods he experiences at the hands of his teacher—ad infinitum—constitute *his* learning experiences.

How This Guidance Philosophy Influences the Selection of Learning Activities

This chapter is concerned with the learning opportunities which the teacher makes available to children. Does the fact that the teacher feels, or fails to feel, that one of his most important functions is the guidance of individual boys and girls make a difference in the learning experiences he provides? The writers of this yearbook are quite sure that it does. A teacher who integrates guidance with his classroom teaching is oriented primarily with reference to individual children and knows that whatever the content of his subject field or fields happens to be, the child will learn this content only if the approach used is congenial to him.

The teacher knows that there are many ways to encourage growth toward a given academic objective and that different children will find it profitable to take different routes. On the other hand, a teacher who considers the adjustment problems of individual children solely the concern of a specialist is primarily oriented with reference to the content of the course of study and tends to assume that all the children in his classroom can be given essentially the same learning tasks. In the first instance the teacher is much more flexible than in the second, because he is convinced that the state of mind of a given child, compounded as it is of his feelings, his attitudes, his physical energy and his capacities, has a tremendous effect upon his acceptance of the things the teacher—and in back of him the school and the society—thinks should be taught.

What the Principles of Learning Imply for Guidance

First of all, the teacher who incorporates guidance in his class-room teaching provides learning experiences in harmony with what he knows about how learning takes place. In the following pages some of the implications of certain principles of learning for guidance and teaching as related functions are briefly reviewed.

Learning takes place more readily if the child accepts as useful and important to him the activities in which he is expected to engage. Teachers cannot put this principle into classroom practice unless they are well-grounded in the developmental needs of children at various age levels and unless they know enough about each child to make intelligent guesses concerning the kinds of experiences in which each will find personal significance and meaning. In line with this principle, a teacher who makes instruction inseparable from guidance provides a range of activities which will meet the varied individual needs of his pupils and helps them develop genuine feelings of need for the knowledge, skills and values required to meet societal expectations.

In some classrooms more time and care on the part of the teacher should undoubtedly be given to the applications of learning to practical life situations within a setting with which the youngsters can identify themselves. It would be interesting for a teacher regularly to ask his pupils what they have learned during this day or this week, or in this unit or project which they feel they can really use; and what they have learned for which they can see little or no use. Such direct evaluation might help the teacher see how to bring meaning to things that children do not seem to feel are important to them, and to face the problem of whether some activities might be substituted for others of more significance to the children in question.

A child's learning is both richer and easier if he shares in selecting and setting the goals of learning, in planning ways to gain them, and in measuring his own progress toward them. There is no better insurance that a child will accept a learning activity as important in his life than to involve him in selecting the goals toward which he and his group should be striving, and to encourage him to think about the kinds of activities which will help him gain these objectives. If he is also involved in "taking stock" of himself at appropriate intervals, his experience relative to any given unit of work is four-fold. He gains experience in deciding what, in the light of his own needs and the needs of his group, it is important to "shoot for"; he gains further experience in logical and versatile thinking as he considers the range and variety of activities appropriate for the intended purpose, and in exercising choice between alternatives; his background is enriched through participation in various aspects of the activities he has had a share in selecting; and, finally, he gains in critical thinking and in self-knowledge as he attempts to analyze the variety of experiences he has gained, the level of success he has achieved, and the next steps which seem appropriate for him.

All of these aspects of learning are guided by the wise teacher. The simplicity or complexity of the situation with which the teacher encourages the youngsters to deal depends upon their maturity and their previous experience in planning and evaluating their own activities. There are few school children who are too young, however, to accept some responsibility of this kind.

In a subject centered situation where the teacher typically sets the goal, gives the assignment, grades the papers and issues the marks, the child is not only denied three-fourths of the total learning opportunity but the one-fourth reserved to him is likely to be achieved less efficiently and well since the goal and the methods have been superimposed. Not only is learning less efficient and less rich but such a situation reflects a teacher-pupil relationship in which an essential guidance ingredient appears to be missing. The teacher who guides as he teaches shows his basic respect for boys and girls, his faith in the worth of their ideas, and his confidence in their growing capacity for exercising independent judgment and choice by providing opportunities for his pupils to become progressively more self-directive. Where such opportunities do not exist we have a paternalistic rather than a guidance relationship between teacher and pupil. Paternalism breeds either dependence or resentment or both and is antithetical to the objectives for which guidance strives. A teacher who is striving to relate instruction to guidance in the application of this principle may want to check up on himself occasionally by asking, "How much of the 'doing' did I do today as contrasted with what the pupils did? Might their experiences have been richer if I had shared with them more generously the jobs of goal-setting, planning and evaluating?"

A child learns to solve his life problems—some of which he cannot now anticipate—only to the degree that he is capable of understanding himself and directing his own actions. This proposition

is a derivative of the principle which precedes it. It deserves separate
analysis because it touches upon the whole problem of the evaluation of learning experience.

The major objective of guidance, as indeed of education itself,
is to help each individual to face confidently and to solve intelligently his persisting life problems. The form in which these are
likely to appear cannot always be anticipated. For this reason it
is important to encourage growing boys and girls to become self-
directive. Teachers and counselors would like to help them know
how to choose wisely between alternative courses of action and to
make suitable plans for their own lives. Such intelligent self-direction, however, stems from self-understanding—from fair recognition by the individual of what he can and cannot do, of the progress
he has made to date and the next steps he needs to take. His
knowledge of himself must be far broader than that which relates
to his academic achievement. He must learn to understand himself
as a member of his family, as a friend and companion with his own
peers, and as a worker and cooperator in a wide range of activities
which call for different personal skills. He must gradually gain insight into how such things as his health, his appearance, his character traits and his social adjustment serve to help or hinder him
in gaining his goals.

Growth in self-understanding is progressively achieved through
guided experience in sizing up one's self in many different situations which demand the display of different skills. It is not achieved
in school solely through a monthly or quarterly teacher's estimate
as entered on a report card. In fact, most report card entries do not
contribute much to self-enlightenment. Neither is much development in self-understanding gained from the teacher's grades on
arithmetic papers or English themes. Often such teacher evaluations precipitate no analytical thinking on the part of the pupil
but are merely passively or gleefully or resentfully accepted as
something handed out to him by a teacher-judge. All of this is to
say that the learning experiences gained from evaluation of this
kind may actually be harmful since they may encourage the youngster to shift responsibility and to rationalize his deficiencies. Marks
and grades also may tend to distract him from his major objectives.
It might prove interesting to a teacher consciously to observe the
expressions on the faces of the youngsters at the time he returns a
set of papers or issues the report cards. How many of these boys and
girls respond to their marks with disappointment, elation or a

"don't care" attitude? How many seem genuinely to be stimulated to find out what their present difficulties are and what they can do about them?

Experiences which help the child size himself up with fairness and frankness are, however, important to encourage, and such evaluation should be an on-going aspect of every learning activity. This presupposes classroom and out-of-class situations in which at appropriate intervals a wise teacher helps boys and girls talk about and think about, first what it is important for them to be learning and doing, and then how well or poorly they seem to be progressing with reference to quite specific goals. For a second grade teacher, for example, to take time to discuss with the children such a question as "How are we getting along with our mural?" encourages analytical thinking at an appropriate, second grade level. One child may say, "We get in each other's way. We could do better if some of us worked at our seats while a few worked on the mural." A second may comment that the children are sharing the equipment nicely; or a third may say, "The roof on the schoolhouse looks funny." Using such comments as a point of departure, the teacher can guide a discussion about both the children's methods of work and the quality of the product they are turning out. The children thus participate in one more experience in thoughtful consideration of the measure of their success thus far, and the improvements or shift of emphasis which should be made from this point on.

As the children become older they are able to analyze the results of their efforts on a more mature level and to consider a wider range of factors which might relate to their success or failure. But, whether in the kindergarten or the senior high school, every youngster, at his own developmental level, can and should share with his teacher the task of appraising his own progress.

As with any good principle of learning, guidance in self-evaluation is not foolproof. Seeing himself with all his inadequacies and limitations may be a shattering experience for a person who is not psychologically ready to accept, to evaluate and to learn from what he sees. A sensitive teacher perceives how much a given child is able to "take" in self-revelation without undermining his basic self-assurance. Such a teacher helps each child set standards which are reasonable for him in light of what the teacher can discover about his capacities and his background of experience. Thus the child is encouraged to measure himself against a yardstick which helps to assure acceptable progress and growth. With such a growing backlog of successful experience, the youngster is better able to compare himself with others and to accept the fact that there are some things he cannot do because he is confident of certain things he *can* do.

When we recognize how many children are handicapped by physical defects or by socially deprived homes and neighborhoods, or by I.Q.'s below ninety, we begin to appreciate how important is the guidance role of the teacher in helping each child balance off his liabilities against his assets in a manner that will help him lay plans commensurate with what he can successfully achieve and at the same time preserve and strengthen his self-esteem. With those whose physical and social and intellectual gifts may be many, the challenge to the teacher is no less great. Here self-appraisal involves helping the child set goals which are challenging to his superior talents while guiding him to respect others and to develop perspective regarding the social importance of everyone's positive contribution.

Learning is more efficient if it has satisfying emotional content— if feeling is supportive of thinking. One way of providing satisfying emotional content is to gear learning to the interests of children. Unfortunately there are still many classrooms in our elementary and secondary schools which are woefully drab—if not for the whole class, certainly for some members of the class. The reader may recall the film *The Drop Out* picturing classroom scenes where there was no fun, no excitement, nothing to stir the imagination or tingle the blood of Steve Mitchell.[1] He was left untouched by any wholesome emotion. In consequence, there developed the destructive feelings of discouragement, distrust and failure which were sufficient in his case to cause him to drop out of school. The teachers of Steve's classes appeared to ignore the differing interests of the boys and girls, and failed to arouse to any significant degree their sympathy, their sense of humor, their loyalty, their righteous indignation or any of the other feelings which bring meaning to the things being learned. As Nathaniel Cantor said in reflecting upon some common teaching methods, "High school students must acquire knowledge of a sort to pass the subjects before being certified for graduation. They possess facts. The facts, however, do not 'possess' them."[2]

---

[1] Problems of Pupil Adjustment—*The Drop Out.* New York: McGraw-Hill Films.
[2] Nathaniel F. Cantor. *The Dynamics of Learning.* Buffalo, New York: Foster and Stewart Publishing Co., 1946. p. 19.

A teacher who integrates guidance with his teaching is not primarily interested in whether the children can pass a given examination, but rather that what they learn is linked with sufficient concern and interest to be applied to life situations outside as well as inside the school environment. School learning is for the purpose of changing people, and for this to happen in approved directions children must be stirred "where they live." Major reliance on the bookish and highly verbal approach to learning will fail to elicit constructive emotional responses from many boys and girls and thus fail to achieve the guidance purpose of meeting pupil needs.

Firsthand experience makes a deeper impression upon a person than vicarious experience. Active involvement in an activity is almost certain to provide the emotional content which we have been stressing as an important ingredient of a learning experience. It is much more fun, as well as more instructive, to make a tallow candle than merely to read about the process, or to hold a sham meeting of the United Nations Security Council than merely to describe it as reported in the social studies textbook. Pupils feel a much greater urgency to obey the traffic rules when the officer takes them to the intersection and demonstrates how to cross safely than they do when the teacher merely tells them what the safety rules are. There is much more appreciation on the part of young people for the beauty and cleanliness of the city park if they have had a share in planting the flower beds and in deciding where the refuse containers should be placed than if they have merely read a chapter in the civics book on "City Parks and Playgrounds."

It is, of course, undesirable to carry the idea of increasing firsthand experience too far. The accumulated wisdom of the ages is handed down to boys and girls through books. Young people, moreover, are able to identify themselves with people beyond their face-to-face contacts, and eventually to show concern for problems larger than those they can solve at firsthand, only through using second- and third-hand sources such as the newspaper and radio. The reading, listening, writing about, reciting and discussing which constitute the typical classroom activities are themselves firsthand experiences for learning *how* to do these things. These experiences are vicarious, however, with respect to *what* is being read or talked about. The inclusion of these vicarious experiences is, of course, amply justified, especially where such experiences serve to symbolize firsthand experience and to develop general concepts. The proportion of emphasis typically given to them which may deny other equally important activities is, however, open to question. In many classrooms more opportunity could well be provided for boys and girls to learn through selecting, experimenting, collecting, surveying, constructing, role playing, putting theory into practice, participating in solving school and community problems, and expressing creative ideas through various art media.

Learning-by-doing makes life itself the learning laboratory and is therefore an important principle for guidance as well as for teaching. Teachers who provide a range of firsthand experiences for boys and girls and show them how these embody mathematical or scientific principles, or how they grow out of historical background, or whatever the relationship may be, give children and young people opportunity to develop skills and to try themselves out in situations which will have counterparts in their own lives.

Learning is facilitated and reinforced when more than one sensory approach is used. Any good scientist who wants to learn all he can about a substance employs every possible method of investigation of sound, sight, feel, taste and smell. Infants approach the task of learning their environment in much the same manner. The rattle not only gets seen and heard but manipulated and mouthed. This multiple approach to learning is no less important in the classroom. Animals and plants for the children to observe and care for, laboratory equipment to experiment with, films, field trips, radio and television programs for visual and auditory experiences—such activities, with the reading and writing and discussion which normally accompany them, insure more lasting impressions than any single approach.

From a guidance point of view this is an important learning principle because its application makes provision for children's widely differing sensory acuities and especially for youngsters who are handicapped by a sensory defect. In colloquial terms we speak of people as being eye-minded, or ear-minded, or hand-minded. Some children may have difficulty in getting the idea of how a gadget works by reading about it, but if they can handle it—take it apart and put it together and make it work—real understanding develops. Some youngsters may have trouble following verbal directions but if these are written on the chalk board or, better still, if the teacher demonstrates the process while the children observe, the chances for successful learning are enhanced.

This principle of learning ties in closely with the one previously discussed. Observing, listening, tasting, smelling, manipulating are the firsthand experiences which provide a foundation for logical thinking and for intelligent behavior. In a very real manner, they relate learning to life.

A child learns best when he is relieved of too great pressure to compete and when he feels reasonably confident that he can accomplish what is expected of him. It is probably fair to say that much of the primary motivation of children for their school tasks relates to their struggle to pass the test, to be promoted to the next grade, to beat out a close competitor or to win a coveted award. While we do not advocate the elimination of the kind of competition which provides wholesome incentive and adds zest and challenge to a learning situation, it is important to understand and avoid the damaging consequences of over-competitiveness. According to psychologists the effects of many aspects of school competition are more devastating than teachers realize.[3]

Competition between individuals, of course, assumes a single standard of achievement and behavior, which serves to deny individual differences and conflicts with the guidance philosophy. One unfortunate result affects all children except "the top man" by giving even the next to the best a feeling that he has fallen below what he wanted to achieve and hence has failed in his own estimation. From among children less capable than those in the upper one-half of the class, a considerable proportion will experience such persistent feelings of failure as to invade the nonacademic aspects of their lives with similar feelings and thus to handicap adequate performance in activities involved in normal human relations. As indicated in the second chapter, a child who holds a mental image of himself as a failure cannot face the problems of life with the zest and assurance needed to release the best of his creative talents. The inhibitions and frustrations of people who, through failure to compete successfully, have been taught again and again that they are just not as good as the people they want to be like result in an appalling waste of human resources.

Too great emphasis upon competition does other damage as well. Individuals behave in harmony with that which they value most. By employing competitive practices teachers are placing premium value upon grades, honors and awards, and in effect are saying to children that the sacrifice of other values for these ends is fully justified. Emphasis upon beating out the other fellow re-

[3] Donald Snygg and Arthur W. Combs. *Individual Behavior.* New York: Harper and Brothers, 1949. p. 223.

flects an orientation to life which is primarily self-centered. This handicaps children's learning of the attitude which perhaps is more important in a democracy than any other—namely, sensitive understanding of and respect for others. Through establishing a single standard toward which to strive, teachers encourage children to view one another in terms of their success or failure related to this standard and to accept or reject each on the basis of a grossly oversimplified measure of worthiness.

To prepare children for effective participation in democratic group living, the teacher who integrates guidance with his classroom teaching accepts as one of his solemn obligations that of helping children learn that every individual is worthy of respect whether academic work proves difficult or easy for him, and that, while people possess different talents, all are capable of contributing to the group something that it needs. In a school situation in which learning tasks are diversified to suit the level and kind of capacity of each youngster and in which emphasis is placed upon progress and growth toward an individual objective reasonable of attainment, the need to compete is relaxed and the possibility of persistent feelings of failure minimized. Moreover, a child who accepts himself as a reasonably successful individual with respect to the things he sets out to do, and at the same time observes others who are likewise reasonably successful in doing a range of different things, some of which he cannot do nearly so well, is psychologically able to respect other people and to appreciate the importance of everyone's social contribution. His own ambition to improve is in no way pitted against the other fellow's similar effort to succeed.

A child learns best when his failures are viewed constructively by a teacher who likes and respects him, and when appropriate remedial or corrective measures are worked out with him. To say that children should feel reasonably confident that they can accomplish what is expected of them is not to recommend a school environment devoid of the possibility of failure. In a world as uncertain as ours where, for psychological survival, we must develop resilience to such crises as loss of job, family separation or other personal tragedy, boys and girls deserve help in learning how to face failure by experiencing occasional failure. The toughening up process by which these youngsters develop the personal philosophy and the qualities needed to respond constructively to unhappiness and failure can proceed, however, only if such failure is viewed by the individual against a lifetime of experiences in which he has been reasonably successful most of the time. Moreover, for the child to incorporate failure into the warp and woof of his total life pattern in such a way that it strengthens the fibre and enriches the design there must be interpretation and help from a wise and accepting adult.

One of the finest contributions which a guidance-minded teacher can make to the wholesome growth of boys and girls is to guide them as groups and as individuals to gain experience in seeing what their mistakes are, why they are making them, and how they can overcome similar difficulties in the future.

Failure may stem from unfortunate past experience, or from limited capacity or from both. Where experience has been limited or at fault, the teacher, with the help of the cumulative record and the other teachers and the child himself, is challenged to make a careful analysis of the factors which relate to the failing situation and to devise with the child reasonable steps he might take to solve his problem. Where the child is failing in something in which there seems little likelihood of success, then, without "slamming doors," the teacher may need to help the child substitute other learning experiences from which he can derive some personal pride in accomplishment.

Failure for the child, of course, may relate not only to academic work but to his social behavior. This principle of learning, therefore, has implications for the handling of so-called disciplinary problems. The manner in which a child is disciplined is a learning experience for him. On the one hand, an inflicted and unaccepted penalty may bring with it such an avalanche of unwholesome feelings of bitterness and antagonism or fear and guilt as to far outweigh in disastrous consequences any good resulting to the child from "taking his medicine." On the other hand, a self-chosen or -accepted penalty may be experienced by the child with increased respect both for himself and for the teacher who helped him think his way through the problem.

The success of the teacher in providing this latter kind of constructive learning experience relates to his genuine regard for each child as a human being and to his capacity to separate the child whom he respects from his behavior which he condemns. If the teacher never questions in his heart that John is just as appalled and concerned by his own behavior as is the teacher, and that John is just as anxious to find a way out of the mess he is in as the teacher is eager to help him, John's failure can become a constructive learning experience.

Attitudes, feelings, values and appreciations are learned no less than knowledge and skill are learned. Every experience involves a constellation of such learnings. While this particular principle of learning has been rather fully discussed in the second chapter, it is of such primary importance for any teacher who integrates guidance with his teaching that some additional comments may be justified. A good teacher is not so much interested in what a child knows as in how he uses his knowledge or, in other words, how he behaves. Actually the child's behavior—which is likewise learned—is a translation not only of the facts and skills he possesses but of the feelings and values he gained in the process of learning these things. As a child learns the facts about conservation practices in his state, or the skills involved in changing fractions to decimals, he is also learning certain allegiances and refusals of both people and ideas. He is learning to be conscientious about some things and to neglect others. He is learning to fear, to hate, to cherish, to persist against all odds or to capitulate in the face of obstacles. He learns courtesy, self-control, honesty, cooperation, courage or their opposites while he is learning the things which we normally talk about as comprising the content of the school curriculum.

It is dangerous, therefore, for teachers to be so preoccupied with the academic aspects of learning as to be blind to the other things a child is learning along the way. A youngster's attitudes and values are far more potent in influencing his way of life than any given body of academic content. If the classroom situation encourages unwholesome learning in these areas, no amount of subject mastery will offset the corroding effects upon the psychological and social adjustment of the boy or girl concerned.

For learning experiences to have a total constructive effect upon each child, the teacher must plan carefully with respect to as many facets of a learning situation as he can envision. He must likewise be attentive, as the learning activity progresses, to observe the boys and girls as they work, for evidences of frustrations, antagonisms or other unwholesome factors. By adjusting his own methods and approaches and by assisting the child to alter his goal or change his techniques to achieve his purpose, the teacher helps insure the total learning activity as a constructive experience.

A child learns best when his efforts are appreciated by his teacher and his classmates. There is no difficulty in perceiving the guidance implications of this principle of learning. As was indicated earlier, a child's success in both the academic and nonacademic aspects of school learning is, in large measure, contingent upon the state of his mental health. To give conscientious attention to a school task, the pupil must feel right about himself. One of the best ways to develop such ego-satisfaction is to assure each youngster that he is accepted by his group as a contributing member. Under circumstances in which the range of learning opportunities is narrow and is comprised largely of tasks geared to a level of achievement at or above that which is reasonable for the typical youngster, there are certain to be children who are not involved in classroom learning in any real sense and who, therefore, cannot receive the recognition from which personal security stems.

A teacher who integrates guidance with his classroom teaching accepts the responsibility for finding appropriate ways for every child to gain some recognition from his peers. For the least intelligent child, the most retiring, the clumsiest, the untidiest, the most handicapped physically and even for the child whose behavior may be most irritating, the teacher must somehow contrive to provide opportunities for participation so that each may receive appreciation from those with whom he wants to become identified. If the child belongs to his group in this psychological sense, the chances for his success in school learning are vastly enhanced. Moreover, greater success in this area of his life will, in turn, encourage him to make a forthright attack as well upon other life problems which may confront him.

A child learns best when he is freed from the distractions of personal problems. There are, of course, many factors other than his success in gaining the recognition of his classmates which relate to a child's personal adjustment. Any situation in his life which causes divided attention will reduce his efficiency in learning. Although his parents hold a far more strategic position and exercise a far more pervasive influence in the child's life than his teachers, nevertheless there is much that the teacher might do to observe evidences of personal difficulty and to attempt to discover what may be the sore spots in the child's relations with his family or his gang. Especially if parents and teachers can work as partners will the child's needs be more readily discovered and better served.

With the burden of work which falls upon a conscientious teacher today, the suggestion that he should become acquainted with the homes and parents of his pupils, and that he should know something as well about each child's friends and activities within the community, is sometimes dismissed as quite impractical. The authors of this yearbook feel, however, that to spend time in identifying individual needs is an intensely practical goal toward which to strive. There is no disagreement with the contention that the teacher always seems to have more to do than he can handle satisfactorily. He is constantly forced to decide which of a number of ways of expending his energies is most important for the welfare of the children he is trying to guide and to teach. Teachers would probably agree that the major wear and tear of the profession comes from the teacher-frustrations involved in attempting to persuade Betty and Jim to learn when they just cannot seem to make progress, and in trying to get Sue and Paul to behave in ways that will allow them to make progress.

Most of the cajoling, coercing and enticing with reference to an academic objective is done on the basis of too superficial a knowledge of the motives underlying a child's behavior and of the situations in his life which are distracting him from the job at hand. The expenditure of time by the teacher in acquainting himself with the potential or actual problem areas in a child's background will usually pay high dividends in future time- and energy-saving. There seems to be no short cut to understanding a child, yet it is only in terms of such understanding that a teacher can help the child clear away some of the emotional debris which may be blocking his progress.

A child learns best when the rhythm of mental activity, physical activity and relaxation is appropriate for him. A youngster who is fatigued cannot do his best work in school. Often such fatigue stems from faulty organization and management of his classroom. In a classroom situation in which order and quietness are held up as supreme virtues, many children are placed under tension as they attempt to conform to adult standards of control. Such tension takes its toll in fatigue and may eventually lead to an "explosion" which exceeds the limits of approved behavior. At the other extreme, the wear and tear on children who are in a classroom characterized by confusion and disorganization result in fatigue as great as the situation where enforced quiet is maintained.

A teacher who considers the needs of each child with reference to an appropriate balance of rest and activity is able to strike a happy medium between the two extremes described above. Without relinquishing his consistent control of the classroom situation, he can permit sufficient freedom and flexibility to provide adequately for variability. The teacher who acknowledges his guidance responsibility appreciates that each youngster represents a somewhat different energy pattern and needs a somewhat different amount and kind of activity on the one hand, and of relaxation and rest on the other. He will therefore permit the overactive child to get an occasional drink of water and take a walk down the corridor as ways of relieving tension. He will not feel disturbed when one youngster takes more time than another to rest and relax, even perhaps in somewhat unorthodox ways. The eighth grade boy, for example, who is regarded as "lazy" by an unperceptive teacher may actually be fatigued rather than lazy. Perhaps because of the rapidity of his growth or the load of chores he is doing at home he may be in compelling need of a rest period even at such an inauspicious hour as ten o'clock in the morning. If he takes his rest by slouching in his seat and sprawling his legs across the aisle, the wise teacher usually tries not to make an issue of it.

Teachers who guide children as they teach them also attempt to alternate periods of relatively quiet mental concentration with opportunities for some freedom to move about, to converse in small groups, and to engage in construction or art work of one kind or another.

Flexible seating arrangements, midmorning snacks, designated rest periods and recesses, and a daily schedule to permit sufficient time at noon and between classes for a change of pace and scene are some of the ways to help insure an appropriate balance of rest and activity for boys and girls. In general, teachers of the younger children appreciate the need for such variety and plan for it more effectively than do teachers at higher grade levels. It is in the classrooms of many junior and senior high schools, especially, that overemphasis upon the conventionalities of order and quiet needs to be relaxed in favor of a wise permissiveness and of greater variety in learning activities. It is important to remember that the child does not take "time out" to rest and exercise. The relaxation and bodily activity permitted by the teacher are as much a part of the child's learning as his intellectual activities. If the balance is appropriate for a given child, each aspect of his learning will serve to reinforce the others.

Learning opportunities are richer for children when they are not restricted to the things which the teacher already knows. Historically the conventional role of the teacher has been that of information-giver. In the classroom of such a teacher where the respect of his pupils is contingent upon his ability to supply the answers, it behooves him to discourage embarrassing questions— questions which may involve loss of face if he fails to have on the tip of his tongue the information required. If the pupils feel that the teacher should be the authoritative source of information and if his personal security rests upon knowing the answers, there is little likelihood that he will encourage wide reading in references with which he may be unfamiliar or that he will allow the pupils to stray very far afield into the investigative aspects of learning. The classroom diet for children is bound to be restricted in situations in which the teacher plays such a role.

As emphasis upon the mastery of predetermined subject content is reduced, and as greater attention is given to providing a range of firsthand experiences which correspond to pupil needs, the teacher's role as information-giver will become less important. This does not imply, of course, need for less background on the part of the teacher. In fact, to do an adequate job of applying the principles discussed in this chapter the teacher needs, in addition to competence in his own field, sufficient breadth of general background to understand how his subject matter relates to other areas and to know how to help his pupils take advantage of learning situations which utilize knowledge and skill from more than one subject field.

The practical problems of living with which boys and girls need firsthand experience are no respecter of subjects. While the major part of a given learning problem may, for example, utilize geometry for its solution, if it is applied in a practical situation it is almost certain to impinge upon and draw from such other subjects as English, the social studies, science and practical arts. Teachers who would provide boys and girls with opportunities for learning which are as rich as possible will not circumscribe the learning situation by limiting the activities to those which represent their own area of greatest subject competence.

The type of background needed by teachers, however, is not of the encyclopedic variety. Facts and figures and other precise information encompassing a number of subject areas would, for most capable teachers, be both impossible and unnecessary. If the teacher is a generally well-informed person, his acquaintanceship with fields related to his own will be sufficient to enable him to see opportunities for pupil investigation and to give boys and girls some assistance concerning where to go to find the solution to problems which neither he nor the youngsters may now be able to resolve.

In a classroom situation in which the teacher is a learner along with his students and in which the where-do-we-go-to-find-out approach is employed, a rich learning situation is certain to prevail. Moreover, such an approach identifies the teacher as a team worker as well as a resource person, and is evidence of his faith in cooperative effort and of his willingness to carry his share of the load. Such a relationship encourages boys and girls to be frank about what they don't know, just as the teacher has been frank with them on this score. The likelihood is that they will also be frank with the teacher about more personal problems which baffle them, feeling that the teacher will work with them in seeking an acceptable solution. From the standpoint of guidance, the quality of this personal relationship between teacher and pupil is, of course, of supreme importance.

How Learning Experiences Are Varied
To Meet Individual Needs

To put these principles of learning to work with a class group requires a combination of techniques in which teachers should be skilled. Where ostensibly the same experience is engaged in by all youngsters in a given classroom, such as reading a chapter in the geography book or writing a newspaper account of the football game, the teacher who guides as he teaches sets a somewhat different level of expectation for each individual in the light of what he knows of the child's special excellence on the one hand or special problems on the other. Some of the children will be able to do the job more rapidly than others; some will show more insight and imagination than others; some will comprehend more clearly and engage in higher levels of critical thinking than others.

In evaluating the efforts of each pupil the teacher will take these and other similar factors into account and will also consider the type of motivation to which each child will respond most constructively. He will not blatantly underline every spelling error in red if he is sensitively aware that the discouragement involved for a particular child will interfere with a positive approach to his spelling problem. The teacher's comments and suggestions will be phrased in each case with reference to what he knows will encourage the youngster in question to make progress. He will follow up Jim's contribution to the class discussion with a suggestion that he do further reading and try to dig below the surface of the question. With Paul, who perhaps is even more superficial in his comments, he will show only appreciation, recognizing that this child's contribution represents his maximum effort. With one youngster the teacher will take time to point out evidence of even slight improvement; with another he may actually encourage feelings of dissatisfaction because he knows that for this child such an approach motivates him to set higher goals for himself and to mobilize his energies more effectively.

What appears to be the same initial learning experience, therefore, turns out to be a somewhat different experience for each individual largely because of the way the teacher adjusts his expectations, modifies his attitude and varies his approach to harmonize with what he knows about the individual pupil.

It is often unnecessary—and even inadvisable—to have the learning experience appear initially to be the same for all youngsters. Suppose, for example, that a group of sophomores taking European History is about to begin a study of the Industrial Revolution. If a reasonably good library is available, the teacher may encourage each pupil to read a different account of the subject from a list of books and chapters he might recommend. He may supplement this general assignment by suggesting to the slow reader an especially good book for him, and for the mature reader and thinker a reference which would offer him a real challenge.

The discussions and plans which grow out of this type of differentiated reading assignment are far richer in opportunities for learning than when all are drawing upon the same textbook as their source of information. This is a way for boys and girls to see that historians put stress on different things and that sometimes their interpretations also differ. Of much more significance is the importance which attaches to each child's contribution. Rather than reciting on material which everybody who did his lesson knows anyway, and from which he can gain no feeling of personal accomplishment, the pupil now can make his own unique contribution and receive genuine recognition from his peers.

The teacher who has taken the trouble to gather together a shelf of European history books, and who has perused these sufficiently to know what to recommend in the light of the various levels of intellectual maturity and reading skill represented in his group, can do a significant guidance job. He can make it possible for each pupil to experience a feeling of successful achievement and to make a place for himself in his group. He can encourage cooperative effort as the group pools ideas gleaned from different sources. He can make possible not only the learning of a broader array of historical facts; in addition, he can help his pupils gain an understanding of the possible limitations and biases of historical writing. If every youngster had read the same chapter from the same textbook, the learning outcomes would have been meager by comparison.

In the preceding example, although a range of reference material was used, the same general content was covered by all the pupils. There are many occasions when classroom activities can be further differentiated. In the kindergarten where growth in socialization and the development of oral language are two important purposes, the teacher generally finds little difficulty in controlling a situation in which thirty or more children are engaged in a variety of activities. Some may be building a firehouse for the "hook and ladder," each engaged in a different aspect of the job; others may be using crayons to express something they saw on the way to school, each having seen a different thing; still others may be carrying on imaginative play in the playhouse, each acting the part of a different member of the family. When all the kindergartners are seated together on the floor for their news period, the contributions to the conversation relate to the interests of each. Sally's news item is, "I have new pink socks," and she proudly displays them before the group. Billy has news too. "See my short haircut!" Madge tells the children that her Aunt Beth is visiting at her house; Gerth shows the group a jump rope he has brought to school and demonstrates how to use it and still be safe. The fun and freedom of this conversational period encourage learning because the various interests of children are recognized.

At the kindergarten level the teacher expects the children to express considerable individuality and understands that in a relatively free situation children will develop more rapidly and more wholesomely than they would were she to demand the same things of all children at the same time. For the kindergarten teacher, the guidance role is paramount. She is always considering these four and five year olds as individuals, observing the activities of each, encouraging, calming and explaining "why" to each child as he needs such help.

At upper grade levels and in the high school where subject content is more highly organized, it is also appropriate and possible to introduce greater diversity of activity within the class group than is often found. In modern industry the principle of division of labor is universally held. Each man contributes to the final product what, through intelligence and skill, he is best equipped to do. While the purposes of school learning are not the same as those of industry, nevertheless, within limits, the principle of division of labor has something to offer the teacher who is eager to integrate guidance with his classroom teaching.

Let us assume a sixth grade class is going to try to answer the question, "How can we make Milltown a better place to live in?" In the first place the teacher appreciates that this type of study lends itself to cutting across subject matter lines. He can help individual boys and girls develop skills and acquire knowledge in the fields of the social studies, the language arts, the fine arts and even, to a degree, the consumer aspects of science and mathematics. Since he is responsible for the school learning of this sixth grade group for almost the entire day, he can adjust his time schedule to permit temporary integration of two or three subject areas for purposes of this study. The teacher also sees that growth in cooperation, in social sensitivity to those beyond the face to face group, in appreciation for such qualities as beauty and justice, and in the development of basic values of daily living may also be achieved through such a study if activities are cooperatively selected and organized with reference to what they may contribute to the fundamental attitudes and ideals of the children concerned.

In the initial planning period many different approaches are suggested by these sixth grade boys and girls both for appraising the present assets and liabilities of the community and for discovering ways to remedy its weaknesses. There is the question of the health of the community which involves investigations in fields which run the gamut from proper inspection and handling of foods in community stores to safety regulations in Milltown's factories and on Milltown's highways, to building codes for fire protection and sanitation, to hospital and medical facilities for both the economically deprived and the financially able, to community-sponsored programs of diagnosis and immunization. There are also such areas to be explored as the opportunities for cultural enrichment available in Milltown, public and parochial educational facilities, labor-management policies, the wholesomeness of family life, each of which can be analyzed by the boys and girls into many subproblems.

Such a wide range of possibilities for research are brought forth by the class that they may see a necessity for limiting their study in terms of the number of weeks or months allocated to the unit. They also plan some order for attacking those aspects of community life which they have chosen to include. They then face the problem of how to parcel out responsibilities among the various members of the classroom group.

The teacher, of course, is a very important part of everything that is going on. Depending upon the versatility of the group and the freedom of its members to express their points of view, the teacher may suggest ideas for group consideration, or encourage a certain child in the group to contribute his idea when the teacher observes an eager expression but not quite the courage to volunteer. He may suggest places to go, people to see, and books and community surveys to read at points where his experience can add to the suggestions of the boys and girls. And, of course, the teacher is involved in a very important way when the jobs are allocated. Here his knowledge that Frank, aged eleven, with a mental age of fifteen, has a father who has been laid off at the plant, leads him to suggest that Frank might be interested in a study of unemployment problems in the town. The teacher refers him to background reading materials on a ninth and tenth grade level commensurate with his mental age. He likewise suggests that Frank work out a series of pertinent questions for use in interviewing two of the leading industrialists in the town. Two other boys of average intelligence offer to join Frank at the interviewing stage of the operation.

For Gertrude who is mentally retarded but who needs the socializing experience of the classroom, the teacher suggests keeping a clipping file of newspaper accounts of selected motion picture films, concerts, plays, art exhibits, hobby shows and the like as evidence of what the town offers in entertainment and cultural enrichment. Several other youngsters are encouraged to work with Gertrude. They are the ones who actually read the daily papers and mark the articles for Gertrude to clip. They help Gertrude with a classification scheme for the file. Another group of boys and girls who are interested in sports and other recreational hobbies study the recreational opportunities in the town. They locate on a map the public parks, beaches, playgrounds and the headquarters of the various Red Feather agencies which sponsor a recreational program. They divide the responsibility for visiting the head of each of these agencies to request printed material on the program of the organization and the type of service rendered by each. Just to see how some of the population *feel* about their town, everyone in the class agrees to interview three people on his street to find out what they like best about Milltown and what improvements they think ought to be made. They discuss how to hold an interview of this kind, how to phrase the questions and what the etiquette of the situation demands.

Such activities are, of course, only a beginning of the scores of interesting experiences which might be mentioned to show how individual differences can be considered by dividing responsibility for various aspects of a problem. Yet the authors of this yearbook have known of situations where "Our Community" was studied from a textbook of a similar title, where all the children were reading and writing and talking about very much the same things at the same time. They have known of situations where learning about the community actually extended very little beyond the walls of the classroom and failed to use the vast and rich resources which the citizens of the community would have been eager to contribute had they but been invited to do so.

In learning situations in which individual pupils have opportunities to choose the aspect of a problem they would like to investigate and to select the means they would like to use to gather and report their findings, the functions of guidance and instruction are so closely integrated that it is impossible to disengage them. To the outside visitor it might appear that the children are very much running their own show. And actually they *are* being accorded the respect and confidence of a teacher who believes that they have ideas worth expressing and that they are, without teacher imposition, capable of a constructive approach to problem solving. The teacher, however, though seemingly inconspicuous at times, is actually a very important factor in the situation. He is a resource person whose suggestions and help bring beneficial results because they are appropriate in light of the interests and special needs of each child. It may not be as easy to equate one child's accomplishment with that of another as it apparently is in a situation where all are doing much the same things. But the teacher who guides as he teaches is not as interested in comparisons as in how each individual is growing and in what progress along a number of different lines he is making. If the children, as individuals and as a group, have opportunity to figure out, with teacher guidance, where they want to go in the first place—what their goals and purposes are— and to "take stock" at appropriate intervals to see what progress they are making, the chances are that important academic skills and knowledge will also be learned. In addition, and as highly important extra dividends, the boys and girls will likewise have gained greater skill in problem solving, more independence in making intelligent decisions and, in general, will be more self-directive as they face the next, perhaps more difficult, problems.

Good Group Procedures Encourage Wholesome Learning

The range of activities recommended in the preceding pages cannot easily be engaged in if the classroom is permanently arranged so that pupils sit in straight rows facing the teacher and facing the backs of the other youngsters. The application of most of the principles of learning implies flexible classroom organization and some understanding of the dynamics of groups.

In the first place a teacher who integrates guidance with his classroom teaching appreciates that the group of thirty boys and girls who are seated before him represents a pattern of social interaction. In order to foster better social development for each child, it is important to know to what degree and for what things he is accepted or rejected by his group. The teacher's personal reactions to these boys and girls may be quite different from their reactions to each other. The youngster who wants undue attention may, from the teacher's point of view, be engaging in unacceptable behavior, yet actually he may be attracting the loyalty of certain others in the group and be exercising strong leadership, though it be of the negative type. The quiet girl in the back seat who always follows directions may be attractive to the teacher because she is courteous and well dressed, and yet she may not play a role in the child society which satisfies her need for belonging. When a teacher appreciates the fact that adults respond to children somewhat differently from the way they respond to each other, he will be able to observe more intelligently the social forces which are actually operating.

The refusals and acceptances of children for each other show up best in relatively unsupervised and unstructured situations. If the teacher says, "Sit anywhere you please" or "Join the group you would like to work with," the resulting groupings reflect something of the social patterning. Behavior in the corridors and the lunchroom related to who links arms with whom, who bullies whom, who talks to whom or who shares his lunch and equipment with whom, provides added data for picturing the interpersonal relationships and the stresses and strains within the group. The techniques of the sociogram may be used to check on such teacher observations.

Whatever the methods used, it is important for both guidance and teaching that the adult in the group knows such things as the degree to which the youngsters are pulling together as a team, who comprise the divisive cliques, who appear to be the social outcasts, what chum relationships exist and who can be depended upon for constructive leadership.

The teacher will likewise note, as he observes the boys and girls in cooperative undertakings, the role which certain individuals play with considerable consistency. Frieda, for example, may typically be the one who helps the group find a compromise for conflicting points of view. Kitty may be an attention-seeker whose chief objective appears to be to retain the limelight, regardless of the best interests of the group. George may be the one to whom the group turns for the facts to support an argument or to dispel a rumor. Gus may be the "wet blanket" whose sophistication attracts certain youngsters in the group, yet whose leadership is often demoralizing to group spirit.

In the light of the teacher's observations of the group structure and of the roles which individuals play, he will see the directions in which the group, and individuals within the group, need to be guided. These observations will not, however, tell him *why* a given subgroup is operating as a clique or why Kitty is seeking attention. As we have reiterated in other parts of this and previous chapters, back of these behaviors exist situations in the lives of the boys and girls in question which account for the loyalties they are developing and the methods they are using to gain a sense of personal importance. Whether it be failure in school work, poor physical health, economic disadvantage, constant moving about from school to school, rebellion against parental restriction, anxiety concerning parental discord, or a combination of these or other problems, only as the teacher is apprised of these background situations will he know what steps to take and what methods to use to help a child and to facilitate both individual and group learning.

Much has been written in current literature about using the group situation to encourage the wholesome growth of individual members. As applied to groups of children representing a normal range of social and emotional adjustment, this is a subject which should interest the teacher who is trying to integrate guidance with his classroom teaching. Where seating arrangements and discussion techniques encourage free expression of ideas and sharing of the leadership function, children can do much to foster wholesome growth on the part of each other. A teacher as a member of the circle can help boys and girls discover how best to tap all of the various ideas and resources available within the group, and how to help each child assist the group to move along with reasonable efficiency toward its goal. Even relatively young children can be guided to see what is happening within a group—what, perhaps, seems to be holding up progress. The teacher can both demonstrate and talk about the importance of being a courteous listener and of being appreciative of each child's contribution. He can show the advantage of discussion which is "circular" rather than always directed toward the teacher. If Mary will address herself to John in answering a question he has raised, and Bill, in turn, will look toward Mary and John as he raises a further question or amplifies Mary's explanation; and if then Bill will turn to other members of the group for another idea, each participant is helped by his peers to feel that his ideas are important to the accomplishment of the group purposes. Acceptance which comes about in this way, rather than through teacher approbation only, gives the child a feeling of at-homeness which releases the best productive efforts he has to offer.

There are various techniques of group work such as the buzz session and role playing which teachers can learn to use to encourage a greater spread of active participation.

Role playing is especially effective for several purposes. First, it often reveals the thoughts and feelings of youngsters who under normal circumstances would keep them closely guarded. Just as writing under an assumed name gives an author more leeway to express his feelings, so playing the part of someone else can sometimes free a child from the inhibitions and the conventionalities which the teacher or his own group expects him to hold. In his role he can "go to town" and say anything and behave in any way he wants, within reason, without having to accept direct personal responsibility for his words and acts. The drama and fun of this kind of activity are highly motivating and usually bring forth richness of ideas. But from the teacher's point of view, its importance lies in providing clues to what youngsters may think and feel as they express themselves without fear of social censure.

Role playing can also be used as a teaching and guidance device. For the reticent child, for example, who may have good ideas but who is not self-assured enough to express them, playing a part for which he receives group recognition may bring him into the group when other methods have failed. Role playing is also a method of preparing for a novel situation which the pupils must shortly face. Acting out how to behave at the freshman banquet or playing out various approved and unapproved ways of interviewing possible prospective employers for jobs may be much more effective learning activities than talking about these situations or even seeing them in films.

Finally, by skilful assignment of roles in such a way that the thoughtlessly playful youngster takes the part of a dependable, helping person in the group, or the quiet child takes a role which demands that he assume some leadership in the discussion, or the irrepressible talker takes the part of the one who listens and summarizes, youngsters can often be helped to find more constructive roles that are quite possible for them to assume in real life.

In the above discussion we are, of course, talking about role playing and other group methods as they may be appropriately used by teachers for developmental guidance. Boys and girls whose adjustment problems indicate need for therapy—either individual or group—must be referred to specialists who are qualified to give proper treatment.

Space does not permit detailed discussion of the various ways in which classroom organization and the application of what we know about the dynamics of groups can encourage rich and varied learning experiences. Teacher experimentation in this area is, however, very much worth while. Even if classroom space is at a premium and desks are screwed to the floor, there is still a number of ways that an ingenious teacher can utilize democratic group techniques and thereby help the group become happier and more purposeful as its members work together.

This chapter has shown the kind and variety of learning experiences which the teacher who has the interests of each child at heart attempts to provide. In an analysis of important principles of learning, it has shown that wholesome guidance and effective learning go hand in hand. Finally, it has illustrated ways in which a teacher can guide the learning of thirty or more youngsters in a group, and at the same time adjust his methods, vary his assignments and utilize flexible classroom organization both to enrich the total learning situation, and to identify and care for the unique needs of each child.

CHAPTER V

Organizing the School for Guidance

A S HAS been shown in earlier chapters, accepting the point of view of this yearbook that instruction is inseparable from guidance makes the classroom teacher the central guidance worker in the school. How does this position influence the manner in which the school should be organized?

Organizing the Guidance Services

Because instruction is inseparable from guidance, it is sometimes mistakenly inferred that there need be no systematically organized guidance program in the school. This conclusion is entirely unwarranted. If the classroom teacher is to be as effective as possible in relating guidance to instruction, it is imperative that there be a well-organized guidance program which is designed to give him every necessary help in discharging his guidance responsibilities.

It must be remembered that while instruction should be *inseparable* from guidance, guidance is *separable* from instruction. Not only in the classroom is guidance taking place. In all good schools there are certain other provisions which relate to individual differences—provisions which are vitally important parts of a good guidance program, whether or not they are so designated. For example, such schools have a planned testing program comprehensive in scope, individual cumulative records for all pupils which mirror the significant things that are known about them, conferences with parents and pupils, and other provisions designed to identify and to assess the significance of the many important differences among the children and youth who are being served.

All such aspects of a good school program are, in fact, parts of a good guidance program. Yet often they do not contribute what they might to the guidance of individual boys and girls because they are not systematically interrelated and integrated into a program designed to make every classroom teacher a party to the many valuable insights which they afford. If, on both the elementary and the secondary school levels, there is a guidance specialist on the staff—as there should be—it is his responsibility to formulate and submit to the faculty a cooperative plan through which all the separate aspects of guidance will be made to reinforce each other. He should work closely with the teacher, integrating all that is known about each child and unifying around the work of the classroom teacher, as far as possible, all the efforts which are made to teach and guide the youngster as an individual.

The phrase "as far as possible" is used advisedly in the preceding sentence. There are always some pupils whose problems require a species of diagnosis, prognosis and remediation which classroom teachers are usually not qualified to provide. These youngsters should be referred to specialized guidance workers whose technical training does qualify them to deal competently with such deviate pupils. Even here, however, the classroom teacher should occupy a central position in the organized guidance program, since he must be competent to recognize such deviate pupils as cases for referral, and to deal helpfully with these pupils after they are returned to his classroom.

The point to be stressed here is that there should be an organized guidance program in the school, and that this can make its maximum contribution to pupils only if it is so structured that all that is known about them is used to help teachers in their daily guidance of these youngsters. Clearly, one of the most important functions of specialists is that of communicating their insights to classroom teachers—of helping them become sensitive to pupil needs of which they may have been but dimly aware, and of aiding them in meeting these newly discovered needs. It is equally evident that the organization of the guidance program should be such that the reverse flow of information will be facilitated. It should make systematic provision for teachers and parents to inform the guidance specialists as well as one another of the pupil needs which their continuing contacts with the youngsters uniquely permit them to observe.

A review of recent guidance literature indicates that in actual practice the trend is in the direction noted in the paragraphs above. "The concept of the specialized guidance worker, with little contact with either the teachers or the vast majority of students, is rapidly becoming outdated. Guidance *coordinator* has now become much more nearly accurate than guidance *director*, and a most important aspect of this guidance coordinator's work is helping teachers to be more effective in their guidance tasks."[1]

Patterning the Curriculum

The organizational pattern of the curriculum should also be so ordered that it will be possible for teachers to gain a deeper understanding of their pupils and have greater opportunity to guide their development effectively. The "primary block," for example, is one departure from the typical primary grade setup which—given a fine teacher—provides certain advantages for guidance. By eliminating the yearly hurdle of passing from one grade to the next, a three year span of time permits the children who are slower to mature to catch up in learning to read and to accomplish other important developmental tasks without the need for repeating a grade and without the feelings of failure which accompany retention. The primary block also offers children the security of a continuing relationship with a teacher who, in the course of three years, comes to know each child personally, and his parents as well. Through reducing by two-thirds the number of the teacher's contacts with different children and different families, the primary block enables him to do a far better job of guidance than he could find time to do as a teacher of a single primary grade.

On the junior-senior high school level one promising departure from strict departmentalism is the multiple period setup which permits a teacher to guide the learning of the same group of pupils for a two or three hour block and, in some situations, to continue this relationship for more than one year. If, for example, a two hour core course is substituted for separate one hour courses in English and social studies and is continued under the same teacher for two years, the contacts which this teacher makes with different pupils—assuming thirty pupils to a class—is reduced from 120 to 30, and the amount of time spent with this student group of thirty is increased fourfold. Often the teacher of the multiple period course also acts as the adviser of the pupil group. The equivalent of a five period teaching load for such a teacher would be two sections of the double period "core" and one single period elective. This

[1] Dugald S. Arbuckle. "The Classroom Teacher's Role in Guidance." *Review of Educational Research* 14:185; April 1954.

teacher would be able to know well the sixty students for whom he was acting as both teacher and adviser. In the period of two years it would be reasonable to expect that he could become acquainted with the parents of these youngsters, to visit many of their homes, and to observe the children themselves in a variety of social as well as academic situations. The double period block would likewise provide the teacher more time to do something about the needs revealed by his study of the pupils, and greater opportunity to develop the kind of trusting, confidential relationship which is prerequisite to good guidance.

Moreover, many of the suggestions made in the preceding chapter for relating classroom learning experiences to pupil needs can perhaps be more easily implemented when lines of demarcation between certain subject matter areas are erased and when larger time allotments permit more effective use of community resources. Especially when the teacher feels secure enough to depart from the subject matter content typically "covered" in the courses for which the "core" is substituted and to develop with the pupils a course which is genuinely problem centered, will guidance and teaching be more effectively integrated.

The two departures from common practice illustrated above, however, are not foolproof. No changes in time scheduling and no theoretical erasures of grade lines or course lines can *guarantee* better guidance by classroom teachers than that which is possible in the setup which typically exists in our schools today. If the teacher is insensitive to the needs of individuals or inflexible in adjusting to these needs in his one hour English class, he will be similarly insensitive and inflexible in his two hour English-social studies combination. On the other hand, a teacher who meets in all essential respects the personal and professional requirements set forth in Chapter II of this yearbook will guide children wholesomely and teach them well regardless of the subject he is teaching or the length of the class period. The quality of the teacher—not the organizational pattern, is the crucial factor. But having more time with fewer different pupils does enable such a teacher to do an even better job of guidance and instruction.

What difference, then, does the philosophy of this yearbook, that teaching should be made inseparable from guidance, make to teachers in their consideration of problems of curriculum organization? It seems to the authors that if teachers are impressed with the influential position they hold in the lives of the boys and girls and appreciate that their responsibility for developmental guidance is greater by far than that of any other member of the school staff, they will seek to discover and to try out patterns of curriculum organization which may help them do a better job of relating guidance to teaching. They will likewise be generous in giving psychological support and backing to their colleagues in whatever experimental program these other teachers may be involved. On the other hand, while displaying an experimental attitude, teachers who accept the challenge of integrating guidance and instruction will not "rest on their oars" until promising innovations in curriculum patterns have been introduced. There are many ways in which a better job of relating guidance to teaching can be done within whatever the present organizational pattern happens to be. These the good teacher will be anxious to discover and use.

Organization of subject matter *within* the teacher's classroom has already been discussed in the final section of Chapter IV. The problem approach to learning which substitutes for logically organized academic content units of study which tie more significantly into pupil needs and which stimulate more fully an active quest for understanding usually eventuates in better guidance and better teaching. Without forfeiting sound training in the basic skills, many teachers on both the elementary and the secondary levels can undoubtedly become much more alert to situations in the lives of their pupils which concern and interest them. They can also become much more skilful in developing challenging studies which capitalize on these interests.

Organizing Staff Efforts

Earlier in this chapter it was noted that the guidance of children and youth can most effectively be accomplished only if classroom teachers and guidance specialists work together closely. It is also clear that pupils can best be served only if the teachers also work together in this way. Only if they share with one another their awareness of the needs which they perceive in their pupils, and only if they are sensitive to the things which they might unthinkingly do which would handicap their fellows, can such teachers be effective as guides of youth.

This need for the reciprocal reinforcement of one another's efforts is very real at all school levels. In the elementary school, however, it is principally in out-of-class settings in the halls, the lunchroom, the library, the assembly and on the playground that such mutual aid is called for. This is because the teacher in the lower school usually has a given group of pupils under his tutelage for most of the day. Although a few special teachers of art, music and speech may share in the guidance and instruction of his pupil group, the elementary school teacher usually has abundant opportunities to help the youngsters keep in mind throughout the whole day the goals for which they are striving in all the subjects they may be studying. In such a situation the teacher is not likely to undo or to fail to reinforce in the second hour what he taught in the preceding period.

In the secondary school, however, this hour to hour reinforcement is frequently lacking. The work of a given teacher is sometimes unwittingly nullified by his colleagues. In a departmentalized school the pupil is likely to be viewed in a departmentalized fashion with the result that the guidance and instruction he receives may not be as consistent or as effectively integrated as they should be. Because of the seriousness of this too commonly encountered situation, the remainder of this chapter is concerned with the cooperative efforts toward mutual aid which secondary school teachers should undertake.

The teachers of any given subject perceive the needs of youth a bit differently than do the teachers of the other subjects. When all of these teachers share their perceptions, each will very likely gain a much more complete knowledge of the needs of his pupils. As already noted, the teachers of any subject can be unwittingly handicapped by their fellows in other subject areas who either fail to capitalize upon opportunities to reinforce what the "other" teachers teach or who unthinkingly do things which negate their colleagues' efforts. Conversely, the effectiveness of the teachers of any specified subject is significantly heightened when their teachings are consistently reinforced by their colleagues in other subject fields.

It is axiomatic that this business of reinforcing the other fellow's efforts, and of being reinforced by his, can be accomplished only as each teacher makes himself aware of what it is that he should do in support of the efforts of his colleagues in each of the other subject fields—and then proceeds to give this support. Each subject matter department in the school should make known to all other teachers those of its objectives which can be accomplished only if other members of the faculty are aware of, accept and seek to facilitate these purposes.

By way of giving some indication of what this pooling might result in, the funded replies of teachers in each of ten subject fields who were asked to tell what help they needed from the other teachers are given below. It should be emphasized that these teachers were not asked to list all of their objectives. Instead, they were asked to name those among their instructional goals which can be achieved only if the teachers of other subjects are also mindful of them. Here, then, are the helps which these teachers said must be given if their pupils are to be as well served as possible:

How the Teachers of Business Education Subjects Wanted To Have Their Efforts Reinforced

We are trying to engender in pupils those qualities of personality (loyalty, good manners, pleasing appearance, discretion, accuracy, promptness, dependability and tact) which make for success in the business world. Every teacher is unavoidably either fostering these or the opposite qualities, depending upon the expectations which he holds and the "way of life" typified in his classroom or student activity.

We are trying to help pupils see more clearly the role each is now playing, and the role each is likely to play, in the business world. This task of self-discovery and self-direction we cannot successfully guide without the assistance of as many as possible of the other teachers whose work relates in any way to the world of business.

We are trying to help pupils acquire facility in adapting themselves to as many different business situations as possible. To the degree that their work brings students into contact with actual business situations, all of the other teachers in the school either help or hinder depending upon whether or not they consciously try to help students make these adaptations.

We are trying to help pupils gain as much practical work experience as possible. Since the total life of the school is full of potential work experiences, every member of the faculty must share this objective if it is to be achieved.

We are trying to help pupils appreciate the importance of business in our personal, home, community, national and international affairs. To the degree that his instruction touches any of these areas of living, every other teacher in the school will inevitably either help or hinder us in our efforts to do this.

We are trying to help pupils understand common business terms, and to pronounce and spell these correctly. Depending upon whether these terms are accurately or inaccurately understood and correctly or incorrectly pronounced and spelled in all other classes in which they occur, our efforts are either aided or negated by these other teachers.

How the English Teachers Said They Should Be Supported

We are trying to help pupils learn how to express themselves freely, adequately and enjoyably. This important learning cannot be acquired unless all teachers not only allow but encourage the student to express himself freely in whatever the medium, help him to do it adequately and enjoyably.

We are trying to help pupils develop clear, forceful and pleasing expression in speech. Every teacher teaches speech by example whether he wishes to do so or not. All the speech teaching in the school should be directed to the same end. Unless it is, our best efforts may easily be nullified.

We are trying to help pupils learn to write according to accepted standards. We are bound to fail to some degree unless all teachers encourage the preparation of written work so that it meets acceptable standards.

We are trying to help pupils learn to read more effectively, to enjoy reading and to find satisfaction in reading better literature. All teachers who employ written materials are inevitably teachers of reading. Unless all these teachers encourage effective reading with reference to the materials in their particular fields, and make it an enjoyable experience for the pupils, our accomplishment is certain to be limited.

We are trying to help pupils grow in vocabulary power. Our work is handicapped unless every teacher provides satisfying situations which encourage growth in vocabulary.

We are trying to help pupils become more intelligent listeners—listeners who can follow a line of reasoning, identify the good points or flaws in it, draw the most important items from the array of facts or impressions presented and critically evaluate them. Inevitably, every teacher either helps or hinders in this regard, depending upon the example he sets, the expectations which he holds and the procedures which he follows in his class.

We are trying to help pupils to select, utilize and enjoy the best in radio and television programs, movies, magazines and newspapers. Unless every teacher gives guidance in this regard, our success is certain to be meager.

We are trying to help pupils learn to use parliamentary procedures effectively so that they may participate courteously and intelligently in formal group affairs. By the example they set, and by the manner in which the affairs of their classes or their activities are conducted, the other teachers will inevitably either enhance or negate the effectiveness of our efforts.

What the Foreign Language Teachers Asked of Their Fellows

We are trying to help pupils develop an appreciation of the contributions (both past and present) of foreign cultures to world civilization, and of our consequent debt to these cultures. Since these contributions touch every major aspect of our lives (what we eat, wear, do, say, believe; our music, art, literature, science, transportation, communication, religion, warfare, public health and safety, housing, conservation of resources, government, education, industrial arts and amusements), every teacher in the school can and should help achieve this civilizing objective. We cannot do the job alone.

Conversely, we are trying to help pupils become more aware of the contributions America has made and is making to foreign cultures. Again, since these contributions touch every major aspect of life (food, clothing, shelter, beliefs, recreation, music, art, literature, science, industrial processes, government, educational, transportation, communication, public health, safety and housing), every teacher can and should help us in achieving this objective.

We are trying to help pupils appreciate the mutually beneficial effects which flow from the exchanges noted in the foregoing paragraphs. Since every aspect of life touched by any school subject reflects these cultural borrowings, it follows that this civilizing objective should be striven for by every teacher. Foreign language teachers cannot hope to do the job by themselves.

We are trying to help pupils develop an attitude of sympathetic understanding with reference to people of other lands, both abroad and here in the United States. Whether or not he wills it or is even conscious of it, every teacher is unavoidably teaching either tolerance or intolerance every time any allusion is made to any foreign group or person in his classroom. Needless to add, we can never successfully teach tolerance unless all other teachers do likewise.

We are trying to help pupils develop an abiding interest in world affairs. This is imperative if we are to have good citizenship in a rapidly shrinking, highly interdependent world. We cannot do this alone. Every teacher must help if this objective is to be realized.

Reinforcement Requested by
Home Economics Teachers

We are trying to help pupils become intelligently aware of the changed and changing role of the home. The cooperation of teachers in several other fields is clearly indicated when such questions as the following are faced: What changes have occurred in respect to the economic, protective, educative, recreational and custodial functions of the home, and what are the consequent changed relationships among its members? To what new problems do these changed conditions give rise? What economic, protective, educative, recreational and custodial roles does the home seem destined to play in the proximate future? With what community agencies or institutions will the home presumably have to cooperate in order adequately to carry out these functions in the years which lie immediately ahead?

We are trying to help pupils improve the various aspects of their personal family relationships within this changed and changing context. It is beyond the ability of the teachers in our department to provide adequate guidance in respect to these important matters. These problems are likewise the proper concern of teachers of language arts, social studies, biological sciences, physical education, industrial arts and possibly other subjects.

We are trying to help pupils make homelife more healthful. To do this adequately we must have the cooperation of at least the teachers of science, physical education and social studies. This is probably also the legitimate concern of other teachers as well.

We are trying to help pupils make homelife safer through teaching them how to prevent accidents in and around the home, and how to administer first aid. The cooperation of at least the teachers of science, industrial arts, social studies and physical education is necessary if this is to be successful.

We are trying to help pupils make homelife better through wiser consumer buying. Almost without exception, the cooperation of all other teachers is essential if this objective is to be achieved.

We are trying to help pupils make homelife more enjoyable

through beautifying the home. Since this involves problems of design, color harmony, gardening, landscaping, constructing, painting and the like, the cooperation of several other teachers is clearly needed.

We are trying to help pupils to improve home living through making needed or desirable home repairs. The cooperation of the industrial arts and science teachers is clearly necessary if this help is to be adequate.

We are trying to help pupils make homelife more enjoyable through encouraging home-centered recreational activities. This objective implies the cooperation of the teachers of virtually every subject.

We are trying to help pupils acquire the social amenities as to etiquette, dress, dating, boy and girl relationships, and such social skills as dancing, playing party games, and the like. This objective is inherently embedded in the purposes which are operative in several of the other subjects. No realistic home economics department would ever hope to do this job single-handedly.

We are trying to help pupils improve the home as society's child-bearing and child-rearing agency. Again, this objective implies an approach to certain areas (happy marriage, wise parenthood, child care and others) which are likewise the proper concern of other teachers. Unless all these staff members cooperate, the school is certain to fail to provide adequate guidance in this regard.

Types of Cooperation Needed by Teachers of Industrial Arts

We are trying to help pupils become familiar with the industrial world in which we live—with its materials, processes, tools and with its principal manufactured products. This is also the legitimate concern of teachers of science, social studies, mathematics, language arts, home arts, music, art and probably all other areas.

We are trying to help pupils acquaint themselves with the changing nature of industrial occupations, and to choose fruitful exploratory experiences in this regard as a basis for intelligent self-guidance. Teachers who, in whatever manner, infect students with the "white collar virus" are certain to negate our efforts. The active cooperation of teachers of language arts and social studies is particularly needed with reference to this objective.

We are trying to help pupils appreciate the aesthetic qualities of industrial products, and to learn how to utilize these to enrich their lives. This clearly makes imperative the cooperation of the teachers of art, home arts, physical education, language arts, music and probably all other subjects as well.

We are trying to help pupils lay a sound foundation for wise consumer buying with reference to present industrial products and services, and to help them anticipate the new problems likely to confront the consumer because of industrial changes. Here again we have a community of interest with the teachers of home arts, sciences, art, physical education, music, language arts and probably all areas.

We are trying to help pupils develop numerous and varied hobby skills in the realm of industrial materials, processes, tools and products. We are certain to fail in this to some degree if other teachers, whether by example or precept, teach that such hobbies are unworthy or "lowbrow." In a subject matter sense, such hobby interests are the legitimate concern of teachers of science, language arts, home arts and probably of other subjects.

We are trying to help pupils acquire numerous and varied practical abilities with reference to everyday affairs, for example, the care of the family automobile, replacing fuses, repairing electrical and other appliances, et cetera. This objective is also implicit in the functional subject matter of teachers of science and home arts, and of other areas as well.

We are trying to help pupils learn how to avoid accidents through the safe use of gas, oil, electricity, automobiles, bicycles and whatever other industrial products they may be utilizing. Teachers of science, home arts, language arts, physical education, and probably other areas are legitimately concerned with this objective.

Kinds of Assistance Requested by Mathematics Teachers

We are trying to help pupils acquire the ability to select, assemble, classify and interpret relevant data with reference to problem-solving; to develop a valid technique of problem-solving. As concomitants, we are trying to help students develop an appreciation of exactness, a disposition to insist upon strict logical deduction, a respect for the power of reasoning and a faith in the value of sound inference. Whether he does so consciously or otherwise, every teacher is certain to help or hinder us in achieving this objective. We are helped if every teacher typifies this approach in his own behavior and holds it up as an expectation in all problem-solving situations, regardless of the subject matter or types of problems involved. We are hindered when any teacher permits pupils to overlook relevant data, or to include irrelevant data, or to fail to assemble and classify data into usable form, or to draw inferences based only on part of the relevant data, or to formulate conclusions unwarranted by their data.

We are trying to help pupils develop an appreciation of the function of mathematics in contemporary life, of its contributions to everyday living and of its role in the drama of civilization. We are helped to the degree that all other teachers sensitize their students to the role played by mathematics in whatever areas of living their subjects are centered or touch upon. A few examples would be (a) the role of statistical mathematics in the business world; (b) the utilization of mathematical symbols, formulas and equations in industrial processes, in advancing the frontiers of science and in securing data essential to the social sciences; (c) the mathematical basis of music; (d) the mathematical basis of sketching, design, architecture, map-making, and such; (e) the mathematics commonly utilized in games, sports and the laying out of playing fields, courts, et cetera; (f) the mathematics commonly utilized in recipes and patterns; (g) the universality of mathematics as a language; (h) the mechanical and social inventions made possible through mathematical discoveries or applications; (i) the role of mathematics in modern warfare, in government, in transportation, in communication, in public health, in conserving natural resources and in producing, distributing and consuming goods and services.

We are trying to help pupils develop a functional mathematical vocabulary which is part of the everyday vocabulary utilized in other school work, in news accounts of local and world events, and in intelligent discussions and conversation. To illustrate: (a) in various school courses students are called upon to utilize such mathematical concepts or devices as rates, length, area, percent, dependence, equality, similarity, quotient, sum, product, units of measure, statistical graphs, pictograms, height, interest, circle, angle, measurement, horizontal, vertical, et cetera; (b) there are 498 mathematical terms in the 6000 words in the Thorndike list; (c) the newspaper account of a flight around the world contained nine units of measure, eight geometric terms, two mathematical instruments, seventeen scientific terms or phrases, and twenty-two semimathematical terms such as "few" and "all." We are helped to the degree that every other teacher sensitizes his pupils to these concepts, terms, symbols, instruments and such, as they relate to his work.

What the Music Teachers Requested

We are trying to help pupils understand the conserving and the creative roles which music plays in any culture; how it helps "tincture each generation with the dye of the preceding"; how it spreads new hopes and ideas; how it has been known to sweep individuals, groups and even nations into allegiances which sometimes have been misleading and tragic and, at other times, ennobling and inspiring. The creating of deep allegiance is likewise implicit in the subject matter of the language arts, art, social studies, and probably other fields as well.

We are trying to help pupils grasp the relationship between music and human desires; to understand that it is always associated with every human activity, with the way we plow our soil, sow our crops, harvest our wheat, feed our pigs, milk our cows, conserve our soil, swing our partners, woo our sweethearts, rock our babies, play with our friends, fight our enemies, worship our God, bury our dead, and so on and on. And not only do we want our students to understand music in this sense; we are also trying to help them use it more intelligently and enjoyably in all respects. Obviously this is far more than a one department job. Since music is associated with every human activity, this objective is implicit in every school subject that touches human life at any point.

We are trying to help pupils appreciate the forms in which music has been important in the history of culture—in folk song and dance, religious ritual and pageant, mystery play and drama, and instrumental music for concert and home. This objective clearly implies the cooperation of at least the teachers of social studies, language arts, and art.

We are trying to help pupils broaden their views with reference to the relationship of music and the culture by helping them realize that folk music is not of the past alone, but that it still is and always will be in the making. This objective is also implicit in the functional teaching of language arts and social studies.

We are trying to help pupils sense the rudimentary music values in our language, our dialects, our localities, our problems, our needs, our common interests. The cooperation of teachers in virtually all other fields is indicated here, most notably that of teachers of language arts and social studies.

We are trying to help pupils understand how modern technology is revolutionizing music, as indeed it is affecting all forms of communication. We are also trying to help them develop the ability to grapple successfully with the problems which are thus being created, and to make the most intelligent and enjoyable utilization of the new instrumentalities which technology has given us, such as the radio, phonograph and television. This objective involves the cooperation of teachers of language arts, social studies, science, industrial arts and home economics.

We are trying to help pupils enrich their leisure time through acquiring skills and appreciations with reference to vocal and instrumental music. This objective is also implicit in the functional teaching of the language arts, and possibly of other fields as well.

How the Health and Physical Education Teachers Wanted To Be Helped

We are trying to help pupils acquire organic power, which is the essential foundation of all physical fitness and good health. This necessarily involves vigorous big muscle activity for virtually all pupils. Both by example and precept, teachers frequently depreciate big muscle activities as being "lowbrow" and engender similar attitudes in students. When translated into behavior, this attitude can only result in lessened physical fitness. Carried to an extreme, it will inevitably undermine good health. We cannot possibly succeed in this objective unless all other teachers typify, and hence teach, the directly opposite attitude toward big muscle activities.

We are trying to help pupils establish many other sound basic health practices. By their very nature, as the following breakdown will attest, these practices must be a continuing concern of all teachers if they are to become habitual.

We are trying to help students safeguard their eyesight. Every teacher can assist in this as he sees to it that his classroom is properly illuminated at all times. This objective also involves the securing of certain understandings which are the proper concern of the teachers of science, of home arts, of industrial arts, and probably other fields as well.

We are trying to help pupils make habitual the breathing of

fresh air. This implies certain understandings which are the legitimate concern of other teachers, notably those in science, industrial arts and home arts. Also, this objective can be achieved only if every teacher sees to it that his classroom is properly ventilated at all times.

We are trying to help pupils acquire a healthful posture. Both by his personal example and by the seating and other arrangements which he provides in his classroom, and, no less important, by the nature of the expectations regarding posture which he holds up to his students, every teacher is unavoidably a teacher of posture. His only real choice is whether he will teach good or bad posture. Further, if students are to know the why as well as the what of good posture, we must have the cooperation of at least the science teachers.

We are trying to help pupils acquire habits of physical cleanliness. This (or the opposite) is also inevitably taught by example in the classroom. Nor is there any subject area of the curriculum which does not legitimately embrace this objective.

We are trying to help pupils learn how to maintain a proper balance between work or exercise and relaxation. This can be learned only as it is lived in every classroom of the school. Again, if students are to understand the why as well as the what of such a proper balance, we must have the cooperation of other teachers, notably that of the science teacher, in their direct teaching.

We are trying to help pupils learn how to provide for their physical safety through accident prevention and the care of injuries to prevent infection. This is a proper concern of every teacher as far as what he teaches by example is concerned. In a subject matter sense, it is also a proper concern of teachers of science, home economics, industrial education and probably of other subjects as well.

We are trying to help pupils become intelligently aware of the changed and changing nature of leisure and recreation in our culture. The cooperation of teachers in several other fields is clearly indicated when we face such questions as the following: What forces are changing our leisure time situation? What important changes have already occurred? What changes seem likely in the immediate future? What new recreational needs are emerging? What kinds of recreational skills will students probably need after they have left school? Through what school and out of school activities can these needed skills best be acquired?

We are trying to help pupils acquire a rich variety of enjoyable recreational skills, many of which will be suitable for after-school years. Obviously, this is an objective which must be striven for by teachers in every subject matter field if it is to be achieved, and certainly every subject area potentially has in it many rich and varied recreational outlets. Still another type of cooperation is necessary: we cannot succeed if other teachers depreciate physical play by labeling it "lowbrow."

We are trying to secure physical health test data (vision, hearing, heart, lungs, general physical tone, and others) concerning all pupils, and to put these data to work as a basis for the better guidance and instruction of these youth. Obviously, this calls for the full cooperation of the entire faculty, both with reference to collecting certain of these data and with reference to putting all of the data to work.

Types of Support Solicited by Science Teachers

We are trying to help the pupils develop an appreciation of the role of science in everyday life, of its contributions to daily living and of its role in the unfolding drama of civilization. Since science has profoundly altered every aspect of living (producing, distributing and consuming goods and services; conserving human resources; conserving nonhuman resources; transporting; communicating; spending leisure time; governing and educating), every teacher whose subject matter touches life at any vital point can and should help us in achieving this objective.

We are trying to help pupils make habitual the scientific attitude. Inevitably, every teacher either helps or hinders in this regard. In the example which he sets by his own behavior, and in the expectations which he holds up to his students, each teacher either typifies the scientific attitude or its opposite—and this regardless of whether it be done consciously or unconsciously on the part of the teacher.

We are trying to help pupils recognize the universality of cause and effect relationships. Unavoidably, every teacher either typifies this recognition or its opposite in his teaching and in his own behavior, and hence inevitably either implements or negates our work.

We are trying to help pupils see through the fallacious "reasoning" which lies at the foundation of claimed racial superiorities, and by so doing to help them become sympathetically understanding of other racial and language groups. Depending upon the nature of the attitudes typified in their own personal behavior, all teachers by example unavoidably teach either tolerance or intolerance toward other racial and language groups. The selection of the subject matter in whatever the subject field also has an important bearing on the teaching of tolerance.

We are trying to help pupils increase the number, variety and depth of their interests in and to acquire an operational understanding of the many and varied phenomena of the physical environment. Unavoidably, both by precept and by example, every teacher either encourages or discourages the nurturing of active interests in this regard and either helps or hinders us in achieving this objective.

We are trying to imbue pupils with a desire to improve various aspects of the physical environment to the end of a more abundant and secure life for all. Every teacher is certain to reflect some variant of this attitude in his classroom and in his personal behavior, and hence helps or hinders in the achieving of this objective.

We are trying to help pupils acquire command of a working vocabulary of scientific terms commonly encountered in everyday life; to have an accurate understanding of these terms, to use them properly, and to pronounce and spell them correctly. We are either helped or hindered, depending upon whether these terms are accurately or inaccurately understood, properly or improperly used, correctly or incorrectly pronounced and spelled, in other classroom situations in which they occur.

We are trying to help pupils become skilled in and habituated to the practice of applying simple but fundamental research techniques in solving their problems, and the more these can be centered in real life situations the better. Our efforts are certain to be negated if other teachers encourage or permit students to draw final conclusions based upon a single approach, upon an uncritical reliance on secondhand information, or upon the pronouncement of a single authority.

We are trying to help pupils learn how to interpret scientific data of the types commonly encountered in everyday experience, and how to apply these interpreted data to life situations. We are either helped or hindered by other teachers, depending upon whether or not they correctly interpret these data as they are encountered in their classes, and whether or not they are intelligently applied by the students in these other classes.

We are trying to help pupils recognize the unfounded assumptions, and to inoculate them against the superstitions, which are commonly encountered in everyday living. To the degree that any of these superstitions and unfounded beliefs underlie any aspect of the observed behavior of any other teacher, our work is more than likely to be undone. Conversely, we are helped to the degree that all other teachers, both by example and by precept, sensitize pupils to the fallacies underlying the unfounded assumptions and superstitions which are prevalent in our community and world.

What the Social Studies Teachers Asked of Their Colleagues

We are trying to help pupils gain an intelligent understanding of contemporary society, of the heritage which it carries, of the historical roots of this heritage, and of the unsolved problems with which we are today confronted. This is also a legitimate central objective of most of the other teachers in the school. Unless these teachers also strive to accomplish this objective, it cannot be achieved adequately.

We are trying to help pupils develop an allegiance to democratic values and processes—to discover how our funded experience has taught us that these are productive of the good life, and to discover what behaviors are and are not sanctioned by these values. The school can engender an allegiance to democratic values and processes only if these are lived in every classroom and extracurricular activity. As opportunities to do so naturally arise, each teacher should also help students to intellectualize these values and processes.

We are trying to help pupils gain proficiency in using techniques for cooperating in the solution of social problems. Since this objective implies developing interest in human welfare, sensitivity to social problems, the habit of working cooperatively with others, skill in investigating social problems, the habit of collecting and considering appropriate evidence, facility in interpreting pertinent data, and facility in applying significant facts and principles to social problems, it is clearly apparent that every teacher must make this his objective if it is to be achieved to any adequate degree.

We are trying to help pupils familiarize themselves with and to immunize themselves against the devices of unscrupulous propagandists. This objective must also be shared by virtually all other teachers—most notably by those in the language arts, in music, art, science and mathematics.

We are trying to help pupils make their leisure time count to better advantage through helping them acquire an interest in reading about and discussing social problems of every type and description. This calls for close cooperation with the teachers of language arts and of most other subjects.

One very significant omission will have been noted by the reader; the teachers of art are not represented. This omission does not stem from any lack of appreciation for the importance of art in the curriculum on the part of the yearbook committee. Rather, it derives solely from the fact that there were no teachers of art in the summer school groups from which the preceding statements were solicited.

Instructional Goals Become Guidance Goals

As teachers help each other gain such objectives as those listed in the preceding pages, they do it with reference to individual boys and girls. It is at this point that instructional goals become guidance goals. The English teacher, for example, accepts his responsibility for the health objectives set by the teachers of health and physical education by seeking to observe and understand the somewhat different health needs of each pupil, and by then providing learning experiences in his classroom in the health areas which are appropriate for each pupil. While he may reinforce the efforts of the teacher of business education by helping *all* his pupils in English develop qualities of personality which make for success in business, his approach is varied in light of a given youngster's need for improvement in such qualities as courtesy, personal grooming, tact or dependability. If the English teacher's assistance to the home economics teacher in achieving the objective of helping pupils improve personal family relations is to be of maximum worth, he must know something about the problems of family relations faced by particular pupils and help each on an individual basis. To illustrate, he might help one pupil to gain insight through reading a novel concerned with family problems similar to his, help another to seek an outlet for his pent-up feelings about his family through creative or autobiographical writing, and encourage a third to seek his counsel on a problem of family discord through establishing with him a relationship of trust and support.

By way of further partial illustration, one teacher, Mr. Brown, quickly noticed that among the twenty-five pupils in his mathematics class, Bill and Sam seemed particularly to lack the ability "to express themselves freely, adequately and enjoyably," and Pete and Sadie quite obviously did not "write according to accepted standards." In dealing with Bill and Sam, Mr. Brown was careful not to involve either in situations in which embarrassing attention would be called to their inadequacies in oral communication. He bided his time and capitalized upon every opportunity to have them either explain to or tell the class about their successful resolution of problems concerning which most of their classmates desired help. By virtually guaranteeing that their first experiences in communicating with the class would be both successful and valued, Mr. Brown helped the two lads to overcome at least some of their reticence in speaking out. And by seeing to it that their help was sought by their classmates, Mr. Brown made it both easy and pleasurable for Bill and Sam to become more proficient in expressing themselves.

Pete, Mr. Brown discovered, was reasonably conscientious but simply did not know what the accepted standards for written work were. Sadie, it was soon apparent, knew but did not care. Mr. Brown's few words with Pete's overworked English teacher helped her to "spot" the youngster's difficulty much sooner than her large number of pupils might otherwise have permitted, so the help this transfer pupil needed he soon received. The improvement which soon began to be apparent in Pete's written work was approvingly noted by Mr. Brown in brief conversation with him.

Sadie's problem was more difficult to resolve. From the guidance counselor Mr. Brown learned that she came from a somewhat unfortunate home situation where standards in regard to things academic were sadly lacking. Good-naturedly but firmly, Mr. Brown let Sadie know that anything either markedly or consistently less than her best would not be acceptable to him. Later, when the class was broken into subgroups in connection with an early unit of work, Mr. Brown arranged for Sadie to join the group that was attacking the part of the work in which she was most interested and in connection with which she could probably make her best contribution to the class. He then asked the members of each subgroup to appraise their own and their group mates' written work. By this device Sadie was helped to see that the way she expressed herself had more than a little to do with determining her effectiveness—and the esteem in which her contribution was held by her classmates as well as by Mr. Brown.

One of the most rewarding ways for teachers to help each other in guiding boys and girls is to exchange information about individual pupils—just as Mr. Brown passed on his observations of Pete to his English teacher. In some schools staff conferences for pooling information about a youngster and for cooperative planning to meet his needs are part of regular guidance procedure. In this manner the composite of general objectives set up by the teachers of each subject area is focused and interpreted in light of the needs of a given pupil.

Thus, even in a strictly subject-centered approach such as that depicted in this section, teachers may assist one another in making their classroom guidance more effective: first, by informing one another of objectives which, though primarily related to one subject area, are a proper concern of all teachers; second, by pooling information about an individual pupil to discover his needs with regard to these objectives; and third, by providing in every classroom the help youngsters need in making progress toward these objectives—this to the degree and in the manner which each boy or girl shows a need for such assistance.

The yearbook committee does not recommend that the statements of needed reinforcements which were recounted earlier in this chapter be accepted by the faculty of any school. Instead, it is recommended that the teachers in departmentalized schools utilize the process here indicated to work out for themselves their own answers to the question of what they should do to reinforce one another's efforts. If the statement of needed reinforcements which is thus formulated is an accurate reflection of what the local faculty genuinely believes to be necessary, the likelihood that such reinforcements will actually be supplied is of course far greater than could ever be expected in the case of a "foreign" document.

There will be a need for guidance specialists to confer from time to time with groups of teachers to help them gain greater proficiency in meeting the needs of youth. Undoubtedly, too, interdepartmental meetings of teachers will need to be held for purposes of learning from one another how better to do the things which reinforcing the efforts of one's colleagues requires. In these meetings the teachers in each department may offer in turn whatever instruction their fellow staff members may require in order effectively to incorporate in their work the types of reinforcements which are desired. Through the give and take of such meetings, the faculty of a school will in a very real sense be lifting itself by its own bootstraps. In so doing it will be making itself increasingly more capable of providing the consistent and well-integrated guidance and instruction which both the needs of the pupils and those of the supporting society require.

Part Three

Resources Available to Teachers In Guiding Children

CHAPTER VI

Guidance Specialists as Resource Persons

C HAPTER V showed how the organization of the guidance services, the curriculum and the instructional staff can help a
teacher make his classroom guidance more effective. The major portion of the chapter described ways in which teachers can aid one
another through reciprocal reinforcement of efforts. Part Three
is concerned with the resources—other than fellow teachers—which
the teacher is most likely to utilize in guiding individual boys and
girls. Resources within the school are discussed in Chapters VI,
VII and VIII. Those which are outside the school are described in
Chapters IX and X.

There are additional sources of help for teachers with which, because of space limitations, we are not attempting to deal in Part
Three. Among these are state departments of education, colleges,
universities, special agencies and consultants of various kinds. This
yearbook, however, stresses resources which usually have more
primary or direct influence upon teachers as they guide children and
youth. In this chapter *guidance specialists* are considered as a resource available to teachers at both elementary and secondary
school levels.

Preschool and Elementary School Guidance

It would seem logical for the school consciously to engage in
guidance as early as possible in the life of the child, beginning at
least with entrance into school at kindergarten or the first grade.
Yet, "guidance" as an organized movement began, strangely enough,
as vocational guidance, with emphasis at the secondary school level.
It began as a specialized field, with a separate department or bureau,
staffed with specialists to whom a child was sent when in need of
"guidance." As indicated in earlier chapters, this sort of setup still

exists in all too many places. But the viewpoint of this yearbook—that instruction is inseparable from guidance—is being increasingly accepted by schools at all levels. In such schools, the guidance program is an integral part of the whole school system. It is concerned with staff morale, pupil-teacher ratio, curriculum, "emotional climate" of classrooms, tensions of pupils and teachers, relations with school administrators, physical setup—in other words, it is concerned with the total program and functioning of the school. It is likewise concerned with the home and community backgrounds of children because these too affect the development of the individual pupil in school as well as out.

In this new concept, vocational guidance takes its proper place as a very important but highly specialized aspect of a broader guidance, which is *guidance for living*. The key persons in such guidance of children are parents and teachers. In the newer concept of guidance, however, a guidance director and other specialists are even more necessary than formerly. The director plays the role of coordinator of all those phases of the school program which contribute to individual guidance. He and other specialists are essential "resource persons" available to parents, teachers and others to help them in guiding children.[1] It is the purpose of this chapter to clarify the role of such guidance specialists.

Guidance Begins

It is customary to speak of "twelve years of general education," referring to the elementary and secondary school years. We should learn to think of at least thirteen years of general education, since research has clearly demonstrated the educational importance and values of kindergarten. This is already being extended downward as many public and private schools are providing junior kindergarten for four year olds and as some are providing nursery school units for even younger children. Our accepted concept of general education should include at least one year of kindergarten experience in which the child learns to live and work with a group of his peers before launching into the basic "school learnings" usually expected in the first year of the elementary school.

[1] In a major study of guidance in elementary schools, conducted by the National Association of Guidance Supervisors and Guidance Trainers, 611 elementary schools in 19 states were polled by questionnaire. Of the schools responding, 81 percent expressed the need for a "director of guidance." See Dugald S. Arbuckle. "The Classroom Teacher's Role in Guidance." *Review of Educational Research* 14:185; April 1954.

If schools are to meet the needs of children adequately, they must be able to help parents when parents need guidance. Just how extensive this service should and can be will depend upon the philosophy and the resources of the school. A fundamental preventive program would begin in the child's preschool years, extending opportunities for parent education and counseling for parents to the school's future patrons. Either a guidance specialist, trained in child development and psychology, or a broadly trained kindergarten teacher of the regular school staff, might serve as a resource person to parents of children of preschool age. Since for every individual the foundations of personality and the basic patterns of behavior are laid in the earliest years of life, the school could best serve not only the individual and society, but also its own purposes, by doing what it can to see that these foundations are soundly and satisfactorily established.

Few schools, however, can at present extend guidance services to the preschool levels; until they can, schools may wisely concentrate their major guidance efforts on the child's earliest years in school. It seems obvious that the strategic area in which public schools should launch their guidance services is at the kindergarten-primary level. Guidance is based upon recognition of individual differences, many of which may be apparent from birth. Many other individual differences are very apparent by the time the child enters school. The earlier these are recognized, the better the chance of successfully adjusting the school to the child and the child to the school. Thus from the beginning instruction is inseparable from guidance. Efforts to prevent maladjustments during the early years constitute a much more constructive and significant mental health program than do attempts to find remedies for serious problem situations which have been allowed to develop. Each child should, therefore, be studied from the time he enters kindergarten or the first grade.

Guidance in the Elementary School

Since every good teacher guides children, every good school has guidance going on within it, whether the program is so called or not. The good teacher observes and studies each child in order to understand him as the unique individual that he is. The teacher keeps careful records—a cumulative folder for each pupil. Individualization of instruction and treatment of each pupil are the results of all these efforts on the part of teachers dedicated to their tasks.

To help teachers with these heavy responsibilities in their dual role of teacher and guide, the school should, and often does, provide resource specialists. Included among these are: school psychologists, remedial reading experts, school nurses, visiting teachers, speech correctionists and social workers. Increasingly one finds in schools a specially trained worker who serves as a guidance specialist for the elementary level, just as the counselor serves as the major guidance resource person at the high school level. In small schools, this may be a part time worker who serves several elementary schools, or even several small school systems, as a consultant in child development and guidance.

It is this guidance specialist whose functions we are considering here. The primary responsibilities of such specialists are:

To help plan and supervise the gathering of such facts as are essential to the understanding and guidance of each individual pupil in the school system.

To help teachers interpret and use these facts (assembled in individual cumulative records) in solving their problems in the guidance of children.

To assume direct responsibility in the guidance of a child only when principals and teachers are unable to solve the child's problems.

To coordinate and integrate the work of the teacher and the various specialists who deal with the child—that is, the guidance consultant should be the liaison worker who unifies all the efforts which school personnel put forth for the child's welfare.

To help teachers and parents plan and carry on a continuous program of education to increase their knowledge and understanding of children.

To help parents and teachers discover the implications and applications of such knowledge for ways of dealing with children in homes and schools.

To help teachers and parents understand the dynamic interrelationships between guidance and instruction, to the end that mutual adjustment of school to pupil and pupil to school may be a continuously evolving process.

Let us consider these major functions one by one.

Helping to plan and supervise the gathering of facts. In the chapter on the "Cumulative Record," it is emphasized that if a teacher is to individualize classroom instruction and provide satisfying experiences that meet the needs of each individual child, a great deal of information is essential. Such information is of two major types—facts which apply to children in general, and facts about the individual child. The chapter on cumulative records describes ways of recording facts about the individual pupil, the use and interpretation of such facts by teachers for guidance and curriculum adjustment, and ways in which teachers can contribute additional facts to cumulative records of individual pupils.

But the world is full of facts. Who can guide the teacher who needs help in deciding which facts are essential to the understanding and guidance of each individual child? It must be someone who is familiar with research findings about how children grow and develop, what is known about the causes of different kinds of behavior, and how behavior can be modified to help a child develop in certain desirable directions. This is a major responsibility of the guidance specialist.

Since guidance is based upon individual differences, the school needs to gather significant facts which are unique for every child— facts about his home and family background, developmental history, physical health, capacities, needs, interests and achievements. Previous school experiences may be very significant. To understand Robert, it is necessary to know among other things that his father was in service when Robert was born and that they did not see each other until the son was almost three years old. To try to understand why Mary constantly clings to teacher's skirts and follows her teacher about the room instead of pursuing typical kindergarten activities, calls for considerable background about this child's life. Certainly it is vital to know that her mother died very suddenly just before Mary entered kindergarten. As at least a partial explanation of Tom's aversion to reading, one must know that he was really not ready for reading when he entered the first grade, and that here he encountered a teacher who felt that every child who did not learn to read in the first grade constituted a reflection upon her teaching ability. Since he did not read, he "failed" the first grade.

In other words, to understand the behavior of any child we must try to discover the *causes* which underlie that behavior. All behavior is caused, but rarely is there only one cause for any particular behavior. The way a child behaves is usually dependent upon a number of factors—a "constellation of causes" they are often called—in each situation. If the factors all tend to operate in one

direction, they strengthen each other; if they tend to produce opposite results, they weaken each other's influence. Sometimes a
very strong factor dominates and cancels out the apparent effects
of a weaker opposing one.

This means that the more information a teacher has about a
pupil, the wider is the basis for his understanding of the child. However, there are a tremendous number of facts that might be gathered
about any person, while time, energy and record space are limited.
What facts shall be gathered, how shall they be gathered and in
what form shall they be available to teachers? The services of a
guidance specialist should be available to help teachers answer
such questions.

Since many facts which should be recorded about a child are
based upon teachers' own observations in the classroom, it is important that teachers become skilled in observing and recording
significant behavior. Guidance specialists may be helpful to teachers in learning how to observe and record in the classroom without
being distracted in their first and primary responsibility for teaching well.

Helping teachers interpret and use these facts.   Some teachers
have had little training which helps them to interpret concrete
facts about child growth and development and about personality
traits and behavior patterns. As these teachers increasingly recognize that they do guide as well as teach children, they find themselves face to face with facts which they need to interpret and use.

What is the significance of the fact that James is extremely large
for his age, has good intelligence, but appears socially and emotionally quite immature? Why are these six children, now entering
the first grade, not ready to learn to read, according to a reading
readiness test, while the twenty others entering the grade test
"ready"? Susan has an IQ of only 98 on a group intelligence test,
but her intelligence quotient on an individual Stanford-Binet Test
is 138; how does one account for such a discrepancy? Julia is a bright
child according to all tests; yet she does poor work in school and
seems convinced that she cannot do better no matter how hard
she tries. What might be the explanation?

In using facts such as these—and countless others of great variety
—teachers should feel that they can turn to a resource person who
has been specially trained in fields dealing with human personality
and behavior. Many—if not most—of the problems which such facts
present can best be met through wise and understanding handling

of the child in the classroom and other school situations. Teachers are the logical persons to do this, with assistance from specialists when they feel the need for such help.

In consciously assuming their inseparable roles of teacher and guide, teachers inevitably find themselves having more frequent and extended contacts with parents. They need to get facts from parents and to report and interpret facts to parents. In these situations teachers should have the assurance that the guidance specialists are ready to help them. Specialists may also assist teachers to plan a program of in-service training on how to conduct and evaluate teacher-parent conferences. Some teachers want to visit the homes of their pupils but are hesitant about how it should be done. They may welcome the assistance of a trained person who can help them make their friendly approach to the child's family and turn their visit to the most constructive account for the welfare of the child.

Many teachers feel the need for help from a school psychologist or a psychologically trained guidance consultant in interpreting test results and in learning how to report these interpretations to parents. Teachers may get such help through individual conferences with specialists. In some situations short in-service training programs have helped teachers gain basic understandings of the testing program. These training periods have resulted in more constructive use of tests throughout the school system.

In general, the guidance specialist should be constantly available as a resource person to help teachers and parents who are striving to understand and wisely guide a child.

Assuming direct responsibility in the guidance of a child. Although the classroom teacher is in a key position to help a child in solving his problems, there are children whose problems are much too complex to be solved without intensive work beyond the classroom. There may be a need for counseling directly with the child or with his parents, or both. Such therapy may require both time and special skills which the teacher does not have. In such cases, guidance specialists may properly relieve teachers of these responsibilities.

Problems may be of such a serious nature that specialists or agencies beyond the school guidance workers are needed to solve them. In such cases, children may be referred to child guidance clinics or other social agencies available for special treatment of individual children. In some instances, parents take children to specialists in private practice. In these relationships the school guidance specialist usually serves as a liaison person between the school and the agency or private practitioner, interpreting the child's school situation to the agency and in turn interpreting the agency's recommendations to the principal and the child's teachers. Only when principals and teachers themselves seem unable to solve a child's problem should a guidance specialist assume such direct responsibilities for his guidance or refer him to outside agencies. The guidance counselor is responsible for maintaining confidences involved in such individual study and treatment of a child.

There is a tendency in some schools for interested teachers to use therapeutic techniques without having had the special clinical or equivalent training which should be required for the administration of therapy. As was pointed out in Chapter I, this yearbook committee believes that the application of therapeutic techniques should be in the hands of persons trained especially in psychology, guidance and therapeutic work. Such training is not expected of a classroom teacher. There will be wide scope for the teacher to exercise his guidance functions if he limits them to the normal and natural contacts which a teacher-pupil relationship provides.

Integrating the work of the teacher and various specialists who deal with the child. It has been pointed out that in some schools numerous special services are available as resources to teachers. In some instances these include school nurses, visiting teachers, speech correctionists, remedial reading experts, school psychologists and social workers. Rarely, however, does any school make available even the occasional services of all of these specialists. In some schools, one of these specialists may be expected to co-ordinate guidance services if there is no provision for a specialist trained in school guidance as such. Whatever member of the school personnel is given the major responsibility for coordinating the school's guidance services, he should function as a liaison worker who unifies the efforts which school personnel put forth for the welfare of the child. This may involve various responsibilities.

There is, in the first place, a need for all specialists dealing with the child to be aware of the other specialists who are working with this pupil, and provision must be made for circulating among them important information concerning the child. If the school nurse has certain medical findings of importance, not only the classroom teacher, but all other school personnel who deal with the child, should be informed of these findings. Neither the teacher nor any specialist should work either in ignorance of or at cross-purposes with what others may be doing for the child. Usually the best way of integrating such services is through occasional case conferences in which the teacher and the specialists meet jointly to consider the needs and the treatment recommended for the individual child with whom they are dealing.

Ruth is one of those good, trustworthy children whom teachers are likely to seat toward the rear of the room. However, she is doing poorly in schoolwork, despite good intelligence and diligent effort on her part. Hearing tests reveal that much of the time from where she sits Ruth does not hear what the teacher is saying. This hearing handicap can be minimized in the classroom by placing Ruth at a desk near the front of the room. However, so simple a remedy will not meet all of her special needs, and Ruth is being carefully observed and studied. Harry has asthmatic attacks which make it unwise for him to engage in strenuous physical exercise. It is important that both his classroom teachers and the director of physical education should not urge Harry to enter games or activities of a strenuous nature. Whether there are psychological factors in the asthmatic attacks has not been determined, and a case study should be undertaken to learn more about Harry. James is having difficulty with reading. His teacher has been prodding him, believing that he is capable of reading up to grade level. Intelligence tests given by the psychologist and diagnostic tests given by the remedial reading specialist indicate that he is doing as well as he can if he reads two grades below his present school placement.

We must bear in mind that rarely, if ever, is there only one cause for any particular behavior. Only when those who are dealing with Ruth, Harry and James put all their facts together and consider these youngsters as *total persons* can wise decisions be made in regard to them. In any such decisions, parents, too, must be consulted and considered. Their attitudes toward the school problems of their children will be factors in determining whether or not the children adjust successfully in specific school situations. These are only a few of the countless illustrations any school situation affords, which indicate the importance of a unified approach to the problems of any child.

Carrying on a continuous program of education for teachers and parents. Up-to-date knowledge of child growth and development is essential to successful teaching, but as yet only a limited number of teacher-training institutions provide adequate background in this area. Not only teachers, but also parents, principals, superintendents and school board members (who, in a final analysis, determine nearly all school policies), should have such information, because all valid programs of education and guidance are based upon an understanding of how children grow and how they build healthy personalities. Those who guide children, whether as parents, teachers or in any other relationships, should know what can reasonably be expected of each child at *his* stage of growth. They should also understand what needs he is seeking to satisfy and what tasks he is striving to accomplish during each period of his development.

Up to now, a considerable number of parents have had little opportunity to gain this background; many teachers, likewise, feel they have had inadequate opportunity to do so. Furthermore, there are always new parents and teachers, and also new facts uncovered by research. Continuous opportunities for in-service training of teachers and parents in the area of child growth and development should be provided, therefore, through the services of a guidance specialist. This may be done in a variety of ways, such as organized programs of lectures followed by discussion, or through informal study-discussion groups in which teachers and parents participate. One of the most valuable types of in-service training is carried on informally as teachers seek assistance over the weeks and months from a genuinely helpful guidance consultant.

Helping parents and teachers discover the implications and applications of such knowledge. Knowledge of child growth and development will be of little avail in either classrooms or homes unless teachers and parents understand the implications and applications of such knowledge as they deal with children in homes and schools. Knowing what can usually be expected of twelve year old children will not help either his parents or teachers in dealing with William unless they also understand his own unique patterns of growth and personality development. True, he is like most other twelve year olds in many ways, yet he differs from them in many significant aspects of his personality and behavior. How he should be helped in the light of these particular likenesses and differences is what both his teachers and his parents need to know.

The fact that research indicates a wide range of differences in development among so-called *normal* children of the same age has important implications for schools and homes. It means, for example, that a third grade teacher should expect some children in that grade to read at first grade level, while others may have achieved a fifth grade level of reading. All these children must receive instruction adjusted to these individual differences. Research also indicates that within an individual child there may be a wide range in different aspects of his development. Ten year old Barbara comes from a family of small stature; she is no larger than an eight year old. Psychological tests, however, indicate that she has the mental ability of a twelve year old. If she were put in the seventh grade, her intelligence would enable her to do the work of that grade level, but her small size and social immaturity would make it difficult for her to be happy there. What kind of school program can be set up for Barbara that will best take care of her during this period when unevenness of development presents a problem? Where should she be placed in school?

This matter of school placement for each child presents some of the most difficult and baffling questions in the field of guidance. Such problems arise out of the wide range of individual differences found in the development of children. Should children automatically "pass" or be "retained" at the end of the school year in terms of arbitrary standards of scholastic achievement? Should every child automatically progress from grade to grade, year by year, regardless of his school achievement or other factors that might be considered in deciding upon his grade placement? From a guidance viewpoint, no promotional policies are sound that do not consider individuals and provide the maximum benefit for each child. Yet relatively few schools have promotional policies carefully based upon consideration for the welfare of each child. What school placement will be of greatest benefit to this child next year? This is the key question that should be considered in every case. Only upon the best answer which the school can suggest should the child's "passing" or "retention" be decided.

Obviously, school promotional policies are a concern not only of school administrators but of the entire staff and of the parents. A decision regarding the best placement for the individual pupil, however, is a matter of guidance. In making such a decision, knowledge of each child as an individual must be considered against a background of knowledge of the group of which he is—or may become—a member. Numerous factors must be reviewed and intelligently analyzed before the decision is made. Parents should also be consulted. As teachers and other members of the school staff make such decisions, the guidance specialist should be available to help them reach the best possible decision in each individual case.

The guidance specialist should also be available to parents, teachers and other school personnel to help them discover the implications and applications of knowledge—knowledge of children in general, and knowledge of the individual child. Ways in which children are alike are important, but the ways in which each individual child differs from his fellows are even more important. Every child is a unique personality, and it is this uniqueness, this individuality, which is of paramount importance in a democratic society. We do not desire "robots" in a free society. To help teachers discover this uniqueness of each child is a major responsibility of the guidance specialist.

Helping teachers and parents understand the dynamic interrelationships between guidance and instruction. Traditionally, most teachers and parents had rather fixed ideas of what children should learn as they go through any certain grade level at school. Teachers who understand individual differences and are able to adjust instructional programs to the needs, capacities and interests of the individual pupil are limited in what they can accomplish if other members of the school personnel and parents of pupils do not share this understanding and accept this viewpoint. Another major responsibility of guidance specialists is to interpret the facts and philosophy which make instruction inseparable from guidance until this point of view permeates the school and the community. This may be done in a variety of ways—through meetings, lectures and discussions, and through bulletins or other reading materials. Any method which brings up-to-date facts to school personnel, parents and other members of the community may be utilized by guidance specialists in accomplishing this task.

Successful school experiences involve a process of continuous adjustment. Sometimes the child must adjust to the requirements and demands of the school; sometimes the school situation and curriculum should be adjusted to meet better the needs, abilities and interests of the child. In most instances, the wisest procedure involves some mutual adjustment of child to school and school to child.

Chapter III emphasizes that in any sound curriculum development *the learners* must constantly be considered. Practically all of the services which are provided by the guidance specialist have implications for curriculum. Whether the guidance activity be a child-study program to study the characteristics of children at various age levels, designed to help teachers and parents know what they can expect of children at different ages, or whether it be a study of individual children the findings are of importance to all who are concerned with the school curriculum. The guidance specialist, in turn, must be concerned with the school's curriculum. If it is inflexible, if it disregards individual differences, if it is not properly geared to what research has shown should be expected of children at various age levels, the guidance services of the school cannot function satisfactorily in meeting the individual needs, abilities and interests of boys and girls.[2]

All guidance is of one piece, so to speak. To understand children at any age level, a longitudinal view of child development is needed. One cannot guide the elementary school child wisely unless he understands the preschool years, in which the foundations of personality and behavior are laid. Also, one must have sufficient understanding of the adolescent and adult years ahead to know what the child needs to accomplish in his elementary school years. Those who guide high school and college students, in turn, need knowledge and understanding of these earlier periods. Counselors and guidance specialists, whatever may be the age level at which they specialize, need full understanding of what happens as the child grows and develops from birth to adulthood.

The role of the high school counselor does not differ basically from that of the elementary school guidance worker. Because of the more complex organization of the high school, with its special subjects and particular fields of study, however, the functions which the counselor performs in the daily program of the high school are somewhat different from those of a guidance specialist in the elementary school. The role of the high school counselor is discussed in the next section of this chapter.

The High School Counselor

The high school counselor holds a key position in the life of the school. A good counselor is something far more than a skilful technician. He must have a well-considered philosophy of education to

[2] Despite this rather obvious dynamic interrelationship of guidance and the curriculum, a review of recent literature indicates "that curriculum books almost ignore mention of the organized guidance program, while guidance textbooks have been written as if what the school teaches is of no concern to the specialist." See Henry B. McDaniel. "Organization and Administration of Guidance in Elementary and Secondary Schools." *Review of Educational Research* 14:109; April 1954.

guide his actions and a carefully formulated philosophy for his own life and for his particular job.

Fundamentally, such a counselor values the individual and believes in his worth and dignity. He respects the uniqueness of human personality. These attitudes toward people are reflected in all of his relationships with teachers as well as in his contacts with students. He has a real appreciation of the importance and value of the teacher in the total guidance program.

The good counselor develops his own technique for establishing a satisfactory relationship between himself and the teachers. He takes responsibility as a morale builder in his relations with all in the school. He is generous in his praise of the fine things which teachers do for boys and girls and remembers that genuine appreciation of the efforts of teachers encourages them to work sincerely in behalf of the young people who are entrusted to their guidance. The counselor's contacts with the teachers typify the best in human relations. His office is a place where anyone may bring a problem no matter how trivial and receive understanding consideration; it is also a place where teachers may receive courage to tackle difficult situations and inspiration to undertake new ventures. A good counselor is sensitive to the fact that teachers live under pressures and often have difficult problems. He knows that these pressures are different from teacher to teacher and from school to school and that his services to teachers should be based on their particular needs.

A cooperative counselor-teacher relationship may be likened to a two way street; while the counselor can be of service to the teacher, the teacher in turn is in a unique position to aid the counselor. He has countless opportunities to observe pupil behavior which are unavailable to the counselor. Together, teacher and counselor may study and interpret these observations and plan a course of action. But it is the teacher alone who must provide the kinds of classroom experiences for the pupil which are appropriate in the light of his discovered needs.

It is one of the primary functions of the counselor to establish a relationship of mutual helpfulness between counselor and teacher and between teacher and teacher, for it is the quality of these relationships which may mean the difference between a successful high school guidance program and a failure. Once this atmosphere of give and take and mutual helpfulness is created there are many specific ways in which a counselor can help the teacher take advantage of his opportunities for guidance.

Conferences as Aids to Teachers

Everyone who shares the guidance function has two major tasks: (a) discovering the needs of a given pupil and investigating situations in his life which may relate to them; and (b) helping the pupil resolve his problems.

To discover the needs of an individual, information is required from a number of sources. One technique for pooling information is to hold conferences of all persons who have had continuing contacts with a given pupil. There are several kinds of conferences. One might be a staff conference in which all the teachers concerned meet to discuss the problems of a given student. Another might be a case conference where several community workers such as social workers, clergymen, visiting teachers, school nurses and recreation leaders are included. Since parents bear an even greater responsibility for the child than do teachers, it is frequently wise to bring parents and teachers together. In all these cases, the counselor should take the initiative to plan the conference, arrange for the meeting place, notify the participants, gather the necessary information, plan the procedure, see that the conference moves in a satisfactory manner, and take care that the best possible public relations are established.

The conference, regardless of the kind it may be, furnishes an excellent opportunity to pool information, to interpret test results and in general to relate various types of available data about a pupil in such a manner that the level and direction of his development will become clearer to all who are concerned with his welfare. Also through these analyses teachers will be helped to become increasingly skilful in observing pupil behavior and interpreting it, and to better understand the significance of test results and other data as they may apply in a particular case.

The following situation may serve to illustrate how a parent-teacher-counselor conference might be initiated and how it might proceed. The Latin and history teachers in a given school complain that Ted is not doing his work; in fact it appears likely that he will fail these courses. They come to the counselor asking for help. The first step which the counselor takes is to gather as much of the background information bearing on the case as possible. This particular school is fortunate to have a twelve year cumulative record on Ted. Among other things, this record contains: family background, health history, behavior descriptions, standardized test results, academic grades and teachers' comments. This sort of record gives abundant material to compare present progress with past achievement. The school also has a folder for Ted, as well as for every other pupil, in which are accumulated the profile sheets of the standardized tests he has taken, several samples of his original work and reports of conferences with teachers. After carefully reading all the materials available on Ted, the counselor confers with Ted's other teachers to ascertain the pupil's current progress in their subjects. In Ted's case the teachers report poor work in all subjects: C in English, D in trigonometry; even a failure in band.

A conference with Ted is the next step to try to discover his point of view and his feelings about school and teachers and any situations which may be troubling him. Then comes the planning of a conference to include Ted's parents, one or both, and the teacher or teachers most closely involved.[3] In this case the conference is held in the counselor's office at a time most convenient for everyone. The counselor has the responsibility for setting the stage, making the introductions, explaining the purpose of the conference and for giving as much background information as seems necessary. In interpreting Ted's records the counselor feels it important to explain to the parents the state-wide testing program and its limitations. In Ted's case there are only the results of two group tests of scholastic aptitude. On these he scored above average. On the basis of the norms provided with the tests Ted's scores placed him between the 80th and 90th percentiles.

The counselor also interprets the achievement test results from the elementary school. Here no deficiency in any basic skill is evident; instead the test results show Ted to be a better than average student. For example, the score from a silent reading test indicated that his reading level at the time he took the test was two years in advance of that typical for his age. The counselor reminds both teachers and parents, however, that test results may not be reliable and will by no means provide the complete answer to any problem.

Another source of information important in Ted's case is his health record. In his cumulative history a heart difficulty was reported in the seventh grade which kept him out of school for several

---

[3] It depends upon the nature of the child's problem whether or not the parents should participate in this kind of conference. If the parents' emotional involvement makes it unreasonable to expect them to be able to discuss the child's problem with a reasonable objectivity, their share in a group conference of this kind may prove a complicating rather than a facilitating factor. While the cooperation of the parents is needed, it may in some cases be better gained through a counselor-parent or a teacher-parent conference designed to gain the parents' ideas and feelings rather than to pool ideas and plan a course of action for the child.

weeks. His mother helped him with his studies at home during this period. The counselor reviews and interprets for the conference participants this background and the whole pattern of Ted's progress over the years.

When all the data have been given due consideration, the remaining time is devoted to a group discussion with the teachers, parents and counselor all contributing. For example, Ted's mother volunteers that he has talked at home about attending the state university and becoming an engineer like his father. The counselor points out that this information appears to harmonize with Ted's interest in working with electrical equipment as a member of the school lighting crew and to verify the findings of an interest inventory given recently which show Ted's high interest scores in science and mechanics.

The mathematics teacher reports that when Ted was confronted with near failure in trigonometry he seemed surprised because he enjoyed that class and thought that mathematics was one of his best subjects. The coach reports that Ted's intense interest in athletics is, due to his heart difficulty, limited to participation as a manager. He also indicates that in spite of his interest he is not always a good manager because he does not seem to sense the needs of the team. One after another, the participants bring out pertinent information relating to Ted. The counselor bears the burden of maintaining the conference on a high plane, keeping comments and criticisms constructive and relationships friendly.

Since this is the first attempt to analyze Ted's difficulties, other conferences will probably be necessary. The discrepancy between his high capacity and interest on the one hand and his low achievement on the other is puzzling. This discussion closes, however, with definite suggestions of "next steps" for all concerned. The parents offer to have Ted given a physical checkup, which may be a very important step in this case. Because of the added insight gained from the conference the teachers suggest ways in which they can relate Ted's classroom experiences to his interest in engineering and mechanics. These arrangements may help to encourage better school work. The counselor suggests that perhaps he should be given an individual intelligence test, as a check on the scores he received on the group tests. The counselor agrees to arrange for this test.

The counselor's duty then becomes that of following up on all of the "next steps" and of keeping informed all individuals who are concerned. It is possible for such a conference to be a wonderfully satisfying, helpful, informative session for everyone and to result in definite advantage to Ted.

Another way in which a counselor may be of service is to arrange a schedule of conferences for all the parents of a certain group of children. In some schools, for example, the parents of every incoming freshman are invited to confer privately with their child's adviser or homeroom teacher either before the beginning of the school year or early in the term. In such a conference the teacher has an opportunity to interpret the program of the school to the parents and the parents have an opportunity to share their greater knowledge and understanding of their child with the teacher. Similar conferences are frequently held with the parents of the tenth, eleventh and twelfth graders in successive years. This results in mutual benefit to the school, the parents and, above all, the pupil. Arrangements for these conferences, of whatever type, are largely the responsibility of the counselor, thus relieving the teacher of this administrative detail.

Helping Teachers To Use Guidance Tools More Effectively

Counselors must appreciate the fact that teachers are frequently asked to do things they do not know how to do. This is largely because their training has been along different lines. The counselor, however, has had specific preparation in personnel work and he must be willing to share his knowledge and skill. All guidance techniques cannot be looked upon as the exclusive property of the counselor. For example, a teacher may need help in interpreting test results or in understanding and using material in the pupil's cumulative record.

In a certain school Miss Quinn, a mathematics teacher new in the system, appeared at the counselor's office in the second week of the term. The teacher had a pack of the cover sheets of an arithmetic test in her hand. She asked, "Just what am I supposed to do with these?" The counselor, genuinely glad to be of help, sat down with the teacher and together they studied the general explanation of the test sent to the teachers and analyzed the results of the test taken by Miss Quinn's 9A algebra class. They discovered that the class as a whole possessed the basic skills of addition, subtraction, multiplication and division but was weak in working with fractions and decimals. The counselor suggested studying the individual elementary school records of these students. The records showed that five of the pupils had been consistently weak in all aspects of arithmetic throughout the intermediate grades. The rest had attained satisfactory achievement. Comparison showed these five lowest to be the weakest of the group on this latest test. The reasons for the low scores of the others in fractions and decimals could not be determined. These operations may have been too hastily covered and inadequately learned in the first place.

Since all of these students were planning to prepare for college, the counselor and the teacher decided to transfer the five with serious deficiencies to a small remedial class which met at the same hour. In this special class the students would receive individual help. Plans were made to give additional review exercises in fractions and decimals to the rest of the group in connection with their regular algebra work. It was also decided to follow up this remedial and review work by administering a similar test on basic arithmetic skills at a later date to see if further steps might be required in order for the class to achieve maximum success in algebra.

Thus it is evident that whenever tests are given the results must be studied and interpreted, and appropriate action must be planned in the light of this analysis. The counselor must be able and willing to confer with teachers singly and in groups to help them to learn how to interpret and to use test data. As they become acquainted with various tests and have worked with the counselor to use them intelligently teachers will have less need for special assistance of this kind.

Another way in which the counselor can assist the teacher is in the use of the material on the cumulative record. Miss Brown brings the problem of Bill Hayes to the attention of the counselor. Bill, who was a most cooperative, likeable and industrious student when Miss Brown had him in her class two years ago, now appears morose and actually belligerent. She is at a loss to explain the change in Bill's attitude. The counselor suggests that they study his cumulative record to see if they can find any clues which might account for his change in behavior. They discover that early the preceding summer Bill lost his father. His mother is now left with four children of whom Bill is the oldest. From his filed work permit and an entry made by his band teacher they discover that Bill is working in a bowling alley. He starts his job immediately after school and works both evenings and Saturdays. Turning to his class schedule, they find that Bill is assigned to band, biology, algebra, history and English. He appears to have given up art, which he carried for two years and in which he showed unusual interest and talent. His band instructor has written the comment that "previous high interest in band seems now to be lacking." The record shows him engaging in no extraclass activities.

Putting all these facts together, the teacher and the counselor realize that Bill has been forced to give up most of the things he used to enjoy in school, such as playing his clarinet at football games and pep rallies and participating in the art club; that his part time job is taking much of his out-of-school time, depriving him of his social contacts and leaving little time for study. Most important of all, he is faced with the difficult adjustment problem of learning to get along without a father. It is small wonder that Bill's attitude has changed! On the basis of such a study, some of the things which might be done to help Bill become quite clear.

This study of Bill's cumulative record is another example of how a counselor can help a teacher become more skilful in discovering the causes of pupil maladjustment. If it were felt necessary to carry this case further, the counselor might ask all of Bill's teachers to observe his behavior for a time and to make written records of their findings. He could also suggest to Miss Brown that she visit Bill's home. This might help to assure the mother of the school's interest in Bill and perhaps lead to better understanding of his problems. When all of this additional information had been accumulated, the counselor might then call a conference like the one previously discussed.

In both of the preceding illustrations, the counselor shares his skill in the use of guidance techniques and tools with the teacher. He thus helps the teacher to deal more effectively with succeeding problems and further cements the feeling of mutual goodwill which should be the underlying spirit of every school guidance program.

The Counselor as a Referral Agent

Teachers are frequently confronted with problems of pupil adjustment and should generally be encouraged to handle these problems themselves rather than to send the students concerned to the counselor. In these situations, however, the counselor is the back-stage helper, providing information and other resources when needed but not intruding into a mutually respecting and helpful teacher-pupil relationship. A suggestion or two from the counselor may be all the assistance a teacher needs to help a given pupil. Usually when teachers know that the counselor will not usurp their important guidance function they will freely confer with the counselor.

When, however, the teacher feels that the situation is too deep-seated and too complex for him to handle directly with the pupil, the counselor assumes greater responsibility for individual counseling. He, in turn, may deem it wise to seek the assistance of other personnel workers with training which he lacks. In this case his referral function includes first contacting the physician, psychiatrist, social worker or other specialist as the case may be; then providing these specialists with the background information available; and finally seeing that their findings and recommendations, as they involve the teachers of a given child, are transmitted to these teachers. If it is necessary to hold a follow-up conference on the findings, it is frequently important for the teachers concerned to be included, for in the final analysis it is they who see the pupil every day and are in a position to carry out many of the recommendations that may be made. When reports are made to teachers in written form it is often helpful to rephrase the detailed and technically worded analyses of the specialists. Teachers should not be burdened with the task of interpreting psychological or medical terminology. The writing of reports such as the following example is an important part of the counselor's job.

The case of Mary Brown who was constantly falling asleep in class and apparently suffering lapses of memory had been referred by a teacher to the counselor. The counselor in turn found it necessary to call in the services of the nurse, the visiting teacher, and finally the psychiatrist. The following is the report which the counselor sent to Mary's teachers:

The visiting teacher called at the home of Mary Brown and found the family in serious financial straits. The father is presently unemployed and the mother is doing janitorial work on a part-time basis. Mary is keeping late hours on baby-sitting jobs, in addition to doing household tasks and trying to keep up with her school work. The nurse reports that Mary's eating habits are poor. She frequently comes to school without breakfast and does not spend wisely the little money she has for lunch. The psychiatrist feels that her classroom behavior may well be related to both poor nutrition and nervous exhaustion.

It has been recommended that Mary's program be reduced by dropping stenography; that a part-time clerical job in school be provided to make baby-sitting unnecessary. Mary has been interviewed and it is partly through her own suggestion that these changes will be tried. She is going to try to improve her eating habits. A follow-up will be made by the counselor and reports sent to all concerned.

It is sometimes said that the findings of psychiatrists, doctors and other specialists are too confidential to be shared with teachers. When such findings are needed to understand a boy or girl it appears to the authors that there is an obligation to share this information with those classroom teachers who are in a position to use the information effectively. The well-trained counselor helps teachers grow professionally by setting an example in the handling of such information. As the teacher sees the counselor respect this confidential material he will be challenged to do likewise, and his faith and trust in the counselor will grow. The authors further believe that working with highly trained professional people is one way teachers may be helped to develop skills in observation, judgment concerning when the services of specialists are needed and trustworthiness in the handling of confidential information.

Teachers Can Use Opportunities for Incidental Counseling

The counselor is perhaps in a position of seeing the over-all program of the school better than a teacher of any one subject and it therefore may be his responsibility, along with that of the supervisory staff, to interpret the general program of studies to the teacher. All teachers whether in the classroom or homeroom assist students in program planning. Sometimes this is done directly in the teacher's capacity of a student adviser, but just as often it is done indirectly in the classroom. It is imperative, therefore, that the teacher develop as broad an understanding of the whole school program as possible so that he can answer questions, suggest alternatives and in general help the pupil to steer a course that will meet his needs.

In addition, each teacher should keep up-to-date on guidance matters pertaining to his particular field of study. For instance, the English teacher should be informed about college requirements in English; the commercial teacher should be acquainted with the employment opportunities and on-the-job problems his students will face when they enter the labor market; and the art teacher should know about the art schools and types of training available to his students. Such information is appropriately available in the counselor's office, but it should also be placed in the teacher's hands so that he may make use of it in his daily contacts with students. The guidance-minded teacher will find countless opportunities to use such information and to do incidental counseling before and after school as the pupils stop at his desk to visit, as they plan their club programs with him, as they talk together at social functions or in the cafeteria. If the teacher has an understanding of child development and what may be expected at a specific age level and then has been given a broad interpretation of the whole school program and the place his particular subject area occupies, there is almost no limit to the influence he can have on the growth and adjustment of his students, especially those who may never see a counselor or a specialist of any kind.

The Counselor's Leadership in In-Service Education

Faculties need to be engaged in constant evaluation of the school program to determine whether its offerings are actually meeting the needs of the students and those of the supporting society. In the light of such appraisal they should be working together on whichever aspects of the school program may need improvement. This is one of the very best kinds of in-service teacher education and one in which the counselor should take a leading role. A committee of teachers could be set up to work with the counselor and the supervisory staff in selecting areas for study and in planning the details of the program.

For example, in a certain school a faculty committee decided that there was need for a study of the health problems of the pupils and of the services and facilities which might be made available in order to improve student health. The entire faculty was divided into committees, each studying a particular problem. One committee investigated various aspects of the school environment: light, ventilation, toilet facilities, sanitation in the cafeteria, safety on the playground and like matters. Another committee ran a questionnaire study of the pupils to try to discover such things as the pupils' eating and sleeping habits, their present sources of health information and guidance, the major questions relating to physical growth and health which bothered them and about which they would like more information. A third examined the content of various school subjects such as biology, physical education, home economics, and problems of American democracy to see what health information was now being taught and to what segment of the pupils it was available. A fourth studied factors in the school situation which contributed to the good or poor mental health of students. Their study involved examining methods of handling discipline, policies relating to membership in school clubs and grading and promotional policies. A fifth group worked with parents on problems of nutrition both as related to meals at home and to the school lunch.

The counselor worked with all the committee chairmen in planning procedures, gathering resource materials, securing speakers, arranging field trips to some of the other community agencies which shared responsibility for the health of boys and girls, and generally in keeping the program unified and operating smoothly. After the findings and recommendations were made by the committee members, the counselor helped to prepare the final report and to follow up on the suggestions made.

Most of the counselor's efforts directed toward accumulating and interpreting data about individual pupils are to no avail if there are then no curricular avenues through which discovered needs can be met. It is for this reason that the good counselor is vitally interested in curriculum study and assumes some leadership in order to make the curriculum richer and more flexible. He keeps abreast of the current curriculum studies and of new publications and materials. Whether the study is in the field of mathematics, industrial arts, social studies or English, the counselor has an opportunity to serve, together with department heads, as a resource person on current trends. He can provide up-to-date professional materials on child development, assist in the conduct of needed surveys and in general encourage the committee to meet youth and societal needs more adequately.

The counselor may also assist in the development of units of study dealing with guidance problems which are common to many boys and girls, for use either in the classroom or in the homeroom. Units on orientation to high school or college life, on personality study and on choosing a vocation would fall into this category. In addition, he should be willing, if requested by a teacher, to help initiate such units as these or to assist the teacher at some points in their development. For example, for a given group of students, he might discuss job placement and other personnel services available to students. Or, for another group, he might present certain aspects of mental health or of family relations.

A counselor can help teachers, often in informal and unobtrusive ways, to become more sensitive to the opportunities for guidance in every subject area—science, foreign language, English, mathematics or whatever it may be.

There are other types of problems in addition to those which relate primarily to the course of study which counselors can assist teachers in attacking. Developing the cumulative records, learning to observe child behavior more objectively, gaining experience in making home visits and improving the system of reporting to parents are some of the things which often need study by teachers and in which the counselor can become an important resource person.

It is sometimes said that the good high school counselor will try to work himself out of as much of his job as he can. While counselors will always have too much rather than too little to do, there is much truth in this statement. The counselor who centers his major effort in helping teachers acquire the background and gain the assurance needed to handle directly many of the personnel problems which arise in the classroom will find that his own case load will become materially reduced. He is then in a position to give better service to those who need his special background of competence. He will also be able to shift somewhat his former emphasis upon remedial counseling to the preventive and developmental aspects of the guidance program. More adequate informational services regarding colleges, special schools and jobs, better testing services, and more creative leadership in curriculum revision may be some of the outcomes. Greater benefits to boys and girls will thus accrue.

This chapter has discussed the guidance specialist in his role as a helper of classroom teachers. It has presented certain of the problems which teachers face in trying to guide children as they teach them. It has also suggested ways in which counselors and other guidance specialists can help teachers with these problems through assisting them in skilful and efficient use of the tools of guidance.

The chapter has not attempted any presentation of the diagnostic, counseling, therapeutic or other aspects of the specialist's job which require his special training and qualifications and for which he is alone responsible. The point of view presented by the authors is that guidance is a function both of classroom teachers and guidance specialists. There are certain things which each is uniquely equipped to do for children and youth. Almost all, if not the full range of the activities of both, however, can be more adequately accomplished and children can be more effectively served when teachers and specialists work closely together—pooling background information, reporting methods which seem successful in working with given children and, in general, developing a coordinated approach in helping them. In situations in which guidance specialists are generous in giving teachers the benefit of whatever special experience or skill they may possess, and in which they serve as liaison officers to develop morale and to unify the efforts of all school personnel in behalf of a given child, both guidance and instruction are almost certain to bring maximum benefits to children.

CHAPTER VII

Superintendent, Supervisor and Principal As Resource Persons

THE superintendent, supervisor and principal should give strong support to teachers as they provide an atmosphere of wholesome group living for children and youth. In order to guide as well as instruct, a teacher must feel confident that he will receive generous help from the administrative and supervisory staff. From the supervisor should come support for procedures used in the classroom as long as these are educationally sound and beneficial to children and youth. The principal who is most closely associated with the teacher can help to build his security by supporting him in his relationships with his fellow teachers, with pupils and with parents, if his performance warrants such support. The superintendent, as the chief personnel officer as well as administrator, sets the tone for the whole school system so that every staff member can operate freely within a value system which places the good of the individual pupil in the central position. All these leaders will aid a teacher greatly by establishing fine working relations with him and by holding him in genuine respect.

Whatever the administrative and supervisory pattern under which a school system is operated, the leaders can do much to help all who work with children to accept a philosophy of education which is guidance-centered. Only on the basis of such a common framework of values can educational policies and practices serve the needs of children and help them, in turn, to handle their lives intelligently.

The Role of the Superintendent

The good superintendent will have a clear idea of the functions of guidance. Each teacher will be assisted by such an administrator

127

to insure that the part of the curriculum for which he is responsible will yield its guidance potential. The school as a whole will be so organized that the teachers are able to coordinate their best energies toward making the total curriculum well adapted to individual children. If these things are done, then the guidance values inherent in the subject matter of the school curriculum will accrue to the advantage of each child. Children fortunate enough to attend a school led by such an administrator will be greatly benefited. Those who attend a school that is not led by a good superintendent may well have unfortunate gaps in their educational experiences.

As fully as the school can afford, the good superintendent will provide such special helps as (a) the services of a psychologist, (b) an adequate testing program, (c) the services of counselors who give aid to teachers, parents and children in solving their problems, (d) the services of a school physician, a dentist and nurses, and (e) special instruction for the physically and mentally handicapped. Further, he will make these aids available in such a way that they are truly accepted by the teacher and not merely superimposed.

The superintendent needs to understand how the physical aspects of the school and the system bear upon the guidance of children. Many fine teachers and specialists in the field are frustrated because their classrooms, class equipment, playgrounds and some of the materials of instruction do not adequately serve. The superintendent can do much to relieve such frustration through assuring the teacher that he appreciates the limitations under which he works and through planning with the teacher for the best use of the available facilities.

The administrator is in a position in which he is called upon to make many choices between alternative expenditures and courses of action with full knowledge of budget possibilities and limitations. One superintendent, when equipping new classrooms, asks the teachers who are to work in these rooms to make two lists of equipment to be supplied. One list comprises items for a de luxe classroom; and the other gives items less expensive yet adequate for a good educational program. In conference with the teachers both lists and available funds are carefully considered and a practical purchase order for equipment is developed. The teachers are helped as they consider what will bring greatest dividends for purposes of instruction and guidance. In the final analysis, of course, the superintendent is responsible for seeing that services and facilities will "buy" the most in terms of pupil growth and enrichment.

The superintendent should be alert to the importance of keeping the recommendations for instructional materials of all kinds in the hands of those who understand the educational objectives of a school rather than in the hands of a business-trained purchasing agent. Bargain prices on textbooks, on writing paper, pencils, science equipment, kindergarten toys, and health and physical education supplies should not be the sole criterion for judging the value of materials to be used in the classroom. Unsatisfactory equipment can hinder a good educational program. Cooperation between the educational and the business department is essential. On the other hand, while the recommendations for educational materials should be made by instructors, limitations of the school budget must be respected. The administrator who has the understanding and perspective of the total educational program is the one to see that these things are considered and done. If he operates within a sound system of values his wholesome influence as a resource person in this area will be greatly enhanced.

It should be understood that when a person acts as an administrator he draws his salary largely because of what he is able to inspire other people to do. If the superintendent is to be a resource person, he cannot stay in his office and play solitaire with the record cards. He must maintain face to face contacts with his staff members and provide encouragement, suggestions and advice.

This means that a superintendent must have a sensitive understanding of what constitutes good human relations. The organization of school personnel must be efficient enough to insure cooperative effort but also flexible enough so that each individual teacher personality will have freedom to grow and even to make mistakes.

In order that the teacher may function as a guidance worker, the superintendent must sincerely practice the principles of democracy. Democracy implies respect for every human being. A school situation which is democratic provides a setting in which each teacher can make the best contribution of which he is capable. No matter how large and complex the school organization, his identity is not lost and his integrity is not violated. He is respected and he gives respect. He and his fellow teachers have opportunity to pool their ideas with those of the administrative staff in the formulation of school policy and practices. The fact that a school has such things as an advisory council, a student council and an organization which in theory provides for faculty participation in policy making is no guarantee that democracy really operates. The forms of democracy may be there but genuine opportunity for group thinking and participation may be lacking. The superintendent who believes that the needs of children can best be met when every teacher is free to express his ideas and to perform as he best can, will utilize his leadership to see that democracy really functions in all aspects of the school. The connection between the democratic spirit and guidance is so obvious as to need no lengthy discussion. The following two considerations, however, might be stressed:

An autocratic superintendent operating through the outward forms of democracy will tend to regard those forms as sacred. When this happens, teachers and children must fit the forms. The chances are that the curriculum in such a system will not be adjusted to the children and that guidance and instruction will not be appropriately related.

If the superintendent is too directive, the teachers will not feel they can safely go all the way in being friends and guides of children. Teachers will probably be held strictly accountable for measurable results of their teaching—say in terms of pupil performance in reading, spelling and arithmetic, or in terms of rigid obedience to the regulations of the school. By being autocratic the superintendent actually dries up the resources which should be available to teachers. However, by being democratic, he not only makes possible the release of the best efforts of teachers but in turn makes every teacher a better resource person for his pupils. Schools which are autocratic are very hard on children. Schools which are truly democratic encourage children to grow to their fullest capacities.

The good administrator will effectively coordinate the work of all members of a school staff. He will avoid situations in which undue pressure made by one department causes difficulty for teachers and children in other departments. He must possess a clear knowledge of the basic function of each part of a school system and work out a sensible scheme for putting those parts together in such a way that they will all work harmoniously. Perhaps we may say, therefore, that the chief function of the superintendent as a resource person is to insure that all of the other resources of the system actually become fully available. Perhaps his work as a resource person is much like that of a catalytic agent in chemistry. The substance of the catalyst does not become part of the new compound but unless it is there, the chemical reaction will not take place and the new compound will not be formed.

The Role of the Supervisor

In order to be a good resource person the supervisor must possess a wholesome interest in people. He must be sensitive to human characteristics, desirable and less desirable. He may be a perfectionist for himself but needs to be understanding and charitable toward those with whom he associates. Actually, the supervisor is in the same relationship to teachers as teachers are to pupils; for just as pupils function better if teachers are sensitive to their needs, so teachers can function better if supervisors are sensitive to the needs of teachers.

Good rapport between supervisor and supervised can be engendered only through mutual respect and confidence. A friendly, helpful attitude on the part of the supervisor will do much to open the way for the teacher to seek supervisory guidance. This relationship is very essential for beginning teachers and for those who may lack confidence in themselves.

The supervisor can secure good rapport with teachers if he has the self-assurance which comes from practical knowledge and understanding of work in the classroom. Experience as a classroom teacher is not only helpful but virtually essential as preparation for the work of the supervisor. Without such experience it is difficult for the supervisor to be sensitive to a classroom situation. The supervisor who has not been a teacher will find it hard to gain the respect of the teacher and, therefore, to be a true resource person. Memory of his own classroom experiences of success and failure will make the supervisor both more understanding and more helpful with the ups and downs of teaching.

Respect for the supervisor by teachers will be increased in direct proportion to the degree to which the supervisor carries his share of the work. He must be ready to work hard and cheerfully if he is to inspire teachers to successful enterprise.

Teachers as a group are very fine people. They work hard and are extremely serious and conscientious about their guidance of children. No new gadgets have been developed to make life easier for the teacher. He cannot press a button which will release electric or atomic energy to give pupils so strong a desire for learning that motivation by the teacher will not be necessary. As more and more knowledge concerning child development and methods of instruction is learned through research, the work of the teacher is increased. The teacher is not a keeper of school, but a professional person interested in his pupils as human beings, in new information about instruction, and in local and world affairs. Many a teacher has found it necessary to become a television fan, for example, in order to understand the thinking and reactions of his pupils.

The wise supervisor will guide the teacher to adjust to new life patterns that affect pupils rather than to resist these. A slow learning group of children suddenly became greatly interested in television. Instead of opposing and resisting this new phase in the life of her pupils, the teacher helped them build a television set, similar to their play movie apparatus, for use in the classroom. The names and numbers of local channels were used and scenes on the screen were new words to be learned, number facts to be assimilated and other items in the curriculum to be mastered.

The supervisor learns much from the teacher. It is not his function to give, from an encyclopedic knowledge of facts, recipes for classroom situations and methods of instruction. Instead, he helps teachers to solve their own problems and to do their own thinking. From the creative teacher he often learns methods which he can offer to other teachers. To keep the respect of teachers, due credit must be given to each individual. No supervisor loses the respect of teachers by admitting he does not know the "answer" if he demonstrates his willingness to try to learn the solution of a problem.

The teacher must feel that the way is always open to seek advice from the supervisor. No problem should be regarded as trivial if it is of concern to the teacher. Sometimes a teacher is confused about organizing the classroom procedures for effective learning or is worried about how to prepare reports. Such problems are important and their solution with the aid of the supervisor will often free the teacher to become a better instructor and guide.

The teacher will seek help from the supervisor and follow his leadership if he is confident that the supervisor is sincere and intelligent about the work. The supervisor must possess a comprehensive view of the educational program in order to point the way to new goals as well as to be realistic about present needs and practices. As a teacher accepts pupils as individuals, so a supervisor must accept each teacher where he or she is in attitude, in ability and in training.

An example of such leadership is that given by a music supervisor who was aware that the school staff in her community needed to become more interested in child development and guidance.

She knew an expert whose services were available. She approached the school administrator regarding the project. The administrator was enthusiastic about the program, but saw no way in which school funds could be used for such in-service training.

Disappointed but undaunted, the music supervisor took her problem to the association of teachers in her community. The association, after a clear explanation of the proposed activity, decided to sponsor and finance the program. Many teachers, principals, supervisors and parents became active in the project. As a result the children gained through wiser and more understanding guidance in the classroom.

This forward looking music supervisor enthusiastically told supervisors in other communities of the success of the project. Her enthusiasm was contagious. These supervisors secured the interest and support of their superintendents who in turn were able to secure funds to finance similar projects for their schools.

From the inspiration of this leader's vision and courage, a comprehensive study of child development and guidance was launched in four urban and two rural communities in the state. The program was an in-service training project in the field of child development and guidance, enthusiastically participated in by staff members, parents and some members of civic organizations. Parents welcomed the opportunities offered to work with teachers for the good of all children. Study groups of teachers and parents constituted the general pattern of operation. Membership in the groups was voluntary. In most groups teachers and parents of children from kindergarten through senior high school were enrolled. All principals were active in the project. Adequate library material was furnished and made easily accessible to members of the study groups.

One phase of the project was a series of evening public meetings each year. At each of these meetings members of a study group presented the results of their work. Audience participation through questions and discussion was always an interesting and valuable part of the evening session.

In one Midwest community (Rock Island, Illinois) in which such an in-service program was conducted for five years, the following changes in relationships, attitudes, practices and procedures were credited to the project:

There are noticeably friendlier relations between teachers and parents, teachers and children, teachers and administrators, teachers and teachers, and parents and parents than before the initiation of the project.

Teachers have become more cautious in passing judgments, more concerned with the background of the child, more eager to know the causes underlying behavior than before the study of child development.

There have been opportunities for professional fellowship.

Parents and teachers have become more objective in dealing with problems of children and more considerate of others' opinions.

There are no more "problem children" in that city but rather "some children with problems."

A wholesome attitude has developed among junior and senior high school students toward parent-teacher relationships.

The area psychologist who serves that city has expressed the opinion that teachers understand children's problems better because of the child development and guidance program.

Individual teacher-parent conferences for all children of a class have been initiated. Three half-days of school time are allotted for the conferences.

In-service training of members of the school staff through participation in study groups which include helpful discussion of pooled readings has been continuous.

One week workshops at a nearby university during four summers and a three day workshop at a state park were attended by teachers, administrators and parents.

Many teachers and parents have attended scheduled one day sessions at this university at which all communities participating in the project presented reports.

Public meetings have been held at which members of a study group presented the results of the research which was studied. Valuable audience participation in discussion was secured.

Comprehensive and detailed records have been kept of the activities of each study group. These records include the enrollment and attendance, the purpose, plan of organization, meetings held, public presentations, conclusions and recommendations, a bibliography and an appendix.

Five study groups for parents of preschool children have been formed.

Members of the school staff are released from regular duties to serve as consultants to parent study groups which meet during the school day.

A study group has been organized at the senior high school level. Parents, teachers and students take part in the meetings.

Lay leadership training courses are given.

Parents are serving on curriculum planning and textbook selection committees.

A system-wide study of the reading program in the schools as related to research in child development and guidance has been made.

A statement of policy was formulated for uniform practice in the use of test data and the interpretation of school records.

Resource libraries of materials in the field of child development and guidance have been supplied to each elementary, junior and senior high school for use by teachers and parents.

Significant modifications in practices and procedures were also reported for the same school system:

Increased home visits in the interest of children have been made by teachers.

There is a growing public interest in school activities as evidenced by newspaper publicity, television and radio.

Many more group conferences at which teachers discuss with parents methods of instruction, teaching materials and school activities for the new year have been held than were held before the studies in child development and guidance were begun.

Rich rewards of the in-service activity reported above would not have been possible without the leadership of the supervisor who worked cooperatively with teachers each step of the way. The leadership for in-service training is generally assumed by the supervisor. Work in this field is helpful in developing and in keeping a professional spirit among members of a staff.

A number of practices may be used by the supervisor to assist teachers. It is essential that all planning for the best interests of children be cooperative. The successful supervisor understands that all who are interested in the child must feel free to express their views and to help in solving problems. The practice of encouraging such free expression of views and even of accepting critical comments will make easier the cooperative solution of problems.

It is important for teachers to value the parents of their pupils as resource people. A good supervisor will help teachers to look to parents for the kinds of assistance which they can best give in providing information which will benefit the child. If the teachers and the parents are all sincerely interested in helping the child, barriers often existing between teachers and parents will disappear.

A conference with all teachers new to a community has been found to be an important means of aiding teachers. One supervisor in a school system which employs approximately thirty-five new recruits each year follows the practice of inviting each new teacher to her office for a conference before the opening of the fall term.

Most of the conferences are held during the summer months and are scheduled at the convenience of both teacher and supervisor. The philosophy of education under which the school operates is thoroughly discussed and ample opportunity given for raising and answering questions. Materials and methods of instruction are discussed. Materials are given to the teacher in order that he may prepare himself well in advance of meeting his students. For the inexperienced and timid, many opportunities for conferences are available. The orientation of such teachers must of necessity be a step by step process. All necessary information for successfully integrating teaching with guidance cannot be communicated in one conference. One timid young teacher, for instance, is known to have requested seven individual conferences before the opening of school. She learned to solve her classroom problems independently because of her new confidence in herself and in her supervisor.

With ever changing community and world conditions, and with an increasing amount of research in child development and guidance and methods of instruction, it is becoming more and more urgent that teachers and supervisors work to apply in the classroom the findings of this research. When they are invited to participate in such activities as partners and not as pupils, a majority of teachers welcome the opportunity.

The role of the supervisor is well summarized in one of the replies received by a supervisor who asked his teachers to state the kind of supervision they wished. This teacher said, "The supervisor should not only guide and direct the teacher but be prepared to give beneficial and constructive criticism. The supervisor should be qualified to recognize the weak spots in the curriculum and the teaching staff and to guide the teacher in such a diplomatic manner that he will have a constructive attitude toward improvement. If the supervisor is not of the domineering, autocratic type, but instead is friendly, cooperative and informal, all the teachers may profit tremendously through his help."

The Role of the Principal

The principal is in a strategic position to be of great value as a resource person to teachers. He is closely associated with members of his faculty. He is readily available at the time when a problem arises which requires immediate attention.

The principal helps the teachers develop the policies and philosophy under which the school operates. He is directly responsible for aiding teachers in carrying out these policies.

Next to the teacher the principal is most closely associated with children. In the elementary school he probably knows most of the children and his knowledge is of value when helping a teacher solve a problem with an individual child. He knows the parents as well as the children and can help teachers and parents work together. He can view a problem between a teacher and pupil in an objective manner. He can judge a problem in the light of the entire school rather than within the narrower setting of a single classroom.

Perhaps one of the most difficult situations for a principal is when he is performing the function of guidance in a case of so-called "discipline." The following anecdote may serve to illustrate.

One morning Miss Ruth and her class had been greatly annoyed by Bill. Bill was sulky. He was uncooperative with members of the science committee with whom he had been working happily on previous occasions. He persisted in making growling noises, in pushing other boys and in making a general nuisance of himself. Since this was unusual behavior for Bill, Miss Ruth was at first surprised and annoyed. When all her efforts to change Bill's behavior had failed, Miss Ruth sent a hurried note to Mr. Hargrave, the principal, describing the problem and asking for his help in guiding Bill.

Mr. Hargrave felt that Bill should temporarily be removed from the class situation. This would help to relieve Miss Ruth, and might also help them learn the cause of Bill's unusual behavior. He needed to find a way of accomplishing this, however, without causing Bill any embarrassment and loss of face. The principal knew that one of Bill's most recent accomplishments had been building an aquarium with the help of members of his science committee. The principal, therefore, went to the classroom and said that he needed the help of a boy to clean the aquarium in his office. He asked if Bill was free to help. Bill was sulky but said he supposed he could help.

On the way to his office Mr. Hargrave said that he had heard that Bill and his companions had found some unusual specimens of water animals. He was especially interested in the "mud puppies" which the boys had brought to school.

Little by little Bill relaxed and as they worked and talked he revealed to the principal some of the problems bothering him. Bill's pride made it hard for him to divulge the fact that there had been trouble at home. His father had lost his job, and his mother and father had quarreled. Bill had come to school without breakfast.

With this information Mr. Hargrave was able to help Bill at least with the immediate problems of getting some needed food and of calming down enough to view more objectively his behavior in the classroom. Later in the day Miss Ruth and Mr. Hargrave took time to pool their information and their insights about Bill. They anticipated a possible recurrence of poor classroom behavior but agreed that Bill should be given every opportunity to feel secure and accepted in the school situation.

In this example both teacher and principal used a guidance approach in helping Bill. They looked below surface behavior for the real problems which troubled him. He was not blamed or labeled as a bad actor but was helped by adults who gave him friendship and understanding. A principal who approaches all behavior problems in this manner helps teachers develop a guidance point of view and encourages their growth in intelligent guidance of boys and girls.

Thus, the day by day work of the principal as he visits classes, writes bulletins, attends meetings, organizes conferences, and has interviews with children, parents and patrons has an influence upon the degree to which children's needs are satisfactorily met. The impact of his influence upon the atmosphere of the school and the effective work of the school in respect to guidance will be great. Cubberley said years ago, "As the principal, so the school." That, of course, goes for any administrative officer. Cubberley had in mind not that the principal set himself up as a god with infinite power but that the administrative office is so strategic that the character of the person who fills it will inevitably determine the character of the school.

Administrative Officers Work Together

It is the chief duty of the superintendent, the supervisors and the principal together to help teachers provide worth while experiences for children. They must work cooperatively in planning and in leading projects which will provide a good educational program. Some specific ways in which this can be done will follow.

Classroom visits by administrative officers are an important means of helping teachers. Administrators and supervisors in recent years have had so many demands made upon their time by the community and by professional organizations that classroom visits have become a minor part of their work. To be effective resource persons these leaders must choose between alternative pressures the activities which, in the long run, will improve the program of teaching and guidance. Classroom visits should be included in these activities. Advice and help to teachers cannot be given over the telephone unless the administrator and the supervisors have knowledge of the classroom situation.

Classroom visits should not be confined to new and inexperienced teachers. Experienced teachers welcome a professional visit by a supervisor. If the administrator and the supervisor spend all of their time as trouble shooters, they become discouraged and less helpful to teachers. They need the inspiration of visits to classrooms of artist teachers.

Classroom visits must be planned. Some must be on the request of teachers, others as the supervisor sees a need. One method which has proved effective in helping supervisors and principals avoid becoming entangled in nonessential administrative detail is for them to submit to the superintendent an evaluation of their activities during each school term. If an important phase of their work such as making classroom visits has been neglected, they can plan to correct the oversight during the following term.

Good teachers do not all work in the same way, and the intelligent supervisor will view classroom activities objectively. Two third grade teachers are working in adjacent classrooms. One is but little taller than her pupils and is usually found in the midst of a group. A visitor to the classroom finds it difficult to discover the teacher when first entering the room. She may be discussing with the children plans for a trip, a summer vacation experience, a difficult problem in arithmetic, or the most satisfactory way to go from the classroom to the library. At all times she is a member of the group, laughing with them, thinking with them and leading them to express their ideas and to solve their own problems. So she moves from group to group. She is always close to her pupils. She realizes that third graders are not comfortable when sitting for a long time regardless of how modern the desks and chairs may be. So she calls small groups to her as they work together throughout the day.

The teacher in the adjacent room uses a formal approach with her pupils. Her classroom is well organized. Little variation in daily schedule is permitted. She is a kindly person and likes children but does not play with them. She knows that children are not all alike and adjusts learning experiences to their needs. Her pupils learn their basic skills as do those of her neighbor. Demonstrations for visitors in her classroom are smoothly organized and planned. Both teachers are good for children although the methods used are different.

Administrators and supervisors have a duty to teachers in helping them to understand the value of a good testing program in the guidance of pupils. In one school system in which members of the teaching and supervisory staff and parents had studied together the value and use of tests, a policy governing their use was formulated.

It was agreed that all tests were to be administered for the purpose of contributing to the growth of a child and that no scores should be revealed without giving an adequate interpretation of the test and its purpose. It was agreed that it would be wise to give parents information regarding a pupil's performance on a test only in a private conference. The information should be appropriately related to the total picture of a child so that parents might guide him to better ways of living.

Administrators and supervisors must be well informed about child development and guidance. There has been considerable research in the principles of pedagogy which deal with the teaching of subject matter. Only rather recently, however, has much been done in what is known as child guidance. Fortunately, the field has grown tremendously in the past ten years. Many teachers now know what child growth and guidance mean. They recognize the fact that at each stage in the child's development there are several important developmental tasks which must effectively be mastered or the eventual adult will not be a truly grown-up person, governed by a mature mind. They know that school work geared in harmony with the satisfactory handling of developmental problems will be well done. They know, too, that schools which set themselves up as strict subject matter centers and which oppose the natural developmental forces may well make rebels, or docile robots, or frustrated neurotics of their children. If the administrator and the supervisor have a working knowledge of child development and guidance, their influence on the system will be great for good.

As resource persons in this respect, the administrators and the supervisors will function when they hire teachers. They will function when the decision needs to be made as to whether an individual child should have the attention of specialists or whether he should be assisted solely by his classroom teacher. They will know whether or not the operations of the system are contributing to the full development of the children, whether or not the system is in balance, whether it is attentive to developmental tasks, whether

it is as concerned about concomitant as it is about primary learnings, whether it is exhausting children in permitting too intense
competition, or failing to challenge children by not providing
enough competition. They will be able to judge, in reference to
these areas, whether or not the system is building good personalities
and capable citizens. In their capacity as administrators and supervisors they are in a position to be powerful resources for doing something about these matters if the system is ineffective, or for encouraging it to be even better if it is good.

An Illustration of How Supervisors, Administrators and Teachers Can Work Together To Relate Guidance and Instruction

Reference has been made earlier in this chapter to a cooperative
study of child development and guidance and their relation to the
curriculum. In this city-wide project (Rock Island, Illinois) the
general pattern of operation involved the selection of topics by a
planning committee for study by groups of teachers, parents and
supervisors. The object of such group study was to encourage better
understanding of children and youth and better methods of teaching and guiding children in both home and school. The aid of a
well-trained and qualified consultant was secured and the general
supervisor of the schools acted as the local leader.

Only one phase of the program will be reported here to illustrate
how teachers and the supervisory staff can work together on a
project which affects simultaneous improvement in both guidance
and instruction. This was a very comprehensive study of the reading program from "readiness" in the kindergarten through reading
instruction in the senior high school. The superintendent of schools
suggested that the following points be given consideration:

Examine first what we are doing—what our present program is. If
we are going some place, we should first know where we are.

We need to consider what we are doing in the light of what we now
know of child development and guidance. Match what we know against
our experience and see how the two compare.

In the light of what we know of child development and guidance and
what we are providing in the way of learning experiences, list those
present practices which seem to require no change.

Study practices which are potentially good but which are not working
very well and which should be improved.

Then consider what things we are doing that are out of balance.
What phases of the present curriculum can be eliminated? One fault is

that many new items are added to the curriculum but nothing is removed to make room for the new. New things have been added, layer on layer, until the curriculum has become an indigestible mass. Youngsters simply do not have time to absorb it all.

Attempt to discover those things in the curriculum that are completely inconsistent with what we know of child development and guidance. Some things are being done just because they have always been done and some of these may be definitely harmful. Such practices should be discontinued. At no time does the school want to do anything that will hurt its children. A school is set up only to assist in the development of its children.

List in the order of their importance the changes you believe should be made.

An elementary school principal and the general supervisor were co-chairmen of the project. Representatives were elected by the faculty in each school to serve as members of the study group. All principals of elementary and secondary schools, all counselors and the coordinator of special education were active in the project.

At an early meeting of the study group the members voted to divide into two subgroups: elementary and combined junior-senior high school. This arrangement facilitated the work. Each subcommittee elected a chairman and meetings were planned. Sessions of the committee of the whole were held throughout the year at which progress reports of the work of each subgroup were presented.

The comprehensive reports of the study group in child development and guidance which dealt with needs and developmental tasks of children were reviewed at a meeting of the whole committee. All teachers were invited to this meeting and teachers new to the system were urged to attend. Five members of the staff presented their concept of the needs and developmental tasks of children on the following age levels: preschool, primary, intermediate, early adolescent and later adolescent. These reports provided the committees on reading with a child-centered orientation. Eventually each study group presented a report of its analysis.

ELEMENTARY SCHOOL REPORT

General Principles of Child Development as Applied to Reading

The physical, mental, emotional, environmental and social aspects of the child's growth must be recognized.

All children pass through similar stages in the development of reading abilities and this development varies from child to child.

The ability to learn to read is closely related to personality adjustment.

Individual differences and needs among children influence the development of reading abilities and the development of these abilities is gradual but continuous.

The child should be accepted by the teacher at his particular level of achievement and materials and methods should be adjusted to each child.

The evaluation of a child's achievement in reading must be made in terms of his own growth rather than through uniform grade standards of achievement.

Every child should experience often a feeling of success.

Good Practices Which Need No Changes

The basic philosophy underlying our reading program is to take the child at his particular level of achievement and proceed from that point with instruction best suited to his needs.

The home background, the physical, emotional and social needs and the necessary information concerning academic achievement of each child are derived from a study of several sources:

> Cumulative records
> Tests and test results given in previous grades
> Results of physical examinations by physicians
> Periodic check-ups made by nurses
> Home visits made by teachers, nurses and guidance director
> Individual parent-teacher conferences.

Individual needs of a child are provided for through:

> Flexible grouping
> Providing materials on various levels of difficulty
> Variations in assignments
> Counseling and guidance.

The reading program provides:

> Continuous growth in interpretive skills and abilities
> A sequential plan for teaching the study skills, such as use of table of contents, index and dictionary, classifying, summarizing, outlining and relationships
> A variety of experiences for developing good habits in oral and silent reading
> A sequential plan for teaching word perception, such as use of clues (pictures, context, configuration), structural analysis and phonetics
> A gradual growth in reading habits and skills
> Much material related to a child's immediate environment
> Enrichment through use of all types of visual materials.

Teaching is aimed toward prevention rather than correction of reading difficulties.

Provision is made for remedial teaching when prevention is impossible.

Provision is made for the measuring of a child's progress in reading through an adequate testing program.

Many opportunities are provided for the child to develop an interest in reading.

Flexibility is practiced in adjusting the reading program to individual classroom situations.

Opportunities are provided for parent-teacher conferences and parent visitation in the classroom.

Educational trips provide a background of meaningful experiences.

Orientation of new teachers is provided through conferences with supervisors.

Suggested Changes for Improvement of Practices

In parent education more stress should be placed on the needs of the school child.

There should be a less abrupt change from kindergarten to first grade.

Classroom enrollments should not exceed twenty-five to thirty in order that provision may be made for sufficient individual help.

An enlarged library should provide for a variety of interests at the different reading levels.

Individual testing should be done soon after referrals are made.

Group test results should be returned in time to be of value to the teacher.

JUNIOR-SENIOR HIGH SCHOOL REPORT

Some Principles of Child Development
As Applied to the Adolescent

Adolescents differ in mental and physical characteristics and in rate of growth.

Adolescents sometimes return temporarily to habits of the younger child.

Daydreaming is a common characteristic of adolescence.

The adolescent usually has a high interest in a search for ideals. He is a hero worshipper.

He feels a strong need for acceptance by his peers.

He needs unobtrusive adult guidance.

Often his fear of ridicule is keen.

Adolescents need opportunities to express themselves.

Good Practices Which Need No Change

Use of visual materials. They supplement rather than replace reading.

Employment of a diagnostic testing program. This could be expanded. A test might be given at the end as well as at the beginning of the year and the results compared.

Much use of unit system with considerable supplementary material, fairly well adapted to various reading levels.

Encouragement of various kinds of reading for specific purposes.

Remedial reading, including special help, use of diagnostic tests with follow-ups, employment of "accelerators" and other such devices.

Stressing of individual participation and development of independent thought on reading material.

Efforts to make use of school libraries for reading and reference work, rather than as study halls.

Current events reports; weekly news magazines subscribed for by classes; use of other magazines, newspapers, radio and occasionally television.

Practices We Are Using Which Are Out of Balance

Use of considerable reading material unsuited, either in difficulty or in subject matter, to the mental age of the child. This is largely due to a lack of sufficient suitable material.

Use of a textbook, in some cases, which is too difficult for students on the lower reading levels.

Reading comprehension could be stressed more.

Some classes too large to allow the best reading procedures and desirable individual expression.

Not enough attention given to bright pupils who are poor readers.

While our visual education program is comprehensive and well set up, more attention might be given to avoidance of duplication between various grades.

It must be recognized that reading instruction and guidance are not only the job of English teachers, but of teachers in *all* areas of subject matter.

More can be done to tie in our reading instruction with the current child development and guidance program.

Recommendations of the subgroups were considered by the administrator and supervisors in securing the types of materials requested for an adequate reading program. To be of real help to teachers a supervisor must see that proper teaching materials are made easily accessible.

The work of the successful supervisor is one involving many and varied opportunities for service. The supervisor must be fair in dealing with his colleagues. As a resource person he has many opportunities to express sincere friendliness, to encourage those who are working directly with children and youth, and to create opportunities for professional growth for himself and his colleagues.

The supervisor's effectiveness as a resource person to teachers is conditioned by the quality of support given by the superintendent or other administrators.

This chapter has discussed in some detail the manner in which administrators and supervisors can support teachers in their efforts to integrate teaching and guidance. The standards which these leaders set and the values which they hold determine in large measure the things which teachers will work hardest to achieve. If administrators and supervisors are single-minded in their devotion to the welfare of boys and girls and view in broad perspective all of the factors in a school which relate to wholesome personality growth, teachers will very likely be inspired to approach the problem of classroom teaching with sensitive regard for children as people and with vital interest in serving their highest need.

Administrators and supervisors are important not only in helping to provide a good setting for learning, adequate instructional materials and appropriate guidance services but, more important, in developing wholesome staff morale. A spirit of mutual trust and respect among staff members does more to free a teacher to work helpfully with children than all the other aspects of a school put together. This spirit exists primarily as it emanates from those in positions of leadership. Given a situation relieved of fears and tensions between supervisors and teachers, the adventure of relating teaching and guidance will challenge the best effort of both the teachers and their consultants and will result in professional growth for all.

CHAPTER VIII

The Cumulative Record as a Tool

JOHN'S teacher wonders why she is unable to draw him out and make him a truly contributing member of her class. Jean's teacher feels Jean has an unexplainable resentment toward him as an adult, which blocks learning in the classroom. Both these teachers, and thousands of others like them, feel the need to understand the underlying causes of behavior—the motives, the emotions, the personal relationships, the environmental factors, which keep children from accomplishing their classroom tasks and from developing their full potentialities.

How can a busy teacher, even though he is interested and professional in his attitude, hope to know and understand the many young people with whom he comes in daily contact? How can he possibly accumulate the wealth of essential information about each child, and glean and sift from all of this the data pertinent to the child's present situation and needs? Certainly no teacher can be expected to "start from scratch" to build such a background for each of his pupils. Yet, without such information, he cannot hope to individualize classroom instruction and plan satisfying experiences for and with young people who are as different from one another as their fingerprints.

The Cumulative Record Is an Asset to a Teacher

How Staff Cooperation Saves Time for Each Teacher

One solution to the problem of individualizing instruction lies in the development and use of a good cumulative record for each child. Such a record offers opportunity to the teacher not only to serve each child better but actually to save time in his professional job. The teacher may obtain from such a record a developmental history of the child; he may observe in that history interrelations of factors which seldom come to light in his classroom. Included in this information may be items which offer the key to the fulfilment of a current need of this child. For example, the cumulative record may give us the explanation for John's problem in the picture of John in his family; in the picture of his gifted brothers and sisters, with whom his "average" intelligence seems low by comparison, and of his equally gifted, dominant and outgoing parents. Realizing these facts, the teacher may place John in group situations in which he can become more adequate and where he is encouraged to feel that his help is needed for the success of whatever is to be accomplished.

The same teacher, benefiting thus by entries made by others, may, in turn, contribute his observations and firsthand experience to John's record. As John gains in self-confidence through working in the group selected for him, he reveals a genuine interest in nature study and an astonishing fund of information about birds. A teacher notation about this hobby, and the contribution John has made to his classmates through it, may mean time saved for other teachers who will continue to use the record to help John grow.

Through the cooperative efforts and professional skill of many teachers, the cumulative record can thus become an invaluable asset to the individual teacher. The growing edge of each pupil's personality can be traced in the notations of successive teachers on individual cumulative records. Each teacher hands on to the next a torch to light the way for pupil growth.

Guidance Situations in Which Teachers Find the Record Helpful

As emphasized in other chapters of this yearbook, a school curriculum which is intelligently planned attempts to anticipate needs and provide the most favorable growing conditions for all children. Varying developmental levels are anticipated and plans made for corresponding variations in learning experiences.

Final selection of curricular learning experiences suited to the capacities and needs of each child, however, is the ultimate professional challenge of the good teacher. This planning for the child's individual learning experiences represents the type of skilled teaching for which the cumulative record serves as an indispensable resource tool.

On the record of each child the first grade teacher finds such items as a report of the initial pre-entry conference held between his mother and his prospective kindergarten teacher. It indicates some of the child's developmental problems in preschool years as well as certain of the special concerns of the parent. The kindergarten teacher's estimate of the child's level of social maturity, his reading readiness, his motor skills and his energy pattern may likewise be indicated. Results of screening tests for hearing and vision may also be noted. The use of these and other data on the record, along with the teacher's own observations of the child, speeds up the process of his adjustment in the first grade. His teacher is saved much trial and error in selecting learning experiences appropriate for him because of the recorded information *already* available.

As each successive teacher receives the record with its added entries, it becomes increasingly valuable as a basis for providing the learning experiences most beneficial for this child.

With the cumulative record in their hands as a tool, therefore, teachers can focus their efforts in terms of the problems of particular boys and girls. Sam's record, for instance, reveals for a period of four years high scores on general aptitude and achievement tests, but poor social adjustment. These data, plus the observations of the teacher and his analysis of a sociogram, result in his providing opportunities for Sam to improve his skill in getting along with others. Step by step, Sam becomes less anxious in social situations and better able to accept his classmates and be accepted by them.

Twelve year old Jane, whose elementary school record indicates that she has adjusted well in social relations with other pupils, is so low in academic aptitude that her achievement in the regular school subjects probably could never fully satisfy her. Responsibility for watering the plants, adjusting the dark shades for visual education, and reporting daily attendance helps to give her the feeling of adequacy she needs. This, in turn, helps her to advance slowly but surely in reading and in other basic skills. A conference with her parents instead of a "mark" report card of the conventional type helps her further. Thus the record assists teachers in selecting learning experiences appropriate for each child.

The record is also of value in deciding whether or not a specialist should be consulted. The teacher who has exhausted his every resource and skill in classroom teaching without effecting the desired changes in a pupil's development realizes that more specialized professional help for the child may be needed. If the pupil's cumulative record for the current year, and the long overview of his history during previous years, reveal persistent unsolved problems, this need for special help is further substantiated.

Even after all the care the school has taken in setting up a good learning situation for Ben, he just cannot read. Special help, summer tutoring and all the usual efforts have been made. His cumulative guidance record shows above-average intelligence on the Revised Stanford Binet and reasonably good social adjustment. The record also includes an entry by the school psychologist. While she reports good eye-fusion, right-handed right-eyed dominance, and good motor coordination involving the finer muscles, she comments that Ben seems to become emotionally upset whenever he is expected to read. On the basis of these recorded data, the teacher seeks once more the help of the psychologist. At her suggestion the multisensory method of teaching reading is tried. Within three months the teacher is able to bring Ben up to the reading level of his grade. Much time and effort would have been wasted by both teacher and child if the recorded information had not been available.

Beth develops such headaches during her math class that it is often necessary for the teacher to send her to the medical room. Health check-ups reveal no physical basis for the trouble. The cumulative record, however, indicates a history of difficulties in arithmetic. The school counselor suggests giving Beth some diagnostic tests in arithmetic fundamentals. A specific subtraction difficulty is discovered. With a little remedial work in this fundamental process, the math problem is corrected, some measure of success becomes possible for Beth in the math class, and the headaches disappear. The cumulative record history in arithmetic fundamentals helped the mathematics teacher to locate the difficulty.

Sometimes the developmental record of a child reveals problems which grow in seriousness from year to year to the point where the teacher and the school counselor feel that an outside specialist must handle the problem. Jim has such a record. No longer simply timid and shy, he has developed a fear so great that often he refuses to come to school at all. Malcolm is another boy whose seeming purposeless stealing continues despite all that his parents and teachers can do. The combined help of the school guidance staff is needed in studying these boys, and in then referring them and their troubled parents to some community clinic that can provide psychological or psychiatric service. When outside assistance is needed, the record is often of great value in providing the basis for confidential reports to these specialists.

The cumulative record can also assist the classroom teacher in helping high school pupils select their courses and make their plans for further education and for vocational life. Planning ahead for advanced educational training or for on-the-job experience becomes a crucial problem for high school youth. With developmental data on the interests, hobbies, achievements and capacities of individual pupils at his disposal, the classroom teacher can be of great help to pupils in these choice-making situations.

Greta cannot make up her mind in her senior year whether to become a librarian or go into YWCA work. From the kindergarten level her cumulative record has consistently shown that she has marked ability in getting along with other children and interest in serving them. The teacher confers with the counselor and together they help the girl further explore each of these occupational possibilities. Books on vocations are made available, visits to experienced people in these fields are planned, and practice in working first as a playground helper and then as an assistant in the children's wing of the public library is arranged. The records have assisted the teacher and counselor in arranging the kinds of experiences to help Greta make a wise choice.

Thus the classroom teacher, who is the key person in guidance and curriculum adaptation, finds the cumulative record useful for revealing the history and characteristics of the growing, changing pupil.

Features of the Cumulative Record Which Teachers Find of Value

Content of the Record

Since a teacher with the guidance point of view has concern for the best possible intellectual, emotional, physical and social growth of each child, it is apparent that a cumulative record of his development in all of these areas will be most helpful in furthering the child's progress. In general, the scope of the cumulative record material should include such data as family background, physical and mental health history, social and civic competence, academic records, general and special aptitude and achievement test records, vocational and avocational participation and interests, and other personality characteristics.

The assistance a cumulative record can give to a teacher depends, among other things, upon the selection of items to be recorded within each area mentioned above. Especially important are data which shed light on the degree to which the child's school experiences are satisifying his basic personality needs.

Four types of basic needs are recognized. First, each individual has certain physiological needs which must be satisfied, such as the need for an adequate diet and the need for alternate periods of activity and rest. The portion of the cumulative record allotted to health information should reveal data pertinent to these needs. Second, the individual must have a sense of belonging to, and of being appreciated by his family, the school and other social groups. The degree of satisfaction of this need for warm human relationships can be indicated in data on the cumulative record in a variety of ways. Anecdotal comments concerning the child's group experiences and reports of conferences held with him or his parents are among the entries which may shed light on his acceptance by others. Third, the individual must feel adequate to adjust with a reasonable degree of success to the forces which surround him and to the demands made upon him. The record of academic success or failure and of adequacy in the curricular aspects of the school program should reveal how well this need is being satisfied. Fourth, the individual must have some goals which seem worth while to him. It should be possible to gain some idea of the motivation underlying a child's living and learning from an over-all synthesis of the varied data on the record. Particularly, records of conferences with or about the individual child should help to provide data about the child's goals.

Among all the record content, the section which describes the child's personality should represent one of the school's most important resources for wise guidance. Such data on personality development are most helpful if they are recorded as paragraph summaries rather than as ratings on a check list. A year by year "picture" of the child-in-action reveals his characteristics and needs at successive stages of growth and also provides a cumulative history of his personality development over the period of his years in school.

Longitudinal and Cross Sectional Pictures of the Child

It is possible to include in the cumulative record a wealth of important information about a child and still have the record difficult to interpret. The organization of the data should make it easy for the reader to reconstruct a picture of the child at any given developmental level and to follow the direction of the child's growth over the years. Thus it should be possible by reading across or down the folder, as the case may be, to gain a cross section view of the child—his academic achievement, his social adjustment, his special interests, his health status—and the reflection of these things in his behavior at home, in the neighborhood and at school. Similarly, by reading in the other direction, it should be possible to gain a developmental picture of the child both in terms of any single category of data, such as his health history, and of his total personality growth.

No record is adequate unless data are arranged to emphasize the unitary nature of child growth—the whole child each year, and over the years. The kinds of pupil accounting which stress isolated aspects of child growth present as meaningless a picture for guidance purposes as the unassembled parts of a jigsaw puzzle. They do not justify the professional effort involved in keeping records. The quiet graves of unused cumulative record files bear eloquent testimony to the waste of teacher time and effort on material which carried no conviction to teachers as to its value in the teaching process. The educational challenge of the record lies in content which shows a unified picture of a pupil growing from immaturity to maturity at different rates and in different ways. The records that are alive are those which help teachers perceive growth trends in the light of which each pupil can be helped to develop his strengths and to live constructively within his limitations.

Accessibility of the Cumulative Record

The interpretation of data on the cumulative record is a task for trained educators. It calls for a high degree of professional skill. Obviously, then, the records should be so located in the school that they will be protected from examination by the untrained and the curious and yet be readily available to all qualified school personnel. Cumulative records should never be accessible to any person other than teachers, administrators and other staff personnel. The same ethical standards regarding the confidential status of records should apply to the cumulative records in the school office as apply to records in a doctor's office, a lawyer's office or a clergyman's study.

Educators should become acquainted with the regulations of state departments or local boards of education regarding the use of school record material. Whether or not to honor requests from people outside the school for information from the record or for examination of a record depends both upon these local and state regulations and upon the philosophy of the school. Since the cumulative record is a confidential and professional resource requiring a trained professional reader, it is certainly wiser not to show records to those who are untrained in record use. Even though there are no two people more interested in a child than his parents, this general standard should apply also to parents. While they certainly deserve to know the kinds of information about their child which will help in their guidance of him at home, these data should be interpreted for them by the teacher or the counselor *from* the record, rather than making the record available for the parents' direct perusal.

It becomes clear, therefore, that every administrator or guidance director should be responsible for developing understanding among his staff of the state regulations and of the local standards which should be used to determine the kind of material which should or should not be recorded, and the personnel to whom it should or should not be made available. A manual on records is often developed for the staff to help them understand these matters.

How the Record Should Be Interpreted by Teachers

Safeguards in Use of the Record

A thorough understanding of the directions for using the cumulative records is essential before any attempt is made by teachers to contribute to them or to interpret data already available. In one school system the manual on records is introduced by clear statements of philosophy and purpose. The value of various types of record information is discussed and suggestions are given for writing personality descriptions so they will be constructive and helpful for understanding the individual child and assisting him to overcome his difficulties and build upon his achievements. The directions stress the value of suggestions which might be given by one teacher to the next for making a sympathetic contact with a particular child. The confidential nature of the record is likewise clearly discussed in the manual.

The cumulative impact of the record should not serve to develop a fixed attitude toward any child. Records are not designed to catalogue children and if they are thus used they may set up additional roadblocks for children rather than help clear away those which are now impeding their adjustment. As a child grows he changes. Often what appear to be rather serious personality defects moderate or disappear as the child matures and as his learning experiences are more wisely guided. The picture of a child gained from the record must, therefore, be accepted only for the help it gives teachers in knowing how to guide him to grow and change in desirable ways.

Professional use of the cumulative record, likewise, requires that no single type of information, such as scores on general aptitude tests, be given undue importance or be used except in relationship to all other available data. Since a single item refers to but one small aspect of the child's life, the teacher who uses it in isolation is bound to draw false conclusions.

No matter how excellent a record form appears to be, revisions should be made from time to time to meet changing conditions and to guard against having the record, or any part of it, outgrow its usefulness. Teachers who are eager to discover how the record may be of greater value in child guidance will be alert to give suggestions for improvement.

Most important of all, wise and skilful development and use of records require continuous leadership by counselors, supervisors and principals in orienting and reorienting teachers to the philosophy underlying the use of the record, to the data obtainable from the various areas on the record, and to techniques for relating items from these areas so that the *whole picture* of an individual will emerge.

Factors To Consider in Making Differential Analyses

In the field of medicine, the most fruitful understanding of children's growth problems lies in the ability of the doctor to make "differential diagnoses." The pediatrician observes, for instance, that the skin rash is only the outward evidence of the disease, that the true causes—which might, for example, be scarlet fever, food allergy or poison ivy—must be determined by skill in differentiating complete symptom patterns. Only then can proper treatment be prescribed.

While the teacher is not a diagnostician and does not wish to pose as one, through intelligent use of the individual record he can apply the principle of differential analysis as it relates to his classroom. The ability to analyze children's behavior or achievement patterns on a differential basis so that causal factors may be discovered is guidance of a high order. Low grades, for example, can be merely a symptom of trouble—like the skin rash. Whether, in the case of Ruth, the cause fundamentally is low intelligence, a special reading disability or an emotional and social problem may make a great difference in helping this youngster in the classroom.

Below are listed some questions frequently raised by teachers in their efforts to understand certain children. Under each question are indicated some of the factors which should be considered in trying to analyze the behavior of a child on a differential basis. In reading the suggestions related to each problem area, it is important to appreciate that a given behavior may relate to any one of a number of causes or to a whole complex of causes. Similarly, a given adjustment problem may reveal itself in any one of a wide range of behaviors or in an intricate pattern of behavior. The author, therefore, warns against oversimplification of the problem of understanding a growing child and of discovering his needs. When used with discretion the following suggestions concerning where to look in the cumulative record for possible light on certain questions relating to a child's development can be useful. These suggestions may enable the teacher better to help children build on their strengths, overcome or compensate for their weaknesses and grow into their fullest power as persons.

Does the child's trouble stem from a reading difficulty which might be remedied?

The first grade is the setting for the initial reading experiences. What was the child's response to these experiences as judged by the teacher's evaluations, by the child's status in his group, and by his personality traits? Were these responses different from those noted in kindergarten where the child's experiences were all of a nonreading nature?

Did the child score higher on the primary grade picture mental test than on the primary grade written mental test? If so, be alert for possible reading difficulties.

Do standardized test scores show marked differences from one area to another? For example, if scores in reading are markedly lower than those in arithmetic computation and reasoning, be alert for special vocabulary and reading disabilities.

Is achievement in subjects which require the reading mastery of a textbook consistently lower than achievement in shop, art, music, physical education? If so, search for the possibility of a special talent or a reading disability.

Does the child do better on "performance" tests than on group intelligence tests?

Have personality patterns developed which hamper achievement in person to person situations?

Is achievement in school subjects, as indicated by standardized achievement tests, higher than one would anticipate from the child's activities in the classroom? If so, observe the child for evidence of possible social and emotional maladjustments as an explanation.

Is the child's personality such that he might be markedly underrated or overrated by others? Studies have indicated that the "conforming" child is often overrated by teachers in academic achievement; the emotional or social "problem" child is often underrated. Be alert for this possibility by comparing all achievement test scores with class marks. For example, a bright child who tests well may be underrated by a teacher who observes only that his habits of work are poor in daily routine activities.

Is the capacity for academic work, as indicated by scores on general aptitude tests, or by the teacher's subjective judgment of a child's capacity, higher than actual achievement as measured by standardized achievement tests? If so, analyze the class situation and investigate the home training as these affect the child.

Have the early kindergarten personality characteristics exhibited by the child radically changed by the secondary school years from recessive to aggressive and bullying tendencies, or the opposite? If so, look for the possibility of academic and personality inadequacies.

Has the child failed to find satisfaction for his needs for success and appreciation in the school environment?

Can you find on the school record evidences that the school has explored and utilized his potentialities in nonacademic, practical interests?

Does he have at least one area of school activity which gives him personal appreciation and satisfaction?

Can you find on the record evidences that he is attempting to get success and appreciation along lines not approved by the school? Can the school provide situations to encourage approved substitute behavior?

Do the child's problems seem to stem from limited intelligence?

Perhaps no other single item on the cumulative record calls for greater care in interpretation and use than scores gained from general aptitude tests. Much damage can be done by teachers in the use of data about intelligence unless they exercise professional skill in considering such points as those in the following list.

Has the individual an observable "timing" which makes him a slow-moving person? If so, only a test with no time limits has a chance of indicating his power.

Are scores for this individual gained from group general aptitude tests reasonably consistent from year to year? If they fluctuate widely, arrange to have an individual test administered.

What relationship does the score on the general aptitude test administered within a given year have to all the other items entered on the record for that year? How does the child's aptitude level compare with his reading and vocabulary levels? If these do not support each other, search the record for possible causes for the discrepancies.

Compare scores gained from group general aptitude tests with those gained from individual tests. The distractions of the group situation hamper certain children from doing their best on group tests. Compare the scores on verbal test items with those on nonverbal test items. If there are appreciable differences, investigate other aspects of the child's life for possible reasons.

Is there the possibility that the child who scores at a low aptitude level may be slow in maturing but will show future gains? The findings of certain studies suggest that dull children continue to show growth in intelligence for as long as do normal and bright children.[1] No measurement of a child's scholastic aptitude should be accepted with anything but wholesome skepticism. A human being is different from a "product." There are aspects of his growth that cannot be measured or predicted.

Is lack of home training or of satisfaction in the home environment a factor in adjustment?

Does the record indicate that the first adjustment from the home to a nonacademic environment such as the kindergarten was a difficult one? If so, investigate early home training for possible causes. Does the record show that family relationships have changed in any radical way? Be alert for possible effects on the child.

Are there recorded data to indicate that brothers or sisters are much more gifted academically? Is there evidence that they get the lion's share of parental approval? Is the child in question gaining his approvals along the lines of his own talents?

Is there evidence in the record of a specialized aptitude or interest upon which the school can build?

Do levels of general aptitude which represent abstract, academic capacity differ markedly from scores on special aptitude tests, such as musical, clerical and mechanical aptitude tests? Or, do the general scholastic aptitude levels differ markedly from the actual classroom achievement which might indicate special aptitude in such areas as art, typing or shop work?

What special aptitudes are revealed in the secondary school through the pupil's participation in clubs and in other student activities? Does

---

[1] F. N. Freeman and C. D. Flory, "Growth in Intellectual Ability as Measured by Repeated Tests." *Monographs of the Society for Research in Child Development.* Washington: National Research Council, 1937. Vol. II, No. 2. p. 69.

National Society for the Study of Education. "Differential Mental Growth." *Adolescence.* Part I, Forty-third Yearbook. Chicago: University of Chicago Press, 1944. p. 166.

the record show continuing participation in special interest activities over several years?

What was the child's reaction toward kindergarten nonreading experiences, and what may this reaction mean concerning his skill in dealing with things and people? How does his experience in later years, as revealed in the record, give supporting or contradictory evidence?

Are there evidences of such withdrawals from reality that psychiatric services or help from a department of child study might be needed?

According to the record do other children consider this child peculiar or "different"?

Have the early kindergarten personality characteristics of quarrelsomeness, excitability or destructiveness changed to those of shyness and fearfulness by secondary school years? If so, the pupil may have personality difficulties of a character that might be more serious from the viewpoint of mental health than those evidenced by continued aggressive characteristics.

Does the record indicate that the child has special trouble in adjusting at each point of radical change, such as from elementary to junior high school or from school to work?

How persistently does he talk about certain interests and goals? Check these expressed desires against his actual school experience for the reality of his feelings.

Is there marked overinterest in reading—perhaps as a retreat from social contacts or from the realistic demands of living?

Has he changed markedly during the past years in the direction of unhappiness, solitariness, inefficiency, prolonged absences for indefinable reasons, or truancy?

Does he appear to be an overconscientious "grind"? Is he apparently achieving on a markedly higher level than his general scholastic aptitude would appear to warrant? If so, be alert for possible personality changes as work becomes more difficult and competition keener.

Does he try to escape from the school or class situation through offering hazy and indefinite complaints of physical illness? Is there a history of excessive absence from school on an illness basis, despite records of good physical health?

What is the general direction of the child's growth as a unitary organism?

Does the record indicate that his effective power as a human being is on the upgrade over the years?

On the downgrade over the years?

Trying to understand the causes which lie behind the behavior of a child is essential for his guidance. The first steps in such an analysis generally may be taken by his classroom teacher.

How Teachers Can Be Helped To Contribute
Effectively to the Cumulative Record

Teachers are people. The quality of the personal relationship between teacher and pupil is as much a subjective matter of "feeling" as any other personal relationship. In addition, the teacher is an adult, trying with adult eyes to see clearly a growing child who is certainly not a "little adult." The teacher is trying to observe with this perspective in a relationship essentially friendly, but still associated with ultimate authority, and with the necessity for teaching subject matter. Further, this relationship takes place within a dominantly academic environment, which does not interest or appeal equally to all children, and in which children can never be equally secure by reason of their differing accomplishments along academic lines. It is for these reasons that it must be kept in mind that pupils who enjoy academic work will appear to their best advantage in the scholastic situation. The pupils who are unhappy in academic work may be misjudged or underestimated more frequently when the teacher-pupil relationship is restricted chiefly to academic situations. Teachers need to be aware of these limiting factors in their relationships with pupils, so that the recording and interpreting of personality comments can be done with full understanding.

Teachers come closest to knowing pupils as they really are during those moments that are most "natural"—in a friendly conference, for instance, when each is really himself as a person first, and a teacher or pupil second.

The factors which limit the teacher-pupil relationship are not so evident in the pupil-pupil relationship. Here the teacher, a professionally trained person, has a peculiarly excellent opportunity to observe with reasonable objectivity a pupil's personal characteristics in concrete situations involving many other personalities of the same level of development and somewhat the same interests. Unhampered by great differences in age or experience or authority, pupils seem most nearly "themselves" with other pupils. Probably the most accurate judgment of the lines of direction in growth from immaturity to maturity can be obtained from observation of what a pupil says and does, and how he acts and reacts to other children of his age. Further, the opportunity to observe the individual pupil's personal relationships with another pupil and the opportunity to observe his relationships with groups of children are many and varied. Entries on the cumulative record of significant observations of this kind enhance the value of the record for making appropriate curriculum adaptations for the child in question.

When and Where To Observe—A List of Suggestions

Behavior should be evaluated in terms of the forces which motivate it. It must be considered as the means used by an individual to accomplish his purposes. These purposes develop from a definite background of experiences, environmental influences, personality needs, and immediate and remote goals. One must realize that the individual is responding not only to the stimulus apparent in the immediate situation, but to a complex set of stimuli which are meaningful to him.

To analyze and evaluate behavior in a valid manner presupposes skill and accuracy in observing it. It is important to observe pupils in both nonacademic and academic situations for their characteristic personality qualities. The nonacademic situations (a play rehearsal, or a homeroom meeting, or the advertising and selling of the school paper) are probably more revealing of a pupil's personality make-up than are strictly academic situations.

Listen and look at pupils when they are alone; when they are in a group situation; when they are busy, or at leisure. Observe the child's reactions at the points at which academic tasks become difficult, or teacher supervision is lessened. Such observations may provide significant information about a child and valuable background for discussions with parents and with the pupil himself.

Large areas of activity and experience form the matrix within which growth toward maturity takes place. Some of these areas are noted below. They overlap, of course; the terms used to identify them possess no magic, for they could be expressed or reorganized in other ways. They are indicated in this chapter only to serve as points of departure in a teacher's thinking about a child, and as areas in which observation of a pupil may reveal trends of direction in his growth. Illustrations of the kinds of general observations which might be made of certain children are noted below each area.

Adjustment to Informal Social Groups (such as his family, his "gang," his neighborhood, his circle of school friends)

Mingles freely with others
Is fair in judging the work and
  play of others
Is helpful to the group; shares
  willingly

Enjoys companionship of both
  sexes
Gets along nicely with other children at home
Seeks only his share of attention

Enjoys leadership   Is a willing follower when the oc-
Is cooperative   casion demands.

Adjustment to Formal, Organized Groups (such as his class,
his school, student government and other organized groups where
authority and conformity to group standards are involved)

Is loyal to school and class   Usually is agreeable
Tries "to makes things go"   Feels himself a part of the school
Suggests ways and means of im-   Lends himself to suggestion
  proving things   Sees things to do
Shows good sportsmanship   Enjoys formal leadership
Works for the good of the team   Raises tone of group standards
Has respect for constituted au-   and activity
  thority   Practices democratic ways of
Takes care of group possessions   living.

Behavior Patterns in Work, in Play, in Leisure

Is sensibly conscientious about   Exercises reasonable self-control
  work   Completes reasonable tasks
Shares honors   Enjoys routine or creative level of
A self-starter   activity in work, play, leisure
Meets difficulties with courage   Makes his plans and carries them
  and control   through
Sustains effort and attention a   Busies himself constructively in
  reasonable length of time   free time
Works when he works, plays   Stands up for himself.
  when he plays

Values and Interests (includes the practical, the nonacademic
and the out of school areas)

Likes to work with tools   Enjoys dramatization
Enjoys music, literature (the   An inquisitive, pioneering interest
  aesthetic)   in many fields
Athletically inclined   Enjoys exercising authority
Willing to give some service with-   Has dominant interest in people
  out pay   Can be counted on; stands for cer-
Some appreciation of different   tain positive things
  values   Enjoys material possessions
Enjoys company—loves people   Has found some definite purpose.

Self-Understanding and Self-Management

Feels sure of himself   Appears self-reliant
Is sensitive to own personal needs   Has some insight into his capaci-
Has a sense of humor   ties and limitations
Feels personal pride   Takes care of own possessions

Accepts friendly criticism constructively
Faces real problems with active attitude

Budgets time well
Has confidence and courage and self-respect
Seems happy and full of purpose.

What To Observe and Record—A List of Suggestions

Pupil growth toward maturity takes place in different areas. To observe and record such growth on the cumulative record can be very helpful.

Some Developmental Guideposts Toward Academic Aptitude and Achievement: Habits of study and work, which depend upon direct training, emotional attitudes, experience, and physical and nervous stability have much to do with the transmutation of academic aptitude into solid academic achievement. These habits vary with different children at different growth levels. There is no "grade standard" or standard of any kind against which the child's habits of work or study can be judged at any one time. The direction and rate of development and progress are the important things. They should be toward maturity. Indications of trends can be gained from observations recorded in such phrases as these:

Attends to his tasks, completes a reasonable number of his tasks, attentive, persistent, independent; completes jobs within his capacity, orderly, prompt, purposeful, independent; span of attention equal to that of most other children of his age, uses time well, orderly methods, persistent in the face of difficult work; self-directive, sustained interest and effort, independent; businesslike methods, mastery of home study problems, budgets time well, has techniques of preview and review, orderly, accurate, persistent; good reading techniques; plans well; possesses initiative in organization; understands use of library and reference material.

Some Developmental Guideposts in Health and Physical Growth: The positive, constructive aspects of growth need attention as well as the negative aspects which too frequently are the major emphasis of school medical records. It is far more important to help pupils grow toward full physical health and power than merely to keep check lists of diseases and defects. As a matter of fact, in a democratic society the cumulative record emphasis on health should have more to do with functioning levels of physical well-being than the usual medical examination reveals.

In his elementary school life, the matters of left-handedness, motor coordination and eye fusion have much to do with a child's early adjustment to other children and to reading and writing.

Throughout all the elementary school years when fundamental skills are being taught, a child's sporadic absences due to physical frailty or to frequent feelings of illness have a close correlation with his level of learning and with his general attitude toward the school. Later on, mastery of such physical recreational skills as basketball, golfing, bowling, tennis, ping pong and baseball is important since these skills contribute to positive enjoyment of physical well-being in adult life.

The health part of a cumulative record should bring into prominence physical growth trends and reveal those health problems, assets or defects which are important enough in a child's adjustment to warrant definitely recommended school procedures. The record should guide the teacher and the school in determining what they can do to make physical well-being a source of energy, endurance and happiness for a given child.

Where services of a school physician are available the medical department record can contribute additional health data.

Some Developmental Guideposts in Group Living and Civic Experience: Participation and achievement in organized civic groups in the public school such as homerooms, clubs, student government and service organizations constitute training for activities in adult community life. They encourage later participation in such groups as civic associations, boards of education, welfare committees, service organizations, women's clubs and town or city governing committees.

There is no single standard for age or grade against which a school pupil should be judged in regard to his adequacy in organized group situations. The direction of his growth and the progress he is making are the important factors. Do these point toward immaturity and dependence, and the habit of "leaning on others," or to maturity and independence? Some indications can be found in comments like the following:

Takes some care of group possessions; is quarrelsome, cooperative, likeable, excitable, shy, sensitive when with other children in the group situation; sees things to do for other children; group relations friendly; seems isolated and rejected; knows difference between self-interest and group interest; accepts reasonable authority; takes part in group activities; willing to sacrifice own interest at times for group interest; gives some service to group without "pay"; group relations with others tactful, friendly, influential; makes reasonable personal sacrifices for group good; accepts and raises group standards; accepts inner as well as outer authorities; relations with group tactful; already taking active part in community activities of civic or religious nature.

Some Developmental Guideposts in Avocational and Vocational Adequacy: On the elementary level, interests and hobbies have been springboards to enrichment of experience and growth of personality. With adolescence, however, tryout of new interests and hobbies, and the maturing of those previously enjoyed, bring the additional promise of life hobbies or of life careers. It is important, as an adolescent grows into maturity, for teachers to recognize the hobby or career possibilities of the young person's talents. Developing as they often do from the experiences of the classroom, these talents, noted each year in the records, can give some hint of the presence of vocational aptitudes along either routine or creative lines, and of the levels of skill and training to which pupils may reasonably aspire.

From such knowledge about their talents, interests and hobbies, pupils at the high school level may be helped to set up worth-while educational and vocational goals. While these may change in direction and emphasis each year as interests shift or achievements change, they are nevertheless important in channeling the efforts of boys and girls. Before completion of high school the interests of some pupils may actually be used as marketable skills. Such paid work as operating motion-picture projectors, training pigeons, or developing photographic film and making enlargements may be, for some, the entering steps into their first job.

Some Developmental Guideposts Toward Personality Adequacy: Certain "lines of direction" in growing up are significant indicators of progress toward maturity. These may be expressed as general characteristics, or in simple terms of behavior in concrete situations. Any generalization (about "responsibility," for instance) arises out of many experiences and incidents which have occurred in and out of the classroom. The teacher who deliberately turns his attention away from the use of abstractions in describing a child, toward the actual observation of a child's behavior in many academic and nonacademic situations, will gain a much clearer understanding of the child's needs. Following are some questions which need to be answered to gain information about a child's personal adequacy. Some of the generalized observations which might apply to certain children are phrased below each question.

What kind of person is this child, and what is he like at this stage of growing up?

What does he like to do, and what does he do? (interests and activities)

For instance: He reads much of the time; engages in much physical activity; likes to be constantly with people; likes to be "on the go"; wants to be the center of excitement or create excitement if it is lacking; spends much of his time working on his hobby.

Is he interested in doing and able to do the things that other children of his age do? (maturity)

For instance: He plays with younger children; prefers the company of adults; spends his time with children his own age but usually of the opposite sex; lacks coordination of muscles essential for participation in the physical games which are usually enjoyed by children of his age.

What would he like to succeed in and what has he succeeded in? (his values, goals and achievements)

For instance: Wants material things; seems to need much personal attention and affection; social success is important to him; strives almost too hard for high grades; craves constant praise; doesn't say what he wants, but his behavior indicates some acute need.

How does he react to difficulties or frustrations? (emotional stability)

For instance: He often side-steps his responsibilities for the group; he tends to withdraw into himself; he is frequently critical of others; he often refuses to recognize his problems; he blames himself for his weaknesses but seems to lack the persistence needed to improve; he offers in a pleasant manner some constructive solution; he is usually on the "off side" of an argument or classroom discussion; he accedes to the letter as well as the spirit of the law.

How comfortable does he appear with people of his own age; with adults? (security and sense of belonging)

For instance: Is apologetic in manner; flushes and pales easily; appears muscularly tense; often moves around in a disturbing manner; rarely meets directly another's gaze; appears anxious; often seems to expect to be blamed or scolded; nervous; overeager to please adults.

Does he think other children feel he is peculiar or different, and do other children really think he is "different"? (the need for alikeness)

For instance: He says the other children don't like him; children say he does and says queer things; children seem to resent what he does and says; children consider him "tops."

What does he say he does; and what does he do? (sense of reality)

For instance: He accepts verbal responsibility and stops there; his words match his deeds; his ideas do not conform to his actions; he imagines and daydreams excessively; if he says he will do something it will be done; his reports of incidents are accurate; he is overprecise and overconscientious to the point of being hampered by ideals of perfection.

How satisfied is he to rely upon himself in work and play? (independence, initiative, resourcefulness, creativity)

For instance: He usually wants to make new rules for the game or make up a new game; he prefers routine, mechanical tasks; he usually wants to be told precisely what to do; he enjoys working out his own methods of attacking a school problem; he is a pioneer; he is creative and original; he likes to go ahead under his own steam; he has an abundance of initiative.

What is his characteristic pattern of activity in work, play and leisure?

For instance: He is slow but sure; fast and accurate; has to waste just so much time before he settles down to work; deliberate to the point of exasperation; quick when he wants to be; usually behind in his school work; only slow when it ultimately works to his advantage; restless; can't sit still; his interest is sincere and sustained; works in spurts; must be on the go; goes to pieces under high pressure; works constructively under supervision; destructive when unsupervised.

How has he changed during this year? (With reference to one or more of the areas listed above—his interests, goals, security, and work habits?)

For instance: From a happy child, he has become nervous and unhappy; he shows considerable progress in adjusting satisfactorily to new situations; he is losing ground in subject mastery and in friendships of a desirable nature; his general direction of growth appears to have altered but we are at present unable to judge how; he seems now to have found a purpose and a goal to tie to; for the first time, he appears to care what happens to him.

How To Record Observations—Suggestions and Examples

How best to record and evaluate the many observations of pupils' behavior in school situations is a difficult problem indeed. There are several techniques constituting partial answers, but none is fully adequate. The wisest procedure at present seems to be to use each technique in a place where its special contribution can be made use of without adopting also its special limitations.

The "written anecdote," relating briefly and without interpretation a pupil's actual behavior in a certain situation, can be used to a limited extent to increase the objectivity of the personal comments. To collect hundreds of anecdotes as the sole cumulative record material on personality seems far too burdensome for any advantages gained in increased objectivity. The wisest and most useful procedure now appears to be that of using the anecdote as a supplementary technique for assembling materials from classroom teachers, special teachers, sponsors of extracurricular activity, and homeroom teachers.

The more generalized yearly "personal summary," written for the cumulative record by the classroom teacher on the elementary school level and by the homeroom teacher or adviser on the secondary school level, has made and can continue to make a special contribution of its own. Actually the general summary represents a synthesis of anecdotes sent to a child's teacher by other staff members and the remembered but unwritten incidents or anecdotes experienced at firsthand by the teacher himself.

Some Examples of Recorded Observations Made by Various Teachers in the School:

"Applied for a special scholarship of local origin. Found that needier next-door neighbor had applied also. Withdrew his application, stating that a needier and equally worthy friend had applied. (Who can subsidize this boy? He's worth it. Probably will never push himself into limelight, but he should be there.)"

"At club meeting when a fund for Xmas basket fell short of desired amount, he offered the balance from his allowance. (Characteristic of him.)"

"Voted against trying to raise money by means of a movie. Was outvoted. Personally pulled affair to success by selling ninety-five tickets himself."

"Found out that nominees for Student Council offices were investing fathers' gifts in commercial advertising in school. Asked student council discussion of problem, and possible investigation of campaign expenses."

"Coach considered him excellent football material. Urged a tryout for Senior Squad. Boy accepted. Mother phoned and said she felt boy's condition wasn't equal to it. Doctor O.K.'d physical condition. Mother still objected. Boy gave up tryout."

"Has carried a cripple's books from class to class for a year. The cripple was no special friend of his at the beginning and is not now. When asked if he would like to give the job to someone else, said, 'If someone else wants to help, O.K. If not, I'll do it. That guy's got a lot to fight against that I haven't.' "

Some Examples of Summary Comments on "Personality Development" as Entered on the Permanent Record by the Teacher Who Summarizes and Synthesizes All Material Covering a Year for the Pupil Under His Charge:

"Takes part with zest in nonacademic activities. Has a practical, business hardheadedness. Most uncomfortable in bookwork.

Apologetic and nervous in class. Has put school newspaper on a paying basis. Likes to be with people. Hates to read. Worried about being the doctor his family wants him to be. Has become more nervous this year."

"Very dependent on group opinion. 'Cries with the wolves.' Waits to discover majority opinion before he expresses his own. Too anxious for approval of elders. Artistic, dramatic talents. Uncomfortable with boys. Loves acclaim of girls and gets it often. Avoids hard work. A 'dressy' boy. Wants special consideration to an unusual degree. Sensitive."

"Frank, objective, likeable person. At ease with all kinds of children. Knows what he wants and tries to achieve it. Not too good in academic lines, but is a practical go-getter. Successful in organization and selling. A man's man. You can depend upon him to stand for the things that really count. I find myself looking for his reaction as a check upon my own."

"The majority opinion is always a source of dispute. A nonconformer, against the government no matter what it is, yet will work under pressure. Scholastically brilliant; respected but not liked by other students. An omnivorous reader. Watch for possible pioneering slants that may have great promise."

"Poor coordination in physical games. Always wins in mental contests. Apt to underestimate the value of things he does not do well in. Says he doesn't care about girls' opinions, but I feel that the respect of girls is needed to encourage his maturing. Is too much of an idealist for his own good."

"Both an idealist and a realist. Has support of both progressive and conservative student opinions. Is trusted by all, balanced, likeable, but never caters to sheer opinion. Best kind of constructive leader. Hates academic activities."

"Unusual ability to influence people. Happy-go-lucky; at ease with all; pleasant company. Doesn't want too much from life, but doesn't expect to work too hard for the little he asks. Has his feet on the ground. Fatherly attitude. Loves outdoor life. A born sportsman. A conciliator of opposing opinions. Keeps social affairs going without heat or friction."

The Importance of Constructive and Positive Recording

It is possible to say things in two different ways. One way emphasizes the positive aspects of child growth. The other way emphasizes the negative aspects. On the whole, for the purpose of guiding growing children toward higher levels of maturity, the positive type of comment should predominate. Thus we may build toward the future by emphasis upon what the child can do, rather than upon what he cannot do. The facing of personal limitations and failures along specific lines is essential, but it serves an individual best when it occurs against a background of recognized personal strengths. For example, we can record, "Dick thinks he can always be a winner. He is a poor sport when he loses." Or we can say, "Dick is usually highly successful in games as well as in academic work. He needs help, however, in learning how to accept his occasional defeats with good sportsmanship."

The Importance of Dating and Signing Entries

Dating an entry adds to its significance since it can then be interpreted with all of the other data referring to a particular stage of growth. Lack of respect for other people's property is, for instance, a very different matter at the first than at the twelfth grade level. If the reader of the record cannot tell just when a child revealed a given type of behavior, he will likely be at a loss to interpret it.

Signing entries indicates a willingness to accept responsibility for the data. It also enhances the significance of the data since it indicates the area of school activity concerned. For instance, the entry may mean different things if recorded by the supervisor of the cafeteria, the department head, the club sponsor, or the dean of boys. Moreover, since teachers differ from each other just as children do, the reader of a signed entry is helped to interpret the data in light of his knowledge of the person who made the observation.

How To Encourage Teachers To Contribute to the Record by Use of the "Flow Sheet"

There are moments, as noted earlier in this chapter, on the playground, in the library, in club meetings, in performances, in classrooms, shops or art rooms, when the child's behavior reveals a great deal about him—his characteristics, his talents and aptitudes. Such incidents, especially when they are observed frequently enough to show they are typical of the individual, can be of vital importance to the teacher who makes the final personality summary for the cumulative record.

Since they occur day by day, and in many places, and since they are observed by various teachers, the need is for some way for busy teachers to record these observations swiftly and briefly, and for some way to route the information so that it reaches the person who records the summary on the record.

The accompanying "Source Material Sheet for Cumulative

SOURCE MATERIAL SHEET FOR CUMULATIVE GROWTH RECORDS

(This is to be filled out by teachers other than the homeroom teacher, either voluntarily or upon request of the homeroom teacher. Fill out only such portions as you feel qualified to report on. Keep these in guidance packet for current year only.)
Homeroom teachers use these as an additional aid in making out yearly summaries on guidance packets.

To ....
(Homeroom teacher)

About ....
(Pupil's name)

From ....
(Reporting teacher's name)

In capacity as ....
(Position)

ANECDOTE FROM ANY TEACHER—(Brief summary of occurrence.)

Is this behavior characteristic of the student?

TALENTS AND APTITUDES — (From special subject teachers in Art, Shop, Commercial, Fine and Practical Arts, Science, etc.)

TALENTS
Leader ....
Artistic ....
Social ....
Mechanical ....
Musical ....
Practical ....
Domestic ....
Academic ....
Athletic ....
Natural ....
Organizer ....
Executive ....
Salesman ....

LEVEL
Original ....
Creative ....
Routine ....
Hobby level only ....
Career possibilities ....

WORK HABITS
Accurate ....
Sustained effort ....
Prompt ....
Finishes task ....

PERSONAL QUALITIES
(From any teacher)

	Markedly strong	Markedly weak
Ambition	....	....
Dependability	....	....
Willingness to work	....	....
Emotional balance	....	....
Initiative	....	....
Gets along with people	....	....
Practical sense	....	....
Personal appeal	....	....
Physical vitality	....	....
Sense of social responsibility	....	....

GROUP AND CIVIC EXPERIENCE

(From a faculty sponsor or guide in any extracurricular or intracurricular activity—class groups, clubs, student government, community groups if known, etc.)

JOB HELD BY PUPIL ....

TYPE OF CONTRIBUTION IN:
Organization ....
Management ....
Salesmanship ....

Promotion ....
Creative energy ....
Routine responsibilities ....

RELATIONSHIPS WITH GROUP

MEMBERS:
Reasonable sacrifices for group good ....
Conforms to group standards ....
Helps to raise standards ....
Gives some service without "pay" ....

MARKETABLE SKILLS

Typing speed ....
Stenographic speed ....

As a group member, is:
Tactful .... Isolated ....
Likeable .... Rejected ....
Cooperative ....
Influential ....
Negative ....

Growth Records" is one suggested way to accomplish this pooling of information about a given pupil. An individual staff member can select the portions of the sheet which apply to the observation or experience he wants to make a matter of record. By simply checking the level or nature of talents and aptitudes in the appropriate columns, or by jotting down a sentence or two about an incident under the space for anecdotes; by checking the personal qualities in the appropriate column, or by indicating the type of job and nature of the pupil's contribution, or the nature of the pupil's relationships with other group members, the staff member can contribute to the picture of the individual. These recordings may be filed immediately in guidance packets, to be used later as source material for synthesis and recording.

Any one of these recorded observations or experiences may prove helpful. But the cumulative effect of many such recordings from various sources in the school can vitalize the developmental picture of the child and make dynamic and meaningful the direction of his growth.

How to centralize and record material from numerous individual flow sheets, and what staff member should be responsible are questions which must obviously be answered by individual schools on the basis of their varying personnel and organization.

This chapter has attempted to give teachers some practical guidelines for knowing what information an adequate record should include, how the data might be interpreted to discover factors which relate to some of the adjustment problems children face, and how to avoid the pitfalls which teachers might encounter as they try to gain from the record a valid picture of a growing child. The chapter also suggests the areas of a child's life which are significant for understanding his growth, the types of observations which teachers can make of children, and the way these observations can best be recorded.

Whether or not the cumulative record is a valuable tool for guidance depends primarily upon the teachers who use it and who contribute to it. Unless teachers understand the nature of child growth and are willing to work to become skilful in studying human behavior and in recording in a constructive manner what they observe, the record is of little value and may be of definite harm. Unless teachers study to become more competent in analyzing the record data on a differential basis, the results, likewise, may injure some children rather than help them. It is important to remember that children are constantly growing and changing. There is no single rule of thumb by which to understand or educate them. Behavior means different things at different age levels, and recorded comments, though beautifully apt at a certain time, may or may not be important in the picture of the child several years later.

The cumulative record as a tool in guidance should therefore be used with the wisdom, discretion and understanding which characterize teachers with professional experience and maturity.

CHAPTER IX

Parents as Partners

AMONG the major resources available to teachers in guiding children are their parents. In fact, parents are perhaps the most valuable resource which teachers have, if they know how to work with the parents as *partners*. Parents and teachers are the principal guides of children, and only by working together can either hope to accomplish their objectives. It is essential that there be mutual understanding and cooperation between the school and the home, if the needs of each child are to be met.

No good school curriculum or guidance program can satisfactorily accomplish its purposes unless a two-way avenue of communication between schools and homes is kept open and in fairly constant operation. The school cannot understand the individual pupil and his needs unless it has some knowledge and understanding of the home and family from which he comes. Similarly, the parents cannot fully understand their child unless they know something about the experiences he is having under school auspices. In fact, the major objectives of the school's curriculum are likely to fail of accomplishment if parents do not understand and accept these aims. Such understanding and acceptance may well involve parent participation in determining what the curriculum and its objectives are to be. Certainly the school should seek cooperation and support from parents in establishing its major goals and objectives and should constantly interpret its program—both as to content and to methods—to parents and other citizens of the community.

A mother was having her first experience in a child development and guidance workshop in which parents and teachers were working together. She wrote in her notebook:

I have just reached the conclusion, after five days devoted to studying problems in child guidance, that teachers are "people"—nice, warm, friendly people. They are as deeply concerned as parents that all children, everywhere, have the very best chance possible to grow to the limit of their capabilities and to learn to adjust themselves to their environment. It was a truly revealing experience for me to get a glimpse through the invisible wall that unfortunately often exists in parent-teacher relationships. I had not realized that teachers are frequently as bewildered as fathers and mothers and are anxious to do everything in their power to cooperate with parents to develop the best potentialities of children.

This statement was written by a farm mother. In the workshop she attended there were ten people from rural one-room schools and twenty from city school systems.[1] Some were classroom teachers and some were parents; all were working together for deeper understanding of their children. This is typical of the new day in which the family and the school have at last discovered their interdependence. The invisible wall that the mother referred to in her notebook has in the past separated parents from teachers in many communities. Traditionally, the school was here, and the home was there and "never the twain shall meet" was the accepted order of the day. Fortunately, that wall is gradually being broken down. In fact, there is perhaps no area of education in which there has been greater progress during the past quarter-century than in developing and improving school-home relations. In all up-to-date communities throughout the country, schools and homes are learning to cooperate in many and varied programs.

Guidance Is Continuous

Guidance is a process which begins at birth and continues until death. Parents are the major guides of children. The first and foremost influences in a child's life are his mother and father. Their guidance begins at the birth of the child and continues until he reaches adulthood. Teachers are second only to parents as guides of children, but the individual teacher comes and goes, while fathers and mothers remain a constant influence in the lives of their children.

As a matter of fact, all guidance is of one piece, so to speak, forming a *circle of guidance* made up of segments which are periods of life—preschool, elementary school, high school, college and adult years. We cannot guide the preschool and elementary school child

[1] This workshop was part of the Illinois Child Development and Guidance Project, jointly sponsored by the Illinois ASCD and the University of Chicago, described by Ethel Kawin. "A Cooperative Approach to Child Study." *Educational Leadership* 7:563-67; May 1950.

unless we have sufficient understanding of the adolescent and adult years to be able to evaluate the experience of these earlier periods in terms of their possible effects on the later ones. Nor can we guide an adolescent or adult wisely without some understanding of his earlier experiences and their significance in relation to his present patterns of personality and behavior. For practical reasons, most of us have to specialize, working at least at any specific time primarily with one or another age level. But to work wisely and effectively, one must always see any one age period against the background of the total circle into which it must be integrated and of which it is only a segment.

In fact, we should go beyond this static concept of a *circle*, to a dynamic concept of continuous *cycles*. Here is a child growing up. One cannot work with or guide this young child without also working with the adults—especially parents and teachers—responsible for his upbringing. To a great extent, his personality and behavior are responses to situations which these adults create for him. They, in turn, are dealing with him in ways largely determined by their experiences in their own early childhood. What they do now to this young child will affect what he will do with children when he eventually becomes an adult and in his turn creates the next generation. So is established an endless cycle—a dynamic, continuous process through which guidance runs like an endless chain.

Importance of Early Years

The first five years are, in many ways, the most important in any life. Foundations of personality and behavior are laid during this preschool period. The personalities of his parents and the environment which they create for him are major factors in determining what the child is and what he is likely to become. The family has already determined, therefore, the kind of child who will come to school. The school must accept the child sent to it by the home and do the best it can for him. But the home influences, whether good or bad, are the strongest and probably the most enduring that any boy or girl will ever have. In order to understand a pupil, each successive teacher must certainly have some knowledge and understanding of his home and family background.

Parents are, therefore, indispensable resource persons for the school, both because of the strong determining influence they exert during the child's early years and because of their continuing influence in that major part of the child's life which is spent outside of school all during the school years. Without an exchange of information with the parents and their understanding and cooperation, teachers are not likely to be able to accomplish best results in the education of children.

To help in accomplishing these major purposes, the school should extend its guidance services downward to the preschool years. This may be done in a variety of ways. Some schools have parent study-discussion groups in which teachers or other members of the school staff serve as leaders or resource persons to help parents study and understand young children and the importance of these earliest years. The kindergarten teacher may play a major role in such study-discussion groups. Schools might extend the service of guidance specialists to parents of children who will later become pupils. Most young parents are eager for guidance. Many, if not most, of the problems with which kindergarten and first grade teachers struggle when children enter school might have been avoided if parents had been given help in guiding their children during infancy and the preschool years.

Teacher-Parent Conferences

In a school which has a sound guidance program, provision is made for a friendly conference between the teacher and the parents of each child who is entering school for the first time. As soon as the teacher has had a chance to become acquainted with the new pupil, a friendly interview with the mother, or preferably both of his parents, makes a good first step in trying to know and understand the child and in furnishing data with which to start the pupil's individual cumulative record. Such an interview is very important in initiating a friendly, cooperative relationship between the school and the home—a relationship which, it is to be hoped, will continue throughout the child's school years. Traditionally, a parent came to school only upon request, and usually when a child presented a learning or a behavior problem. This arrangement put both parent and teacher on the defensive and everyone concerned got off to a bad start. When a friendly contact between parent and teacher has been made before there are any signs of difficulty, tension is less likely to arise in those cases in which the teacher later must make an approach to the parent regarding specific problems which have arisen in the child's school progress or adjustment.

This initial conference gives the teacher a background for helping the child make his first important adjustments to the school. The young child's teacher should be familiar with his developmental history; he should know whether the child's development has been "normal" or whether it has been unusual in any way. Slowness in walking or talking may or may not be of special significance in knowing what to expect of a child, but in any event it is information which the school should have. It is equally important to know whether the child has seemed to be precocious in his early development. Knowledge of a child's physical history will help a teacher to maintain and protect the youngster's health. Serious diseases of early childhood may have affected the child in ways which it will be helpful to have the school understand.

The conference will help the teacher to get a picture of the family background, to know what kind of parents, sisters and brothers the youngster may have. For example, the child who has been deprived of either his mother or his father during infancy or the early years may come to school with feelings of insecurity which the understanding teacher can help to alleviate. A child's position in the family may be an important factor in helping the teacher understand his school behavior. Research has indicated that oldest, youngest, and "only" children, and even a "middle child" in the family may tend to react in certain ways that appear to be caused by his particular place in the family constellation.

The parent's report of the child's progress in mental development and in habit training, the range of his previous social experience and his reactions to other children, and his play activities, including those related to radio and movie programs, will all help the teacher in understanding the child's school behavior and in making the child's transition from home to school easier and more comfortable. For example, many children come to school with very little previous play experience with other children, and the understanding teacher who knows this will arrange the environment to help them play first with one or two other children, and gradually to extend this experience as each child becomes ready to participate in larger groupings.

The understanding teacher and the alert parent will want to exchange information regarding any behavior problems which the child may present at home and in school. One of the greatest values of this initial teacher-parent conference is that both parents and teachers have an opportunity to learn whether the child tends to behave quite differently at home from the way he behaves in school, or vice versa. This is mutually helpful to the teacher and the parent in their efforts to find *causes* of the behavior trends which they seek to modify. Each may be helpful to the other in developing more appropriate ways of guiding the child so that the desired changes in behavior may be effected.

From its beginnings in this routine teacher-parent conference designed to establish a friendly relationship between parents and teachers when the child enters school, the teacher-parent conference has developed to serve other very important purposes. From having been almost unknown as a routine part of the school program two decades ago, the teacher-parent conference has now reached a place of great importance. Concrete evidence of this is found in an article published in the autumn of 1950 in *Life* magazine. The article was entitled "How Good Is Your School?" and listed 63 items which could be checked "Yes" or "No" by parents who wished to evaluate the schools which their children attend. The third and fourth items in this list were: "(3) Teacher-parent conferences are arranged for a majority of the pupils; (4) There are at least two teacher-parent conferences per year for every child." According to this test of a "good school," the answer to both of these items should be "Yes."

The specific purposes of these individual conferences vary. Teacher and parent at any grade level may meet just to get acquainted and to establish a friendly foundation for further school-home relationships; or at any grade level the teacher may want to get a developmental history and gain some knowledge of the pupil's home background that will help the teacher better understand him. Probably, teacher-parent conferences are most commonly held today as one method of reporting a pupil's progress to his parents. And, of course, there are still many instances in which a teacher asks a parent to come to school because there is a problem for which a pupil needs the help of both school and home.

How common is the regular conference in which a teacher talks with the parents of every pupil in the class? No dependable figures are available. It is doubtful whether many schools achieve the standard set up by the magazine article referred to above, but the trend toward individual teacher-parent conferences is obvious in the good school systems of our land. The rapidity with which this phase of the school program has developed is no less than amazing when one considers the difficulties that have to be met in establishing such a program.

Problems Involved in Teacher-Parent Conferences

What are some of the problems involved? First, there is the preparation of teachers for new procedures and responsibilities. Since such training has not been a part of teacher education in most institutions, this often means some special in-service training for teachers. Then there is the preparation of parents for such a new relationship to the school. This is often done, in a general way, through a meeting of the parent-teacher association.

Many decisions have to be made as to how the program should be started. Should all teachers and parents participate immediately, or should the program be initiated slowly and allowed to grow year by year? If the latter, how should the school begin—with a few interested teachers who want to try interviews with parents or with teachers of certain grades? Should each teacher begin by having conferences with the parents of only a few of his pupils, or should he try to talk individually with the parents of every child in his classroom? If only a few are to be interviewed, it is important that they should not be parents of children with outstanding problems. Otherwise the new program will seem only an extension of the traditional "we'll tell your father and mother" school threat.

Perhaps the most vexing of all the problems to be met in establishing a regular program of teacher-parent conferences is the matter of time for the conferences. A good conference takes time; there is no getting away from that. Most teachers report that twenty minutes is the minimum period required, and a conference that is mutually satisfying to parent and teacher is more likely to take thirty to forty minutes. When the problems to be discussed are complicated, it may take even longer to talk them through and formulate a constructive plan for helping a child to overcome his difficulties.

Where is this time to come from? Most teachers are already carrying very heavy loads. It is a well-known fact that there is an increased number of pupils and a shortage of teachers in our schools, especially at the elementary level. Can one expect the teacher to add to this burden by staying after school hours to interview parents? Let it be said—to the great credit of America's teachers—that most teacher-parent conference programs have been launched on the teachers' own time! This is a testimonial both to the professionalism and to the spirit of dedication that thousands of our teachers bring to their high calling.

But is it fair to ask the teacher to make this great contribution indefinitely? When the value of teacher-parent conferences has been demonstrated, should not the school board grant teachers some released time for this important part of the school program? Many systematic evaluations made by parents who have experienced such individual conferences testify to the helpfulness of these private talks with teachers. Should not the parents urge school boards to provide released time for this procedure which they believe benefits their children so greatly? Parents can indicate their willingness to have part of their school tax dollars go to the support of such a program.

There are other technical questions to be considered in the planning and development of such programs. When and how often should conferences be held? Should there be an outline of some sort to guide the interview? Should such a guide be sent to parents in advance of the conference? What parts of a child's school record, if any, should be shown to the parent? Should the teacher keep a record of the conference, and should some written report of it be sent to the parents, especially if only one parent can be present at the conference? Should pupils themselves sometimes participate in such conferences? If so, under what circumstances and at what age levels? These are some of the many practical questions that any school staff is likely to encounter in a program of teacher-parent conferences.

The answers to such practical questions will vary from situation to situation and with the specific purposes of the conferences. It is common practice for teachers who are to participate in a teacher-parent conference program to study and discuss the whole matter before any definite plans are formulated. They gather reports of what other school systems have tried and found successful. They try to avoid practices that others have concluded were mistakes. Then they are likely to draft a tentative program that seems to meet the needs and possibilities of their own local schools. At this point it is usually wise to appoint or elect a planning committee upon which faculty and parents are jointly represented, so that parents can participate in the planning of the actual program.

Most committees find that there is no one right answer to all of these practical questions. Much depends upon the ideas and preferences of those who are to carry out the program. Also such a new venture usually must be undertaken step by step. For example, outline guides for conferences and written records of them often evolve after parents and teachers see the need for them, though such suggestions may be rejected as "too much to undertake" in the beginning, when teachers feel a bit overwhelmed at the interview itself. Schools frequently seek the guidance of a special consultant who is experienced in setting up these programs to help initiate teachers into the new techniques and procedures of teacher-parent conferences.

Fundamental Principles and Procedures

There are certain fundamental principles and procedures, however, that should be incorporated into any program of individual conferences to make it successful. Here are some of the more important considerations:

Conferences should take place in privacy, parent meeting teacher in a comfortable, relaxed atmosphere. Each should feel that the other has set this particular time aside for the purpose and that each will receive the other's undivided, unhurried attention.

Parent and teacher should feel that each accepts the other *as a person*. There should be a sense of trust between them, so that each feels free to reveal whatever is essential to his understanding of the child, without fear of misunderstanding, condemnation, or betrayal of confidence.

The teacher should come to the conference prepared to give the parent a report on his child in school situations but should be equally interested in getting the parent's report on his own child. The parent should be encouraged to express his ideas regarding the child and his needs and to suggest what experiences he thinks will further the child's growth and development.

The teacher should always begin the interview with some favorable comments about the child. When weak points are brought up, emphasis should be placed upon those in which improvement is most readily possible, and a constructive plan for home-school cooperation, in trying to help the child overcome his weaknesses, should be agreed upon.

At the end of any such conference, the way should be left open for further friendly, cooperative contacts, to be initiated by the teacher or the parent when either feels that the child's interests will be served by such a contact of school and home.

Is this all worth while? Does the investment of time, effort and (indirectly) money pay dividends? One finds little difference of opinion on this point among those—whether parents or teachers who have participated in such programs. Practically all seem to agree that no single procedure has done more to improve school-home relations than the teacher-parent conference and no phase of the school program has contributed more to the establishment of good public relations.

Interpreting Pupil Records to Parents

In the preceding chapter, the individual cumulative pupil record was discussed. The use of such records, it was made clear, constitutes a very important phase of the school's guidance program. As this chapter has pointed out, the initial teacher-parent conference which takes place when the child enters school should provide basic material for the individual pupil record. Since the record is cumulative, it is constantly augmented with additional information and passed along as the child goes upward through the grades of the elementary and the high school. Chapter VIII described ways in which records serve to help each teacher to understand and to deal wisely with every child who comes under his guidance. It is equally important that such records be used to help parents or other adults responsible for the care of a child to deal with him understandingly and guide him wisely. Such an understanding parent becomes a major source of help for the teacher in the latter's efforts to guide each pupil. Perhaps the teacher's greatest ultimate contribution in using individual cumulative pupil records is to help parents understand the child and to help the child understand himself, because parental guidance and self-guidance continue for the pupil after teacher guidance has ceased.

Records can be invaluable in school-home contacts if the school personnel know how to use records wisely and constructively in dealing with parents. No type of school device is more effective than that which is based on a concrete cumulative individual record when wisely used, yet no material is more likely to antagonize parents when wrongly used. Generally speaking, no school record should merely be handed to parents for them to look over. Selected parts of his record may be reported or shown to a pupil's parents by members of the school staff who are competent to interpret this material constructively. In its whole approach to the parent, the school must be guided by what is known of the parent and by the way he is likely to react to the information given him. Especially must the school consider the effects these parental reactions may have upon the child. For example, a child with limited ability may be trying to do his best and may be achieving all that he seems capable of doing, yet not reach the academic level of most of his classmates or the expectations of his parents. The school should make every effort to help parents accept the child with such limitations and persuade them not to pressure him unduly or treat him harshly for deficiencies which he cannot help. But if parents in such a situation persist in harsh treatment of the child each time academic inadequacies become known to them, the school must be very guarded as to what and how it reports to them concerning the child's academic progress. Such a child may be discouraged from doing his best when confronted with negative parental attitudes.

Much of the objection to records on the part of parents (and even on the part of some school staff members themselves) is based on a fear that an unfavorable impression crystallized in a written record form that is passed on from teacher to teacher may prejudice teachers against a pupil. They even fear that such a negative record may precede a child so that because he once "got off on the wrong foot" with some particular teacher, he will never be allowed a fair, fresh start again. Yet it is not the *records* themselves which cause injustice to a child. The harm occurs when one teacher remarks to another in passing: "Wait until you get that Jones boy! He'll give you plenty of headaches!" Or over the bridge table the mathematics teacher exclaims: "I've got another one of that Johnson family! They're all too dumb to learn anything!"

Such incidents as these occur countless times in schools which keep no special records at all. They occur wherever the teaching staff members are not truly professional in their outlook and attitudes. It is true that records can be wrongly used. The *constructive* use of records is dependent directly upon the professional attitude of the teaching staff. To the extent that teachers see records as tools or instruments to be used to *help children,* they will avoid negative effects of records. In addition to the professional spirit and philosophy of the staff, awareness of the possible negative effects in wrong use of records will help the school deliberately to avoid them.

Certain techniques will prove efficacious and at the same time be reassuring to parents. For example, some positive, favorable comments should be made about a child in every instance before negative and unfavorable facts are recorded. Every child has "assets" as well as "liabilities." Especially in dealing with parents, the favorable items in the record should always be presented first, thus making the undesirable items about their offspring more acceptable to fathers and mothers. Records should be available which will help parents to see their child with reasonable objectivity and follow his school progress and his personality development. They should be interpreted to parents, however, with care and discretion.

Parents as well as teachers may keep records which are helpful in the guidance of a child. Despite the fact that studies of parent reports indicate that sometimes they are subject to considerable unreliability, they still have genuine value. Systematic observations of their own children are extremely revealing to parents. Fathers and mothers often gain insight into their own and their children's behavior in a measure difficult to achieve by any other method. In addition, their reports sometimes furnish important cues about such things as parental attitudes which may prove very valuable to the school in understanding the child.

Readiness

Very early in the child's school life the question of "readiness" comes up for consideration. Most of us think of readiness only in terms of readiness for reading, and that question arises toward the end of the kindergarten year, or very early in the first grade. Readiness, however, is a concept which applies to any learning activity at any stage of life. It is a complex concept involving capacity, maturation, experience and motivation. Appraising a child's readiness or *un*readiness to undertake a new learning activity is vital to successful school experience for the child.

If this matter of readiness for reading, or "readiness for first grade" (as it is often referred to in our schools) is badly handled by the school, the friendly and understanding cooperation of the home may be seriously impaired at the very outset of the child's school life. To help a parent understand and accept the fact that his child is apparently not ready for a certain type of experience for which most of the child's associates appear ready constitutes a genuine challenge to the educator. How can the parent be informed so that he can understand the situation, accept it with equanimity and patiently wait until the child is ready, or cooperate in helping to make him ready? The fact that the child is not ready to do what is expected of most children of his age and his school grade tends to arouse feelings of anxiety and guilt in the parent. He may fear that his child is in some way inadequate because the youngster does not measure up to what is expected of him, or he may feel that he himself is inadequate as a parent and is responsible for having failed to get the child ready. Either of these attitudes imperils the parent's feeling toward the school, and hinders the desired teacher-parent partnership.

There are many things which the school can do to prepare fathers and mothers to understand and to face this problem of readiness. Through various avenues of parent education, fathers and mothers may become familiar with the whole concept of readiness and its significance in education. They can also be helped to understand that if the child's developmental immaturity is due to lack of inner maturation, postponement of learning may be wise because time alone will probably correct that factor. Lack of readiness that is due to a dearth of experiences which contribute to readiness is not likely to occur in a school where young parents have been guided by the school to help prepare the child for first grade and reading experiences. However, where such experiences have been lacking, parents can be helped in planning to provide such experiences and to put such a plan into effect at once.

There is now available a little book that can be very helpful to parents in building a readiness for reading in children of preschool age. *Growing Into Reading,* by Marion Monroe, points out that readiness for reading begins at home.[2] The author describes seven stages of "book behavior" which precede the actual reading-readiness program of the good kindergarten. She considers the mere manipulation of a book by the year-old child as the first stage, and points out that stage by stage a child's behavior in relation to books progresses to an eighth stage of real reading-readiness which we find in many, if not most, children during the late kindergarten period and early months of first grade. Understanding of these successive stages of "book behavior" will help parents to send to school a child who feels that books are to be enjoyed—a child with a love of books based upon many happy contacts with them in his home. This, the author points out, is the best possible preparation for reading.

If a child appears not to be ready for a certain type of learning because he is somewhat retarded in development, the school can help the parents to accept the child as a "slow learner." Such a child can be guided successfully so that he develops a healthy personality only if both home and school help him to feel secure and adequate

[2] Marion Monroe. *Growing Into Reading: How Readiness for Reading Develops at Home and at School.* Chicago: Scott, Foresman, 1951.

when he does the best of which he is capable. Frequently a child's lack of readiness for a certain learning activity is due to specific difficulties or disabilities, such as visual or auditory defects, or emotional problems. Before he can become ready for this new learning experience, there must be a diagnosis of his difficulty, followed by whatever remedial procedures are indicated. Parent cooperation is essential to the school's accomplishment of such a program.

In the school's approach to this whole matter of *readiness*, parents must feel that: (a) The school's program and procedures are based on knowledge of facts, both in regard to the general problem and to the individual problems of their child; (b) The school personnel is primarily motivated by a sincere desire to do what is best for each boy and girl and that consideration of administrative problems and problems of classroom organization is secondary; (c) The school regards every parent as a cooperative person, capable of understanding and anxious to do what is desirable for his child, and that the school turns to the parents as a source of help.

Interpreting Test Results to Parents

Since standardized tests are one factor in determining readiness, it might be well at this point to consider the general problem of interpreting test results to parents. The whole field of standardized objective tests is for parents a relatively new aspect of the modern school program. While it is true that group tests of intelligence, scholastic aptitude and scholastic achievement were developments of more than a quarter of a century ago, organized testing programs have not yet become a regular part of school procedure in a majority of the schools of the country. Most parents of pupils in the schools of today have had no personal experience with such tests in their own school days, and they encounter the testing programs used for their children with almost no background of understanding that helps them to interpret such test results. Even the teachers in today's schools have—many of them—little actual understanding of what particular tests mean or what their significance in relation to an individual pupil's capacity, achievement and future progress may be.

Since tests are important in evaluating the curriculum and the school's progress toward achieving its objectives, as well as in the guidance of every individual boy and girl, it is important that teachers first and parents second be helped to a real understanding of tests, their contributions and especially their limitations. No school should expect a parent to believe that his child is not ready for first grade just because of a score on a paper and pencil readiness test. No school is justified in coming to such a conclusion on the basis of test data only. But how can the school explain to parents why a test does constitute one important bit of evidence? Only if the testing procedure, and the basis on which the results are interpreted and applied, are explained to parents in ways that are understandable to them, can the school expect to gain the parental support and cooperation which it needs in making a plan for the child who has been tested.

This same principle applies to all types of tests which a school gives to its pupils. Whether the tests be used to measure scholastic aptitude, scholastic achievement, vocational aptitudes or other measurable abilities, the school needs the help of parents in planning a program based partly upon these test results. If parents do not understand and accept the bases for a school's decision in regard to their child, there is little hope that the child himself will accept the decision and benefit from the program.

In general, guidance workers should avoid discussing with parents specific scores on aptitude and intelligence tests. It is better to discuss a child's capacities in more general terms. When a child's mental abilities deviate from the "normal," such test results (including all tests yielding intelligence quotients or "IQ's") should preferably be reported by psychologists or guidance specialists who have professional training for interpreting tests and also training and experience in working with parents. If that is not possible, teachers should receive training in how to interpret such tests to parents. In a number of schools there is now a very real attempt to help teachers understand and utilize wisely the test data gathered on their pupils. They do not all approach the problem in the same way, but every school needs to find some method of winning the understanding and cooperation of parents in the development of a successful testing program.

Reporting Pupil Progress to Parents

Closely related to the problem of interpreting test results to parents is the question of how the school should report pupil progress to them. One of the areas of greatest experimentation in education in recent years is in methods of making reports to parents in

regard to their children. The traditional, periodic, stereotyped report card is being steadily supplanted by more informal methods of
reporting, especially at the kindergarten, primary and intermediate
school levels. The purposes of reports will, of course, determine
their nature and content. The newer type reports usually take the
form of individual letters or teacher-parent conferences, especially
at the kindergarten and primary levels. As one goes on into the intermediate grades and the junior high school, the report may be in
the form of a card or folder, but its content is likely to be quite different from that of the report card forms that parents have known
in the past. In addition, the bases for grading are going through a
period of rather constant analysis and change. There is probably no
school in the country which has found a completely satisfactory
method of grading its students. For this reason, this period of experimentation and rapid change is, on the whole, a healthy sign
that the school is trying to improve its marking and reporting
practices.

The parent's role in this whole area of reporting children's progress is, of course, a vital one. Parents have a profound interest in
knowing how their child is getting along in school; they should
also have a chance to participate in deciding what will be reported
to them and on what basis the reports will be formulated. Several
schools participating in the Illinois Child Development and Guidance Project, jointly sponsored by the Illinois ASCD and the University of Chicago, have joint groups of teachers and parents
cooperating in the school's effort to improve methods of marking
and reporting.

Both parents and teachers need time to adjust to new methods.
School grades and reports were traditionally designed to judge a
pupil rather than to guide him. Little attention was paid to personality development, although "deportment" and "effort" were
frequently included as items on the old type report card. Achievement in school subjects was recorded in terms of standards set for
the pupil's chronological age or his grade in school. If he fell below
the standard, he was represented as having "failed," whether or
not the standard set was one possible of achievement by him as an
individual. Achieving above the standard represented success, even
though the so-called successful child might actually be working
far below the level of his capabilities.

To change from these traditional methods of evaluating and reporting a child's school progress, both teachers and parents must be

given time gradually to adjust to newer educational philosophy with its recognition of the importance of developing a healthy personality along with successful acquisition of knowledge and academic skills. They also need cooperatively to work out methods by which a child who does the best of which he is capable can be helped to feel that he is a successful child, whether or not he is able to compete successfully with the group of which he is a member.

This is not to imply that a child's work is never to be compared with that of others. Such comparison is inevitable when any child is a member of a group; and each person must eventually learn the extent to which he can compete successfully in various areas of life. In the process of learning to accept his "liabilities" as well as his "assets," every individual must be helped to maintain basic self-esteem and a feeling of adequacy. There will be many activities, as a person goes through life, from which he can derive enjoyment without successful competition; there are others in which, if he cannot succeed, he is likely to find little satisfaction. The latter is especially true of activities in which one tries to earn his living.

It is very important that parents understand these matters as the child progresses through school. Abandoning the standards and methods with which they themselves grew up and which they expected would be used both by the school and by the home in judging their child's educational progress is a matter of education and of growth for them. It seems evident that, in evaluating a child's growth and development, teachers should consider his progress in terms of three relationships: in relation to the *child's own capacity and previous attainment,* in relation to the *attainments of his own group or class,* and in relation to the *achievements of children about his own age in terms of nation-wide standards.*

The way in which these different standards of comparison are reported to parents and what emphasis will be given to them must depend upon each individual situation and especially upon the parents' understanding of and attitudes toward their child. Schools which ignore all but the child's own growth in reporting to parents often find that at some time the parents are likely to return to reproach the school for not having told them "the truth" about their child's inadequacies at a time when the parents might have seen "that something was done about it." By "the truth," the parent means the fact that the child did not measure up to the achievements of most other children in his grade or class. It is the school's responsibility not only to accept such limitations in the child, if these cannot be overcome, but also to help his parents understand and accept them. This can be done only by facing the limitations, not by denying them.

In projects where parents are participating with teachers in efforts to improve marking and reporting practices, parents are likely to be just as eager as teachers, and sometimes more so, to develop new and better ways of evaluating the child's progress. Among parents as well as teachers, however, there are almost always some "diehards" who cling to rigid standards of marking, with emphasis upon academic achievement and deportment, and who insist upon knowing just where their child stands in relation to the achievements or grades of every other pupil in his group. Schools must exercise leadership and patience in helping such parents to acquire greater insight into the psychological needs of children and to understand why the newer methods of evaluating pupil progress are beneficial to their children. Here, then, is another area in which schools can make progress only as they succeed in getting parents to understand and to support what is best for their children.

Perhaps the greatest innovation in the matter of reporting progress to parents is found in the very rapid growth of the teacher-parent conference as a method of informing the parent about his child's progress in school. In discussing teacher-parent conferences earlier in this chapter, it was pointed out that probably the most common purpose in holding them in present-day schools is to report pupil progress to parents. In some schools, the conference is a substitute for one written report of the school year, with cards or letters serving still as the more frequent method of reporting. In other schools, the conference method of reporting is used several times a year.

A number of communities have circulated questionnaires asking parents to evaluate such teacher-parent conferences after the first year in which these have been introduced into the school program. Responses to the questionnaires indicate that almost all parents are enthusiastic about this method of reporting, even from the very beginning of the practice. Evaluations made by the parents include such comments as: "Deepened my understanding of my child." "Helped me to understand the school's program." "Gave me more helpful information than report cards." "I had an opportunity to become acquainted with the teacher, with freedom to ask questions and discuss problems with her." "It gave me an opportunity to get another's viewpoint on my child, to know my child as the teacher sees him."

Parents and the Curriculum

Progress in curriculum improvement is also ultimately dependent upon the support of parents and other citizens of the community. New developments may succeed temporarily, but unless the community—especially the parents who are the most deeply interested members of the community—understand and support what the school is doing, a reactionary movement attempting to eliminate newer practices and procedures is almost certain eventually to set in. Parents differ greatly, of course, in the degree of intelligence and the amount of knowledge they bring to consideration of school programs and problems. There are *some* parents who have more of both attributes than do *some* teachers.

The role of the lay citizen in general, and parents in particular, in the development of the curriculum of the school is a somewhat controversial matter. Certainly it would seem that parents should have a voice in helping to determine *what* their children should learn in school. Methods of instruction, on the other hand, call for professional training, and few lay citizens have the technical background necessary for deciding how material can best be taught and learned. The school does have a responsibility, however, for interpreting its methods to parents and explaining how and why instruction is undertaken in this or that way. It is extremely difficult for most parents, for example, to comprehend modern methods by which children learn to read, why they are not taught the alphabet at the very beginning of school, and why a meaningful unit, such as a word or phrase, helps the child to learn to read more easily than did a knowledge of isolated letters. It is difficult for parents to understand why script writing precedes cursive in most of the primary schools of today. Parents have a right to expect the school to inform them in regard to these and many other questions that are of vital importance to any father or mother interested in seeing that his child receives the best possible training that a school can offer.

Parent Participation in Specific Projects

Parents can serve as resource persons to teachers in a great variety of ways. There are almost unlimited possibilities for school-home cooperation in regard to specific phases of the school's program, and even in regard to children's activities outside of school. Only a few can be mentioned here.

Most parents have a genuine interest in their children's learning to read. This interest is likely to wane as the child goes upward through the grades. But there are important reasons for keeping parents in touch with what their children are reading and, where it is possible, for enlisting their help in selecting books which their children may wish to read. This need seems quite obvious at the present time, when so many attacks upon the books which schools are using spring from ignorance and misunderstanding on the part of those who criticize. There are important reasons why parents should be encouraged to read the books their children are studying when boys and girls reach the high school level or when they become college students. The gap between the generations is traditionally great. It is likely to be especially so in periods of rapid transition and change, such as we have been experiencing in modern days. Many of the books which students read in high school and college deal with subjects and points of view that startle and sometimes shock their parents. When parents have had an opportunity to participate in the examination and selection of books, they understand why these books are chosen for school reading lists. Such understanding will help to bridge the gap between the generations and to keep parents abreast of the ideas that their children are encountering and the experiences which they are having through modern literature.

In addition to such academic matters as books on school reading lists, there are many practical questions of social behavior which are of deep concern to both schools and homes, and with which parents have little chance to deal satisfactorily except through cooperation with other parents whose children attend the same schools. This is especially true in preadolescence and adolescence, when such issues as the hours children are allowed to keep, the use of automobiles, the types of parties boys and girls attend, and the kinds of places they go for recreation and entertainment become crucial problems for parents and for all other adults with genuine interest in boys and girls of these ages. If the school helps parents to organize and then encourages such groups to discuss these questions, not only among themselves and with the teachers, but also with adolescent groups, many of these serious difficulties might be satisfactorily resolved. The school needs the help of parents in these matters. The individual parent is rather helpless when he endeavors to establish standards or rules for his own boy or girl. But parents cooperating through the school can establish accepted community standards with the cooperation of the boys and girls themselves.

Most parent groups trying to develop a PTA or similar program encounter their greatest difficulties among parents of boys and girls at the high school level. Some of the reasons for this are obvious. Adolescents are struggling for independence and are likely to resist home-school contacts as parental "interference." Parents are less zealous about PTA activities by this time than they were when their children were younger. In addition, they do not want to antagonize their sons and daughters by coming to school when they believe the boys and girls do not want them to.

The most successful high school parent-teacher programs seem to be those which are sometimes called PTS—Parent-Teacher-Student organizations. In these the student himself participates, usually with a very active interest. In this type of program the adolescents' struggle for independence receives a certain recognition which gives them the feeling of *status* so important to boys and girls at this period of their development. Even in dealing with the individual high school boy or girl, it is wise for teachers to recognize this fact. If any member of the high school faculty wishes to interview the parents of a student, the plan should be cleared first with the student himself. There may occasionally be cases in which parents should not be seen over the strong objection of a student; in any event, his reasons for objecting should be given careful consideration. In some instances it may be wiser to give the student a chance to solve the problem himself before his parents are brought into the situation.

Parent Participation in Vocational Guidance

Another area in which the school can accomplish little without the cooperation of parents is in the field of vocational guidance. This seems somewhat obvious, but research studies have indicated that the parental role is even more crucial than most of us have realized. So inadequate has parental guidance been in this field that many young people are openly critical of the failure of their parents to help them make a wise vocational choice.[3] Here, again, is a field

[3] Eli Ginzberg, Sol W. Ginzberg, and John L. Herma. "The Problems of Occupational Choice." *American Journal of Orthopsychiatry* 20:1; January 1950.

in which the organized vocational guidance program of the school should reach out to parents as a resource, enlisting parent cooperation fairly early in the life of the adolescent. Most parents feel quite at a loss to know how to begin to help a child in the challenging and very important matter of choosing his life work. Only with the help of the school is there hope that the parent can begin to meet his own responsibility in this area. The reverse is also true. Whatever the school may attempt in guiding its pupils vocationally, it can do little for them without the understanding and support of their fathers and mothers.

Studying Child Development and Guidance

Parents are dependent upon the school for a full understanding of their children's school experiences and, as indicated earlier, scholastic achievement is only one area in which the school should serve as a source of guidance to parents. Fathers and mothers must look to the school for information concerning their children's reactions to a group other than the family. From the school they should get considerable information about the child's physical and mental health, special interests and abilities, handicaps and disabilities. To the school, also, they must look for much of their knowledge about the child's developing character traits and habits of work as they are observed in school settings.

In order to understand their own children, however, parents must first of all have some knowledge of how children grow and develop. They must know what we mean by the "norms" which we use to measure the individual child. Only with such knowledge can they judge what can reasonably be expected of each child in his particular stage of maturity. There is a common pattern or cycle of growth and development through which practically all individuals pass, and in which physical, mental, social and emotional development are interrelated. A majority of children reach certain points in the developmental pattern at approximately the same age, but there is very great variation in this matter. No two children are exactly alike. Not only is every child a unique personality, every child also has his own pattern of growth and development resembling those of his age mates in some respects and differing from them in others. The wise guidance of every child should be based upon his own individuality, his patterns of growth, his developmental or maturity level at any particular time. In fact, our chief reason for seeking to find ways in which children are alike is in order to become aware of the ways in which each child differs from his fellows.

In the opening chapter of this book, the fallacy of expecting teachers to bring all pupils in a given grade or high school group "up to standard" or "up to the norm" was pointed out. Parents need to understand that a "norm" is a statistical, not a moral term. It refers to the middle 50 percent or to the top 75 percent, or to whatever we wish to call "norm." It does not represent universal development of a certain trait at a given age. Sound and wholesome development may proceed on its own schedule. There are sequences which are predictable, but no one can predict the exact age at which any "normal" child will have developed a given trait.

If the differences found in any child are such that they will handicap the child himself in getting satisfaction from life or in making his contribution to society, home and school should do everything possible to overcome them. If not, parents and teachers should accept the differences, recognizing that in a democracy individual differences have functional values. It is the task of homes and schools in a democracy to utilize individual differences to strengthen and enrich group experiences. Differences which are undesirable in that they will handicap the child himself are all too often characteristics which must be accepted because they cannot be eliminated. Those who guide the child with such physical or mental disadvantages not only must adapt home and school programs to the child's needs; they must also do everything possible to help the child accept his own handicap and make the best possible life adjustments within his own limitations.

Many parents have gained knowledge and understanding of children through keen observation, reading and participation in study-discussion groups. Many others, however, do not have any real knowledge of child development or of what tasks most children strive to accomplish as they go from one period of development to another. Few parents have any agency other than the school to which they can easily turn for help in this area. The school should work jointly with parents to develop opportunities through which all parents can obtain such knowledge and understanding. Study-discussion groups in child development and guidance have been successfully organized and carried on for a period of years in pilot projects. Such programs of school-home cooperation are always possible where schools recognize that they cannot accomplish their objectives in the education and guidance of children unless they secure intelligent and understanding cooperation from the parents of their pupils.

In all of these ways—and others which space does not permit including here—teachers need the cooperation of parents. Since parents are the major guides of children and provide most of the opportunities for experiences which mold personality, teachers can learn much from them. On the other hand, since the school experiences of the child influence his growth in a crucial manner, parents can also learn much from teachers. Certainly the chances for curriculum and guidance to be effective in promoting the optimum development of boys and girls along wholesome lines are greatly enhanced when parents and teachers work as partners in the education of children.

CHAPTER X

Assistance from Other Agencies

THE good teacher today, regardless of the grade level at which
he is working or the subject matter in which he has specialized,
knows that children learn most effectively in the classroom when
their out-of-school as well as their in-school experiences provide
feelings of security and confidence. He knows that effective classroom experiences must be related to the genuine life-interests and
problems of the individuals participating in them, and that effective guidance of children involves discovering these interests and
problems. Such a teacher is constantly looking for information and
clues that will help him gain insight into the reactions of the
young people with whom he is working, although he may feel overwhelmed at times by the enormous responsibility for uncovering the
possible causes that lie behind Sally's daydreaming, Jimmy's cruelty
to other children, or Sam's persistent falsifications. The teacher
may well recognize the principle that what happens to the child in
his out-of-school hours is vitally important in shaping his attitudes
and motivations, yet may feel inadequate in attempting to gather
all the information he needs in order to understand each child.

The preceding chapter discussed how parents can relieve somewhat this sense of inadequacy by helping the teacher to understand
the out-of-school life of the child. Fortunately, there is an additional
resource available to teachers as they seek to know the family and
neighborhood backgrounds of their pupils.

Many communities today either provide or have access to a large
number of casework and character building agencies whose workers agree with teachers on the goals toward which children and
youth in our present day society should be guided. These agencies

often play an important role in the personality development of the children of the community.[1] Fortunately, their resources may be used by the school and their own work with children in their out-of-school activities may be strengthened by the school's cooperation. The problem is to acquaint both teachers and social workers with the values which may be gained from closer working relationships.

Where organized guidance services exist in the school, the special staff will no doubt be utilizing the help of many agencies in the community and will be fostering communication between teachers and these agencies. In one large school system which maintains a central guidance bureau, the staff of the bureau consults with all agencies known to have had contacts with a child who is being studied by the bureau. Workers from such organizations as the public and private welfare agencies, public health agencies, and mental hygiene clinics are regularly invited to staff meetings when a child's situation is being considered. The classroom teacher, in each case, is also invited to participate in the meeting in order that he may contribute to the discussion, hear the facts presented and share in the suggestions made. Teachers in that school system have an opportunity to clarify and receive help from the guidance staff and social workers in interpreting symptomatic behavior and in learning to know the varied forces that may be operating in children's lives. All staff members of that school feel they are growing in their understanding and acceptance of, and in their planning for and with children.

Many schools, however, do not have special guidance staffs to assist teachers in their communication with other institutions of society. How do teachers in this type of school secure the help from workers in the other agencies? In a school system in which a guidance-minded administrator is providing leadership for his staff, contacts with other agencies will be encouraged and facilitated. Social workers, leaders of boy and girl scout troops, youth leaders and staff members from other agencies often are invited by the principal to meet with the school staff to discuss the out-of-school experiences which children attending that school are having through the auspices of particular agencies. In some communities individual teachers may work with some agencies with which they

[1] See: Helen L. Witmer and Ruth Kotinsky, editors. *Personality in the Making*. The Fact-Finding Report of the Midcentury White House Conference on Children and Youth, Washington, D. C.: Harper and Brothers, 1950. p. 357-406.

happen to be familiar. Where an agency is working with a given family or child, a social worker sometimes initiates contacts with a teacher, or the teacher with a worker. In such contacts plans may be set up for the teacher to work directly with an agency in help-ing some child in his classroom.

Communities differ widely in the coordination of the activities of the school and those of the casework and character building agencies in guiding children and youth. In situations in which an extensive effort has been made to coordinate activities and to share findings, tremendous advantages have resulted to the children and youth of the community. But in many schools teachers are unaware of and do not use the vast community resources which are available. It is for this reason that the authors of the yearbook include the following discussion for teachers and other school officials who are seriously concerned with guiding children and who, therefore, would welcome specific suggestions of additional resource help which might be used by the school.

The threefold purpose of the chapter is to summarize and sug-gest: (a) the types of casework and character building agencies existing in various communities and their facilities for coordinated relationships; (b) ways in which children and youth seem to bene-fit from the coordinated activity of school and social service staffs; and (c) steps that are being taken to acquaint teachers and ad-ministrators with the social services being offered in their particu-lar community, and ways in which the information gathered in an individual case may be coordinated.

Casework and Character Building Agencies

Communities differ widely in the extent to which provision is made through both public and private sources to help community members make satisfying adjustments. Despite these differences, there are usually more organized plans for minimizing maladjust-ment, for building character and helping people in trouble than are known to the teachers of a given community. Individual teach-ers may use the help of available community agencies, but groups of teachers by-and-large are rather uninformed about or hesitant to explore the possibilities of working with colleagues in related fields. Likewise, members of the community who work with children in out-of-school situations rarely take full advantage of the opportuni-ties they have to share their experiences with the school staff. While there are many beginning steps now being taken in some communities to coordinate the services to children and youth (such as joint meetings of school and agency boards), so far the success of these steps has depended largely upon the personnel involved rather than upon any basic policy or specific organization.

So important is the need for the development of understanding and coordination between the school and other agencies of a community that curriculum planning at many present day teachers colleges reflects this trend. At many colleges students make complete community surveys of the communities in which they are receiving their student teaching experiences, and the compiled results are discussed and evaluated at the post-student teaching seminars. A number of colleges are including among their required and elective offerings such courses as those provided at one state teachers college: "Human Relations," "The Family and Community as a Resource for Child Growth," "The Sociology of Childhood and Adolescence," "Home-School-Community Relationships," "Community Resources for Programs for Young Children," "Sociology of the Community."[2] The experiences planned for students in these courses include visits to and work with children's courts, social service agencies, mental hygiene clinics, children's church groups, boy and girl scout organizations, YMCA, YWCA, and other groups of the local or nearby communities.

The students of one college sponsored a complete community survey of the recreational facilities provided for children, which resulted in cooperative efforts being made by many of the community's agencies to establish more adequate recreational facilities for children in their out-of-school hours. One college takes its student body on a field trip to a large city ninety miles from the campus, in order to acquaint students with the type of social service resources which they can use or help to develop when they later are members of teaching staffs. Some student groups in teacher-training institutions have increased their own understanding and made important contributions to the teachers of the school district by compiling a resource file and distributing a summary of the social service agencies within a county with which the school can cooperate. Names of personnel in the various organizations who may be contacted are also included. In some communities, similar compilations have been made by other organizations, such as the League of Women Voters. Teachers in one county, through sponsorship of a teachers association, assembled such information.

[2] The State University Teachers College at New Paltz, New York.

It should be noted in this connection that the personnel of social agencies are not always willing to share confidential information about a child or his family with teachers because teachers are not always believed to be able to handle the information confidentially. Unfortunately, this mistrust has sometimes arisen from just cause. But, on the other hand, the growing recognition of teaching as a profession and of teachers as professional people has pointed up the need to train teachers to guard confidential information so that they may be trusted with it. Experience in sharing confidential information and in learning how to handle it has today become a part of the preservice and in-service education of an increasing number of teachers, and many college staffs are continuously exploring ways of working with prospective teachers in such a manner that they will become increasingly more professional in using information about a given child.

Communities also differ greatly in what is considered permissible in regard to cooperative relationships between various organizations and agencies. In a number of communities, for example, the child guidance clinics may not accept referrals from the school. In these communities the referrals may be made only by parents, and reports on the examination and diagnosis of the child's case may be sent only to parents. The parents, in turn, make the decision as to whether the report is to be shared by them with the school. In other communities the referral must come from the school, and a parent may apply for the help of the clinic only upon the recommendation of the school. The report may or may not then be sent by the clinic directly to the school.

Despite the mistrust that unfortunately exists in some communities between the school and other agencies of society, and despite the limitations placed upon the sharing of the case records by various agencies, the best services to children result from the coordinated efforts of the various agencies of society. School personnel should be encouraged to explore and improve ways of working with these agencies. Agencies whose work with individuals is often related to that of the school and from which the school may receive and to which it may give valuable assistance in planning for children and youth are discussed in this section.

Public Welfare Agencies. The Department of Public Welfare, Aid to Dependent Children, and the Bureau of Old Age Assistance, to mention only three of the public welfare agencies supported by city, state and federal governments, provide definite resources to which the school may turn in gathering information about specific children enrolled in the school. The case records of a destitute family such as Carol Sue's, to whom grants of aid had been made for a number of years, were filled with clues concerning this child's approach to life and the numerous adjustments she and her family had had to make in the same years her teachers were trying to find ways of encouraging her to become more cooperative in the classroom. It was not until a teacher in the school who was enrolled as a graduate student in a nearby college used Carol Sue's case in his study of retarded children and sought the help of the public welfare agency which had worked with the family, that the volumes of records became known to any of the school personnel who had worked with Carol Sue through the years. The family had received considerable help in meeting problems relating to lacks in medical and health care, in clothing, in spending money, in financing of haircuts and in helping the father get back on his feet on numerous occasions. The caseworkers' records of visits to the home, including anecdotal accounts of Carol Sue's comments, had important implications for anyone who was interested in learning how Carol Sue was feeling about what was happening to her in school. A worker from the agency agreed to meet with the school staff and discussed with the group many of the possible interpretations of the situations reported in the records. The detailed and careful case records which are prepared in situations of this kind afford many clues that might help a teacher better understand and plan for a sensitive child like Carol Sue.

It should be noted that it is not safe to assume that a child will necessarily have difficulty in personality adjustments because the family is needy and is receiving public aid. But, if a child is having difficulties in making satisfactory adjustments in his school environment, the fact that his family may be receiving public aid, and the way in which such aid is given or received, may be closely associated with the child's inability to cope with relationships in his classroom. Knowledge of the situation by the school and the help of an understanding social worker may prevent many problems of maladjustment from developing or may facilitate the sympathetic handling of those that do arise.

Practically all our states are participating in a plan whereby the mother and the children who are under the age of sixteen are taken care of when the father of the family is dead or incapacitated. When a child is genuinely interested in attending school, as Johnny was, he may be supported through Aid to Dependent Children until he is eighteen. The family is often given help in budgeting allowances and great concern is felt by the agency for the emotional and social development of the child. Just making it financially possible for Johnny to come to school is not enough; it is important for the agency to work with the school personnel to help them develop deeper understanding of Johnny and to learn how best to guide him. The case records of his family, as well as those of other children receiving such aid, include revealing information that a teacher might use in attempting to put together the picture puzzle that comprises the personality of the child in question.

Certain records from the Bureau of Old Age Assistance may also be important to the school. Often the presence of one or both grandparents in the home increases the complexity of family living and may cause problems for children. In certain cases the Bureau of Old Age Assistance may have background information which will make it easier for teachers to help the children involved gain recognition and security in the school situation.

Public Health Agencies. The school has typically worked more closely with public health agencies than it has with some of the other agencies of the community. The public health nurse in some communities carries the dual role of "school nurse" and "community nurse," and the school has long worked with public health officials in promoting good physical health. Increasing efforts are now being made by the public health agencies to encourage good mental health and to provide clinical services for both physical and emotional problems. It has been recognized that physical and emotional problems are often closely related. The progress of the physically ill person may be blocked because of the state of his emotional health; and similarly, good mental health may markedly contribute to the progress an individual is making in raising the level of his physical health. The public health agencies have seen the school as a natural ally in their attempts to encourage better physical and mental health. The public health nurse, too, has come more and more to work with the school in helping its personnel understand the factors involved in a child's life and that of his family which affect health. Since both teachers and public health officers appreciate how necessary to a child's progress in school is his physical and mental health and that of his family members, they usually welcome help from each other in solving health problems.

It is the public health nurse, also, who may facilitate a closer relationship between the school and the home. Often it is she who may be able to arrange an easy entry for a member of the organized guidance staff or for the teacher to visit in the home. She may be able to prepare the visitor for the situation he will find in the home, and to prepare the parent for the visit from the school. The case-work staff in a city hospital, also, may be able to help a school understand the physical and emotional problems of a child or his family when hospital care has been needed by that family.

Child Placing Agencies. Increasing effort has been made during the past quarter of a century to reduce the number of dependent children living in large institutional setups and to locate foster and adoptive homes where these children not only may receive physical care but find substitute parents and family life. These children become members of schools in the communities in which their substitute parents live. As might be expected, studies indicate that many of these foster and adopted children do have serious problems of adjustment in school. For this reason it is important for a school staff to develop clearer understanding of the problems involved in helping these children and to work with their substitute parents long after the child placing agencies have terminated their contacts with the homes.

In some schools representatives of child placing agencies working with parents in a given community have been invited to meet with the school staff members to help them understand the subtle problems of adjustment that exist in the relationships between foster and adopted children and their substitute parents, and between these children and their peers. Although the modern school attempts to work closely with the parents of all the children, the uncertain status of a foster parent and the overanxiety of an adopted child may present problems of how best to gain parent cooperation. The child placing agencies generally have on their staffs well-trained social workers, psychologists and often psychiatrists. These specialists can provide resource help for a school staff so that they in turn can work most constructively with foster parents and gain their support and help in providing the best possible educational opportunity for the children. There are certainly benefits when two way communication exists between the school and the child placing agencies of the community.

Mental Hygiene Committees and Clinics. Under the auspices of county, city and state mental hygiene committees and bureaus, mental hygiene clinics are available in many states. Some of these clinics are stationary; others might be classified under the general head of "roving clinics," since the staff of the clinic travels at regular intervals to various parts of the state or county. Some of these mental hygiene clinics have time and opportunity to make adequate diagnoses of the problems of the children referred to them, to counsel both the children and their parents, and then to interpret to the school staff possible ways in which a given child might be better able to make an adjustment in a particular school situation.

Typically, however, these clinics, whether they are stationary or roving, are understaffed and although the clinicians try to take care of as many referrals as possible, in many cases there is little time for more than diagnosis. If the school staff members do not understand the limitations within which a given mental hygiene clinic seems forced to operate, they may feel dissatisfied when they receive from the clinic little more than a diagnostic summary of an individual child's problems—a diagnosis that may not differ markedly from that made by the school staff. It is clear that the school is often seeking more specific suggestions concerning the school's relationship to the child than the staff of the mental hygiene clinic seems willing or able to give. Under pressure of time, the clinic, in turn, may feel that if its suggestions are couched in any but general terms, misunderstandings may result or comments may be threatening to the school and thus result in little help to the individual child. Such problems of relationship usually develop from failures in understanding.

If the staff of the clinic and the staff of the school with which it works can arrange periodic opportunities for face to face conferences where information may be pooled and procedures cooperatively formulated, time will be saved in the long run and the children concerned will receive more helpful guidance. Relations limited to referral blanks and written diagnoses can never develop the quality of cooperation needed to motivate all concerned to work persistently to help boys and girls with the difficult adjustment problems they may face.

One state-wide mental hygiene committee provided in recent years a series of mental health conferences for the administrators of public schools in various areas of the state. The group therapy sessions which characterized the conferences resulted in planning for better working relationships in the schools represented by these administrators, and clearer understanding of both teachers' and children's reactions and feelings. One teacher who received from a roving clinic valuable help for a child in her group commented on the fact that contacts with clinics of this type actually improved the mental health of teachers; another teacher noted that many teachers would welcome some help from such clinics on the personal problems the teachers face.

In addition to the assistance given in individual cases, many mental hygiene clinics provide without cost, or at very small charge, helpful publications, films, and speakers or discussion leaders for group meetings. Such services also assist teachers and parents to better understand the emotional needs of their children.

Private Welfare Agencies. The private welfare agencies—commonly supported by the Community Chest—and the services supported by various religious organizations offer important sources of assistance supplemental to that provided through the public welfare agencies in the community. Agencies such as Family Service and the Salvation Army are often able to step into difficult family situations involving both the financial expenditure and the time of trained guidance personnel which would not be permitted under the laws governing a public agency. School personnel attest to the fact that assistance has frequently come from such an agency in helping straighten out marital difficulties and unfortunate parent-child relations, both of which situations were influencing the adjustment of the children involved. Such agencies can help in the location of foster and nursing homes and find nursing aid when a family crisis demands immediate help. They are often flexible enough in policy to finance the correction of physical handicaps which may be producing definite blocks to the adjustment of the child in question.

Jerry, for example, who was failing in all his high school subjects, and threatening to quit school as soon as he reached the age of fifteen, was fortunate that a group of teachers in his school were searching for ways to help him. They suspected that Jerry's difficulty in social relations with his agemates was closely related to his feelings about a visual handicap involving a facial disfigurement. A private agency was located that financed an operation, hospitalization, procurement of an artificial eye, and subsequent counseling for Jerry. The final results in Jerry's readier acceptance by his peers and in better use of his potentialities warranted the effort expended. In this case, without the agency and the prior knowledge of where to turn for assistance, Jerry's teachers might have been powerless to help him.

Such also might have been the case in respect to Mary, whose mother was called to school to discuss certain problems relating to Mary's attitude and achievement. The conference with the mother revealed the fact that Mary's chief difficulty probably lay in the general relationships in the home, and particularly in the lack of acceptance of the girl by her father and his expressed favoritism for a younger child in the family. Through the help of one of her teachers, the services of a private agency were provided for Mary's family. With the assistance of this casework agency working in cooperation with the teachers, Mary's whole outlook on life became more wholesome and optimistic.

Peter's problems seemed to stem from worry about his father's unhappiness and depression. The psychiatric help provided through Family Service for his father was probably more effective in relieving Peter's worries than would have been direct counseling of the boy.

The problems of Jerry, Mary and Peter illustrate what teachers and counselors have long recognized—that the child brings his home problems with him to school. The child, of course, is all of one piece, even though he spends part of his day in school, part at home and part in association with various organized and spontaneous groups in the community. Since this is true, cooperation on the part of all who share in the child's guidance and in that of his family is of utmost importance. Certainly, the agencies which are working with families of children in a given school system may provide the school with important clues to an understanding of a child's real interests and drives. Their valuable help should be sought by school administrators and teachers.

Private Counseling and Psychiatric Help. A private counselor or psychiatrist who is working in therapy with some school child or youth may give valuable consultative help to personnel of the school. The counselor or psychiatrist, however, may prefer to work independently of the school and to use the child's reactions in a school situation that is relatively unchanged during the period of therapy as a barometer of the child's mental health. He may, however, do as the psychiatrist did in the case of Jack, a boy in the junior high school of a large public school system. Jack's psychiatrist and parents felt that the boy would benefit from increased understanding of his problems by his teachers and the supporting help it seemed likely they might be able to give him at school when they understood the situation. With the encouragement of the principal, the psychiatrist met several times with the junior high school staff. The teachers expressed the feeling that their increased understanding of the boy's situation made it easier for them to accept his inconsistent behavior and to help him gain acceptance in his peer society.

Help from private counselors and psychiatrists is far less available to school personnel than is help from members of social agencies, mental hygiene clinics and other social services where the team approach is emphasized. The help of private counselors and psychiatrists should be utilized, however, where it is available and where teachers seem to have the readiness to work in such a relationship.

Group Work Agencies for Recreation and Character Building. Community organizations such as the boy and girl scouts, the churches, K. of C., YMCA, YWCA, YMHA, YWHA, community youth centers and 4-H Clubs, to mention only a few, are working with schools in various ways. More and more, leaders in these organizations are becoming interested in enrolling in extension courses of colleges and universities in order to acquaint themselves with recent findings in the area of human growth and development and to learn how they can better use their leadership to help boys and girls with the problems they face. In some cases they are working in classes with teachers of the community and are coming to see the mutual benefit derived through the close relationship of a community organization and the schools.

There are various ways in which the school might work cooperatively with character building organizations of the community. A youngster, for example, who seems to be at loose ends after school hours and who needs associations with a peer group may be encouraged by his teacher to join a boy scout troop in his neighborhood. The approach may be made to the parents and their cooperation enlisted in getting the child interested in joining the organization, or it might be made as a suggestion directly to the child. A third approach, which is used far too infrequently by teachers, is to consult directly with the den mother, the scoutmaster or the Gra-Y leader of the group of youngsters who come from the neighborhood and to indicate that an invitation from one of the boys might encourage the youngster to join in their activities. In such a conference the teacher has an opportunity to give the leader some of the background of the chief interests of the boy through which he might become encouraged to take part in the activities of the troop or club. He can also indicate some of the problems faced by the youngster which wholesome association with his peers might alleviate.

A child who lives in a rural area might be helped by a classroom teacher to participate in 4-H Club work as a means of giving him new interests, of socializing him, and of encouraging activities which will bring the family together in constructive cooperative pursuits. Some children need opportunities for building feelings of competence which they have difficulty in achieving in a school program oriented around academic subject matter areas. Participation in the activities of such organizations as 4-H Clubs, Scouts, YWCA, YMCA, YMHA, and YWHA might provide these young people pleasurable work at tasks along the lines of their major interests.

It should be pointed out, also, that in communities where the leaders of civic or religious organizations working with the youth of the community are especially effective, the school staff can often learn a good deal from them about the reactions of individual children and can work with these organizations in planning for these children. Elizabeth, for example, was a child who met almost continual failure in her later elementary and beginning high school situations. The repeated conferences which her mother had with the school personnel resulted in little change in Elizabeth's negative attitudes and her sullen withdrawal every time she was faced with difficult problems and disappointments. It was through the combined efforts of her mother and her teacher that Elizabeth finally became interested in the activities of a church in her community, particularly in the choir and the Sunday evening club of young people. The director of religious education at the church brought to the attention of the school personnel certain leadership qualities that the girl had shown as chairman of a refreshments committee for one of the functions, and discussed situations in which Elizabeth seemed able "to come out of her shell" and relate herself to the activities of the group, even carrying responsibility for some of these activities. The church worker reported from time to time certain changes that appeared to be developing in the girl's reactions to her school and her family problems, and her growing ability to meet these problems without noticeable frustration. The school personnel, in turn, made certain suggestions that helped the worker utilize still further the girl's interest in the area of home economics. Examples similar to this could be greatly multiplied to show that both guidance and instruction are more effective when teachers pool information and ideas about a child with his pastor, his Sunday school teacher, his scoutmaster or his community center leader.

A teacher who is aware of strong feelings of prejudice within a given group of children may call upon organizations such as the boy and girl scouts, the YMCA and YWCA, or the YMHA and YWHA to assist him in the job of improving relationships, since the programs of these organizations lend themselves to work in this area. The scoutmaster and a seventh grade teacher in one community worked closely together to bring experiences into both the school and scouting situations that would heighten interest in the contributions of various national groups to the development of American democracy and to diminishing the feelings of racial and religious prejudices. When, in the following year, an eighth grade Negro boy was elected student council president in a school attended predominantly by white children, the results of the combined efforts of the school and a community organization were seen.

Service Clubs and Other Community Groups. Community service groups such as the Big Brother and Big Sister organizations may serve an important function which it is difficult for the school to discharge in working with predelinquent youngsters or with those who have returned from a period in a "corrective" institution. Members of these organizations may meet the need of a child for a satisfying relationship with an adult. The workers usually do not profess to be especially skilled in the counseling area, but offer something vital to the child's security as he seeks to re-establish his relationships with his peers and to strengthen his self-esteem. A child's Big Brother may take him to a baseball game, go riding or swimming with him, or in other ways be a trusted friend. A child who comes back to a community after a period of institutionalization may find it hard to accept the attitudes of the community members. Unfortunately, even some teachers may be overly suspicious of a child's conduct if he has been in trouble with the law on a former occasion. The Big Brother and Big Sister organizations help such a youngster weather possible initial rebuffs until he gains assurance that he can make his way and that society is willing to take him back. Often such an individual has greater need for this person-to-person acceptance than for skilled therapy.

Though the services may operate under different names in different communities, the Big Brother and Big Sister organizations represent a growing movement and one which should be used as an ally by teachers in their efforts to help certain boys and girls.

The nationwide Optimist Club is another community organization interested in helping children and youth prior to and after delinquency. It provides services which are definitely supplemental to the authoritarian relationship of a parole setup. Schools have only begun to skim the surface in securing the benefits they could receive from closer relationships with organizations of this kind.

The Kiwanis Club, Rotary Club, Lions Club, Elks Club and various farmers' fraternal groups are organizations which are frequently vitally interested in helping the children of the community. An interested teacher or other member of the school staff can often enlist their help for certain children. It is wise for the school to investigate the field of service in which the local organization is particularly interested. For example, one such organization may sponsor an eye clinic at the local hospital; another may provide funds for glasses for children who need them and cannot procure them by other means. One such organization sponsors a program to provide dental care for children who are not receiving it; another provides hearing aids for some children and youth with auditory defects. Another organization is noted for its great interest in helping the physically handicapped child. Schools have often enlisted the help of this organization to provide facilities and teaching personnel for bedridden children and children needing isolation from group activities. One organization has, on an experimental basis, paid the salary of a guidance counselor for the school and encouraged greater understanding of the mental health needs of school children.

As has been noted in preceding sections, the extent of the relationship between the school and other agencies of a community differs widely from community to community. In most communities it is safe to say that cooperative efforts in behalf of children should be greatly enlarged. If the school staff were better acquainted with the resources for child guidance within its area, the give and take between the organizations of the community and the school would bring rich benefits to many children for whom services are now uncoordinated, overlapping or inadequate.

Acquainting Teachers with Available Services

Throughout this chapter attention has been directed to ways in which school personnel may work with other casework and character building agencies in the community for the more comprehensive guidance of children and youth. The intent has been (a) to suggest areas of team possibilities, rather than a complete list of resources, and (b) to encourage teachers and other school personnel to explore all areas of possible relationship with existing community organizations within an accessible radius of the school and to acquaint one another with the results of the exploration.

Guidance Bureaus. In a number of school systems, organized bureaus of child guidance have worked out plans for orienting new teachers to the services of the bureau and the relationships which the bureau has established with the other organizations of the community. The teacher learns early that he will be brought into the staff conferences and have opportunity to meet and work with other members of the community. In one of these communities student-teachers who are working in the schools participate under the direction of the bureau of child guidance in a survey of the community resources.

State Departments of Education. Departments of public instruction on the state level often provide schools with information concerning the social service resources available to teachers of the state and ways in which the services between agencies and schools are already being coordinated. School personnel can make inquiry of their state education departments for help of this kind.

County and Regional Surveys. In many states and counties teachers' organizations and other interested groups are surveying the total community resources for the guidance of children and youth and are making the results available to all teachers. The teachers of Nassau and Suffolk Counties, in New York State, for example, a few years ago collaborated on such a survey. The League of Women Voters in another community of that state is at present working on such a compilation. In some schools a resource file is available in the principal's office. In large communities, a directory of social services may be available. An agency such as the Child Welfare League of America is also helpful to school personnel in locating directories and in giving suggestions for beginning steps that might be taken by a group interested in making a survey.

Help from Teacher Education Institutions. Courses offered in many teacher education institutions give experience in learning the existence of and possible coordination with the school of casework and character building agencies within the community. As has been noted, prospective teachers and those already in service are being trained by college staffs who are becoming increasingly aware of the advantages that accrue to children and youth when the resources of a given community are tapped for better guidance of youth. Indicative of the importance attached to training teachers to understand and work with community groups are evaluation schedules used in the accrediting process of the American Association of Colleges for Teacher Education.[3] Each faculty member in a teachers college undergoing evaluation is asked to respond to the following:

In what community and civic groups do you regularly take part?

What resources and problems of the community do you use in your own work with students?

Course titles in college catalogues and announcements of special summer programs for teachers and other community members indicate growing awareness of the benefits derived when the school and other community agencies work together in guiding children and youth through the complexities of modern society and into responsible adulthood.

This chapter has indicated some of the important resources outside the school to which teachers may look for assistance in the guidance of boys and girls. The authors of the yearbook feel that teachers should be given encouragement to explore and improve the means of communication between the school and other agencies of society such as public welfare agencies, public health agencies, child placing agencies, mental hygiene committees, private welfare agencies, group work agencies for recreation and character building, and the various service clubs of a given or nearby community. Although communities differ widely in the extent to which the staffs of agencies in the community are available for help to the school, and in the extent to which their services may be coordinated with those of the school, there is a growing awareness that children and youth benefit when the personnel of all the agencies of society trust one another and learn to work together.

[3] American Association of Colleges for Teacher Education. *AACTE Evaluation Schedule.* "Standard III—The Preparation of the Faculty." Oneonta, N. Y.: the Association, a department of the National Education Association.

Part Four

Integrating Guidance with Instruction

CHAPTER XI

Guiding Through
Teaching

AS TEACHERS and parents look at themselves and at each
other, they are probably impressed, as are the authors of this
yearbook, with how far we fall short of the kind of people we are
striving to become; and how far society falls short of what together
we are striving to make it. The complex problems which we adults
face today in our homes, in our neighborhoods, in the nation and
in world affairs frequently find us baffled and confused. We often
lack the singleness of purpose, the breadth of understanding, the
calmness of spirit and the organization of effort needed to find
solutions to our difficulties in ways that bring both to us and to
those with whom we associate genuine and enduring happiness.
That children and young people face, and will continue to face, at
least as complex a world as ours, goes without saying. Our hope is
that they will approach their world and the problems and choices
it poses with more wisdom and courage and constancy of purpose
than their parents and teachers typically display.

This yearbook is an attempt to implement this hope; to show
how the development of a sturdy, democratic citizenry can be more
fully attained. Such a goal will be realized, however, only as parents
and teachers—the adults whose influence upon growing boys and
girls is most pervasive and enduring—accept greater responsibility
and achieve greater skill in guiding children along wholesome lines
of social, physical and mental development.

In this volume discussion has centered primarily upon the guidance role of the teacher in assisting individual boys and girls, each

with his unique pattern of personal characteristics, to develop fully and effectively.

The first section of the yearbook presents a contrast between a school situation in which guidance is considered a special service largely divorced from instruction, and one in which instruction is inseparable from guidance. The case is made for the second of these alternatives. Some of the things that teachers must know, believe and do in order that guidance may be integrated with classroom teaching are then discussed. The point of view presented in this introduction is, in brief, that any curriculum planned prior to the teacher's acquaintance with the individual children who should profit from it, must be continuously replanned with reference to the needs of each child and to his special pattern of strengths and weaknesses.

The teacher is acting in his *guidance* capacity when he attempts to learn about the various social, emotional, physical and intellectual factors in the personality of a child which make him what he is, and when he uses this growing background of understanding to adjust both the content and the methods of his teaching to harmonize with the child's level of readiness. He is performing his role as *instructor* when, through understanding each pupil, he finds the particular ways in which the child's interest may be kindled and his cooperation gained for learning the things which society demands. Thus the teacher who guides as he teaches has a greater chance of finding a congenial reception for that which he is attempting to teach. Because such a teacher appreciates each pupil as a human being and knows something of his thoughts and feelings and of the problems he is struggling to resolve, the chances are that each child will actually learn better the academic work which we typically associate with the instructional program. In addition, and perhaps of even greater importance, he will be gaining, through daily association with a teacher who respects him and cares what happens to him, basic confidence in himself and growing capacity to manage his own life.

In the second part of the yearbook the authors have discussed how teachers who integrate guidance with their classroom teaching go about the task of determining objectives, of selecting learning activities and of supporting and reinforcing one another's efforts in the process of guiding learning. The authors demonstrate that whether or not a teacher believes that one of his important functions is the guidance of individual boys and girls makes a difference in the way he approaches the whole job of teaching. A teacher who views his instruction as inseparable from guidance is concerned that the needs of children and youth be adequately met. He therefore investigates the major sources of human need—contemporary society and the learners themselves—to identify learning objectives. He also utilizes the studies of subject matter specialists as another approach to the discovery of desirable outcomes of learning. He then translates broad and general objectives into classroom learning goals and thence into goals for individual boys and girls. This process assumes a knowledge of developmental sequences and of all the other factors related to readiness.

Similarly, the selection of learning activities to help pupils gain the desired goals implies the basic understanding mentioned above, and especially requires application of the best that we know about how learning takes place. In the first part of Chapter IV some of the important principles of learning are interpreted to show their relationship to the objectives of guidance as well as instruction. This is followed by some practical suggestions for enriching learning opportunities for boys and girls and for varying learning requirements to harmonize with what may well be expected of each pupil in the light of his capacities and of his total personal adjustment.

The problem of evaluating learning experiences is not dealt with separately but runs as a continuous thread throughout the yearbook. One of the major objectives of guidance is to help boys and girls become progressively self-understanding and self-directive. To achieve this goal, pupils must be involved in every aspect of the learning process. They must participate in the selection of objectives, they must participate in choosing among alternative courses of action those which seem most appropriate to advance them toward their goals, and they must then actively share in analyzing and examining how well or poorly they are progressing. The kinds of evaluation which substitute teacher judgment for pupil self-analysis, or which misdirect the energies of the learner from a real to a false objective, unfit the developing citizen for handling present and future problems concerning which the school can give no direct help. The teacher who integrates guidance with his classroom teaching, therefore, provides many learning opportunities which encourage children to understand clearly what they are trying to accomplish, to consider the progress they seem to be making, and to weigh and balance the various methods of work which appear to be holding them back or facilitating their learning.

The final chapter in this section presents a clear argument for a coordinated program of guidance services and for a school curriculum organized to bring both meaning and richness to learning experiences. Especially it urges closer teamwork among all members of the school staff. A teacher who integrates guidance with his classroom teaching appreciates the breadth of his opportunities not only to guide boys and girls to learn those things which are definitely related to his subject matter area, but to reinforce the learning of certain facts, skills and attitudes for which other subject specialists may have primary responsibility. A school situation in which each teacher understands what all the other teachers are attempting to accomplish in their teaching, and in which each consciously tries to help all the other teachers gain their objectives, is one in which pupil learning is both rich and efficient. Only as teachers *share* their perceptions regarding the needs of youth and appreciate that some needs require concerted effort on the part of all teachers will they be discharging their guidance responsibilities and effectively relating guidance and teaching.

Fortunately for the teacher, there are various resources available to him in carrying the dual responsibility of guiding and teaching. In Part Three of the yearbook five categories of such resources are considered in some detail. Counselors and other guidance specialists constitute one of these resources, and their role as helpers to teachers is discussed in some detail. Although such specialists have important services to render directly to certain boys and girls, one of their most important functions is to assist teachers to become more skilful in understanding child behavior and in guiding the development of all boys and girls along wholesome lines. To the degree that counselors can help teachers learn how to appraise and meet the needs of each of the many boys and girls whose problems represent the typical range of developmental tasks, these teachers will be influential in preventing serious adjustment problems from developing. If counselors can also help teachers learn to identify pupils who need the service of guidance specialists and, after referral, to work in close cooperation with these specialists in the follow-up phases of the pupil's readjustment, the process of rehabilitation will be greatly facilitated. When instruction is considered inseparable from guidance, therefore, the guidance specialists serve the teachers. They make easily available the data needed to understand individual pupils; they coordinate the efforts of teachers to help a given child; they advise with teachers on useful methods of child study and adjustment; and, in general, they try to relieve teachers of unnecessary clerical and administrative detail.

Supervisors and administrators represent a second resource. They can do much to assist and support the teacher who considers individual boys and girls and tries to give each an appropriate and balanced educational diet. The equipment which is purchased; the time schedules which are set up; the policies which are established relating to such things as course offerings, school clubs and pupil control; plus the ways in which scores of other administrative and supervisory responsibilities are discharged, have the effect either of helping or hindering the classroom teacher in what he is trying to do for children. Wise administrators and supervisors, therefore, consult and plan *with* their teachers so that whatever expenditures are made or policies formulated will clearly redound to the wholesome growth of the boys and girls for whom the school exists.

The discussion of the role of guidance specialists as resource persons and the role of the supervisor and administrator stresses the importance of genuine appreciation and consideration in the personal relationships of all those involved in the education of the pupils. Where hierarchies exist and department heads, counselors or principals rely on the prestige of position for their security, staff morale is bound to be low and teachers cannot feel psychologically free to accept children as worthy of their trust and help. On the other hand, in staff situations in which counselors, supervisors and administrators are keenly appreciative of the efforts of teachers and respect them for their good will and for the sincerity and value of their ideas, the psychological groundwork exists for making instruction inseparable from guidance. In these situations of mutual trust, teachers do not fear supervision but freely seek and use whatever special staff services may contribute to their growing competence in guiding the development of their pupils.

To integrate guidance with instruction it is important for the teacher to know how each pupil has been developing over the years, as well as what factors are influencing his present adjustment. To gather extensive information of these kinds would be impossible for a teacher without access to a good cumulative record. Even with a good record, organized to provide a developmental picture of a child and to highlight the growing edge of his personality, it takes considerable skill to interpret recorded data and to select and record significant items of current behavior. In Chapter VIII the development and use of the cumulative record as a guidance tool are discussed in considerable detail. The chapter is rich in illustration, especially with reference to the kinds of descriptive data which help in understanding the child's total personality organization.

As reflected in this discussion, the yearbook authors believe that it takes many kinds of information about a child, gathered over a considerable period of time, to begin to perceive him as a *whole person* and to understand his basic motivation. For a teacher to attempt a program of action in behalf of a child on the basis of limited data, or with certain items of data too heavily weighted, is as dangerous to personal adjustment as for a physician to prescribe without a thorough diagnosis. A good cumulative record provides a valuable point of departure for making an adequate analysis of the problems of individual children. Some of the ways in which counselors can best serve teachers are to work with them in the development of a well-organized record form, to assist in keeping records up-to-date and readily available, and to help all teachers become increasingly proficient in interpreting and using recorded data in a professional manner.

There are many resources within the school and its staff for helping teachers carry the combined functions of guidance and instruction, but there are also people outside the school who have important contributions to make to the teacher's competence in these areas. In the chapter entitled "Parents as Partners" a strong case is presented for making the education of children a genuine cooperative venture between parents and teachers. Teachers can learn a great deal from parents if they have opportunities to talk with them and to visit them in their homes. What parents say in these face to face relations about themselves and their children often reveals to the insightful teacher their preoccupations, their standards of value, their methods of child control and the various subtle parental attitudes which affect the basic security of children. Such data are invaluable in helping the teacher approach in an enlightened manner the developmental problems of the children concerned. Moreover, the specific suggestions which the parents of a child give the teacher for his guidance at school are often as valid and helpful as any which the teacher may make to the parents for the child's guidance at home. In their contacts with parents, therefore, teachers should be good listeners and learners, and should fully appreciate that there is no one better situated to understand a child than his mother or father. It is the contention of the authors of this yearbook that only as opportunities are available for parents and teachers to pool their insights and exchange their ideas will the children concerned be guided and instructed in ways most beneficial to them.

Part Three closes with a discussion of a resource area which has been relatively untapped by most teachers. There are many agencies in the typical local or county-wide community which share with the school the guidance of boys and girls or which provide services to their families. Often these agencies have a kind of relationship with a child or his family which the school is not in a position to develop. They often understand the sources of some of the child's problems better than anyone in the school, and are frequently staffed and financed to render services which the school cannot perform. In turn, the school can provide these agencies with background information on the child's school life which helps them view his problems with clearer perspective. Teachers are likewise in a position to reinforce the efforts of welfare workers by assisting a child in school in harmony with procedures recommended by these workers. Yet in most communities, in spite of obvious opportunities for mutual assistance, adequate communication between schools, churches, casework and group work agencies has not been developed. It is the belief of the authors that every effort should be made to develop more effective working relationships between these and other groups which are established to serve children. Chapter X gives much practical information regarding the types of services which each of a wide range of community groups is organized to give. This should encourage teachers and other school personnel to assume greater initiative in promoting fuller exchange of information and help when it can better serve the interests of children.

It is hoped that the point of view presented in this volume and the ideas discussed herein will appeal to classroom teachers as sound and reasonable. The successful integration of guidance with classroom teaching requires skills of a high order. At present many teachers may feel personally unequipped or hampered by teaching conditions which seem to prevent them from fully attaining this goal. Because such integration holds great promise for the welfare of boys and girls, however, the authors hope that teachers will actively strive toward the goal of making teaching inseparable from guidance, in the firm belief that this is eminently worthy of ultimate achievement. They further hope that administrators, supervisors, counselors and all other curriculum and guidance specialists will be encouraged through reading this yearbook to discover ways of being more helpful to teachers. For, of all school personnel, the classroom teacher has the closest and most continuing relationship with boys and girls and, by virtue of this relationship, must assume the major role in their guidance.

Selected References

THE concepts discussed in this yearbook are drawn from a number of areas, among which are: child development, mental hygiene, social psychology, guidance and personnel work, the school curriculum, and teaching method. These concepts are used in this volume, however, to discuss the place of guidance in the curriculum and, especially, the relationship of guidance to instruction. Published materials dealing with this relationship are relatively scarce. Often the most helpful of these materials do not use in their titles the terms "guidance," "curriculum" or "instruction." The following bibliography includes some of the references known to the writers to express a point of view consistent with the thesis of this yearbook and to help, in whole or in part, to reinforce this point of view. It was felt that such a brief listing would be more helpful to prospective readers than a less selective but more comprehensive bibliography.

ASSOCIATION FOR SUPERVISION AND CURRICULUM DEVELOPMENT. *Action for Curriculum Improvement.* 1951 Yearbook. Washington, D.C.: the Association, a department of the National Education Association, 1951.

ASSOCIATION FOR SUPERVISION AND CURRICULUM DEVELOPMENT. *Fostering Mental Health in Our Schools.* 1950 Yearbook. Washington, D.C.: the Association, a department of the National Education Association, 1950.

ASSOCIATION FOR SUPERVISION AND CURRICULUM DEVELOPMENT. *Growing Up in an Anxious Age.* 1952 Yearbook. Washington, D. C.: the Association, a department of the National Education Association, 1952.

AMERICAN COUNCIL ON EDUCATION. *Helping Teachers Understand Children.* Washington, D.C.: Commission on Teacher Education, Division on Child Development and Teacher Personnel, American Council on Education, 1945.

ARBUCKLE, DUGALD S. *Teacher Counseling.* Cambridge, Mass.: Addison-Wesley, 1950.

BAXTER, EDNA DOROTHY. *An Approach to Guidance.* New York: D. Appleton-Century, 1946.

BERNARD, HAROLD W. *Mental Hygiene for Classroom Teachers.* New York: McGraw-Hill, 1952.

BERNARD, HAROLD W.; JAMES, C. E.; and ZERAN, FRANKLIN R. *Guidance Services in Elementary Schools.* New York: Chartwell House, 1954.

BOSSARD, J. H. S. *Sociology of Child Development.* New York: Harper and Brothers, 1948.

BUHLER, CHARLOTTE; SMITTER, FAITH; and RICHARDSON, SYBIL. *Childhood Problems and the Teacher.* New York: Henry Holt, 1952.

CANTOR, NATHANIEL. *The Teaching↔Learning Process.* New York: The Dryden Press, 1953.

COX, PHILIP W. L.; DUFF, JOHN C.; and McNAMARA, MARIE. *Basic Principles of Guidance.* New York: Prentice-Hall, 1948.

CUNNINGHAM, RUTH. *Understanding Group Behavior of Boys and Girls.* New York: Bureau of Publications, Teachers College, Columbia University, 1951.

DETJEN, ERVIN W., and DETJEN, MARY F. *Elementary School Guidance.* New York: McGraw-Hill, 1952.

DOUGLASS, HARL ROY, editor. *Education and Life Adjustment: Its Meaning and Implementation.* New York: Ronald Press, 1950.

ELSBREE, WILLARD S., and REUTTER, E. EDMUND, JR. *Staff Personnel in the Public Schools.* New York: Prentice-Hall, 1954.

GRAMBS, J., and IVERSON, W. J. *Modern Methods in Secondary Education.* New York: Sloane, 1952.

HAVIGHURST, ROBERT J. *Human Development and Education.* New York: Longmans, Green, 1953.

JENKINS, GLADYS J.; SHACTER, HELEN; and BAUER, WILLIAM W. *These Are Your Children.* Chicago: Scott, Foresman, 1949.

KELLEY, EARL C. *Education for What Is Real.* New York: Harper and Brothers, 1947.

KITCH, DONALD E., and McCREARY, WILLIAM H. *Improving Guidance Programs in Secondary Schools.* Sacramento: California State Department of Education, 1950.

LEONARD, EDITH M.; VANDEMAN, DOROTHY D.; and MILES, LILLIAN E. *Counseling with Parents in Early Childhood Education.* New York: Macmillan, 1954.

LINDGREN, HENRY CLAY. *Mental Health in Education.* New York: Henry Holt, 1954.

LITTLE, WILSON, and CHAPMAN, A. L. *Developmental Guidance in Secondary Schools.* New York: McGraw-Hill, 1953.

MACOMBER, FREEMAN GLENN. *Principles of Teaching in the Elementary School.* New York: American Book Co., 1954.

NATIONAL COUNCIL OF TEACHERS OF ENGLISH. *Pupils Are People.* New York: D. Appleton-Century, 1941.

NATIONAL EDUCATION ASSOCIATION, DEPARTMENT OF ELEMENTARY SCHOOL PRINCIPALS. *Guidance for Today's Children.* Thirty-Third Yearbook. Washington, D. C.: the Department, 1954.

NATIONAL SOCIETY FOR THE STUDY OF EDUCATION. 52nd Yearbook, Part I. *Adapting the Secondary School Program to the Needs of Youth.* Chicago: University of Chicago Press, 1953.

OTTO, H. J. *Principles of Elementary Education.* New York: Rinehart, 1949.

REDL, F., and WATTENBERG, W. W. *Mental Hygiene in Teaching.* New York: Harcourt Brace, 1951.

SHANE, HAROLD G., and MCSWAIN, E. T. *Evaluation and the Elementary Curriculum.* New York: Henry Holt, 1951.

SNYGG, DONALD, and COMBS, ARTHUR W. *Individual Behavior.* New York: Harper and Brothers, 1949.

SPEARS, HAROLD. *Improving the Supervision of Instruction.* New York: Prentice-Hall, 1954.

STRANG, RUTH. *An Introduction to Child Study.* Revised edition. New York: Macmillan, 1951.

STRANG, RUTH. *The Role of the Teacher in Personnel Work.* Third edition. New York: Bureau of Publications, Teachers College, Columbia University, 1946.

STRANG, RUTH. *An Introduction to Child Study.* Revised edition. New York: in Rural Schools. New York: Harper and Brothers, 1943.

WARTERS, JANE. *High School Personnel Work Today.* New York: McGraw-Hill, 1946.

WILES, KIMBALL. *Teaching for Better Schools.* New York: Prentice-Hall, 1954.

WILLEY, ROY DEVERAL. *Guidance in Elementary Education.* New York: Harper and Brothers, 1952.

WISCONSIN COOPERATIVE EDUCATIONAL PLANNING PROGRAM. *Guides to Curriculum Building—Junior High School Level.* Madison, Wis.: State Department of Public Instruction, 1950.

WISCONSIN COOPERATIVE EDUCATIONAL PLANNING PROGRAM. *Guides to Curriculum Building—Kindergarten Level.* Madison, Wis.: State Department of Public Instruction, 1947.

WOODRUFF, A. D. *The Psychology of Teaching.* Third edition. New York: Longmans, Green, 1951.

YEAGER, W. A. *Administration and the Pupil.* New York: Harper and Brothers, 1949.

ASCD Board of Directors
(As of November 1954)

Executive Committee, 1954-1955

President, PRUDENCE BOSTWICK, Supervisor, Denver Pub. Schs., Denver, Colo.

First Vice-President, ALICE MIEL, Prof. of Ed., Tchrs. Coll., Columbia Univ., N. Y.

Second Vice-President, VERNON E. ANDERSON, Dir. of the Curr. Center, Univ. of Conn., Storrs.

Field Secretary, MAYCIE K. SOUTHALL, Prof. of Elem. Ed., George Peabody Coll. for Tchrs., Nashville, Tenn.

MARVIN L. BERGE, Asst. Supt., Pub. Schs., Elgin, Ill.

STEPHEN M. COREY, Prof. of Ed., Tchrs. Coll., Columbia Univ., N. Y.

BERNARD LONSDALE, Elem. Consultant, Calif. St. Dept. of Ed., Sacramento, Calif.

Members Elected at Large

HAROLD ALBERTY, Ohio St. Univ., Columbus (1957); WILLIAM M. ALEXANDER, Univ. of Miami, Coral Gables, Fla. (1958); FLORENCE BEARDSLEY, St. Dept. of Ed., Salem, Ore. (1956); ARNO A. BELLACK, Tchrs. Coll., Columbia Univ., N. Y. (1957); PRUDENCE BOSTWICK, Denver Pub. Schs., Colo. (1957); WILSON COLVIN, Weeks Jr. H. S., Newton, Mass. (1955); STEPHEN M. COREY, Tchrs. Coll., Columbia Univ., N. Y. (1957); JANE FRANSETH, U. S. Office of Ed., Washington, D. C. (1958); JAMES A. HALL, Pub. Schs., Port Washington, N. Y. (1956); LAVONE HANNA, San Francisco St. Coll., Calif. (1955); BETTY HUNTINGTON, Union Pub. Schs., N. J. (1956); G. ROBERT KOOPMAN, Mich. Dept. of Pub. Instr., Lansing (1956); EDWARD A. KRUG, Univ. of Wis., Madison (1955); J. MURRAY LEE, St. Coll. of Wash., Pullman (1958); GORDON N. MACKENZIE, Tchrs. Coll., Columbia Univ., N. Y. (1958); THEODORE D. RICE, N. Y. Univ., N. Y. (1956); VIRGIL M. ROGERS, Syracuse Univ., Syracuse, N. Y. (1957); DAVID RUSSELL, Univ. of Calif., Berkeley (1955); HILDA TABA, San Francisco St. Coll., Calif. (1958); KIMBALL WILES, Univ. of Fla., Gainesville (1955).

State Representatives to the Board

Alabama—MABEL C. EDWARDS, Pub. Schs., Hayneville; ROBERT C. HATCH, St. Dept. of Ed., Montgomery; OTTO HOLLAWAY, Ala., Polytechnic Institute, Auburn. *Arizona*—J. LAWRENCE WALKUP, Ariz. St.

229

Coll., Flagstaff. *California*—PAUL C. CLAY, Stanislaus Co. Schs., Modesto; RUTH DODDS, Co. Schs., Sacramento; MERCEDES ERRO, Co. Schs., San Luis Obispo; NEVA HAGAMAN, Pub. Schs., Long Beach; BERNARD LONSDALE, St. Dept. of Ed., Sacramento; C. R. TIMPANY, Santa Clara Co. Schs., San Jose. *Florida*—DORA SKIPPER, Fla. St. Univ., Tallahassee. *Georgia*—JEWEL D. ASKEW, Savannah and Chatham Co. Pub. Schs., Savannah; MARY H. FREEMAN, DeKalb Co. Schs., Decatur. *Illinois*—MARVIN L. BERGE, Pub. Schs., Elgin; NORMAN J. GORE, Pub. Schs., Decatur; PAULINE HOLT, Pub. Schs., Riverside; LORETTA McNAMARA, Pub. Schs., Hinsdale; CHARLOTTE MEYER, Pub. Schs., Decatur; B. L. SMITH, Pub. Schs., Oak Park. *Indiana*—ANNE HOPMAN, Indiana Univ., Bloomington; NELLIE C. MORRISON, Pub. Schs., Muncie. *Iowa*—R. T. GRAU, Pub. Schs., Clinton. *Kansas*—DOROTHY McPHERSON, Bd. of Ed., Coffeyville. *Kentucky*—LOUISE COMBS, St. Dept. of Ed., Frankfort; MELVIN NORSWORTHY, Fayette Co. Schs., Lexington. *Louisiana*—Mrs. J. L. PERKINS, East Parish Sch. Bd., Baton Rouge. *Maryland*—MYRTLE ECKHARDT, Co. Schs., Baltimore; GLADYS T. HOPKINS, St. Dept. of Ed., Baltimore. *Michigan*—THERAL T. HERRICK, Pub. Schs., Kalamazoo; ALVIN LOVING, Northrup School, River Rouge; MAUD L. PRICE, Pub. Schs., Royal Oak; EDITH ROACH SNYDER, Pub. Schs., Pontiac. *Minnesota*—KARL F. NOLTE, Pub. Schs., Hibbing. *Missouri*—RAYMOND A. ROBERTS, St. Dept. of Ed., Jefferson City. *Nebraska*—LEO P. BLACK, St. Dept. of Pub Instr., Lincoln. *New Jersey*—MARY E. FERGUSON, Pub. Schs., Atlantic City; CARL SALSBURY, Pub. Schs., Milburn. *New York*—ADELAIDE W. BAKER, Pub. Schs., Rome; WILLIAM BRISTOW, Bur. of Curr. Research, New York City; MARCELLA R. LAWLER, Teachers Coll. Columbia Univ., New York City; RAY W. SMITH, Pub. Schs., Buffalo; LILLIAN WILCOX, Board of Ed., Buffalo. *North Carolina*—MARGARET FLINTOM, Pub. Schs., Charlotte; H. ARNOLD PERRY, Univ. of N. C., Chapel Hill; MADELINE TRIPP, St. Dept. of Pub. Instr., Raleigh. *Ohio*—ARTHUR W. FOSHAY, Ohio St. Univ., Columbus; PAUL KLOHR, Ohio St. Univ., Columbus; FANNIE JANE RAGLAND, Pub. Schs., Cincinnati; VERNA WALTERS, Kent St. Univ., Kent. *Oklahoma*—JESS HUDSON, Pub Schs., Tulsa. *Pennsylvania*—GERTRUDE BARBER, Pub. Schs., Erie; ETHEL McCORMICK, Pub. Schs., Allentown. *Tennessee*—J.F.RIGSBY, Co. Schs., Lawrenceburg. *Texas*—JEWEL ASKEW, Pub. Schs., Houston; SUSAN CRUTCHFIELD, Pub. Schs., Galveston; ISHMAEL HILL, Pub. Schs., Lubbock; MARGARET WASSON, Highland Park Pub. Schs., Dallas. *Virginia*—ETTA BRANDT, Campbell Co. Schs., Rustburg; ELIZABETH ELLMORE, Pub. Schs., Dinwiddie. *Wisconsin*—MAYO BLAKE, Co. Schs., Waukesha; IDA OALEY, St. Dept. of Pub. Instr., Madison. *New England Region (Connecticut, Maine, New Hamp-*

shire, Rhode Island, Vermont, Massachusetts)—J. EDWARD CASEY, Univ. of R. I., Kingston; J. BERNARD EVERETT, Newton Pub. Schs., Newtonville, Mass.; DONALD MATTOON, Willimantic St. Tchs. Coll., Willimantic, Conn.; KARLENE V. RUSSELL, St. Dept. of Ed., Barton, Vt. *Northwest Region* (*Washington, Oregon, Montana, Idaho*)—CHESTER BABCOCK, Pub. Schs., Seattle, Wash.; NORMAN K. HAMILTON, Pub. Schs., Portland, Ore.; VIVIAN JOHNSON Western Wash. Coll. of Ed., Bellingham, Wash.; JOHN D. McAULAY, Southern Ore., Coll. of Ed., Ashland, Ore. *Rocky Mountain Tri-State* (*Colorado, Wyoming, New Mexico*)— VICTOR HOPPER, Colo. Coll., Colorado Springs, Colo.; VONDOLEE S. PAGE, Pub. Schs., Sante Fe, N. M.

ASCD Headquarters Staff

Executive Secretary, GEORGE W. DENEMARK, 1201 Sixteenth St., N. W., Washington 6, D. C.

Associate Secretary, ROBERT R. LEEPER, 1201 Sixteenth St., N. W., Washington 6, D. C.

Associate Secretary, RODNEY TILLMAN, 1201 Sixteenth St., N. W., Washington 6, D. C.